MW01122059

The Financial Crisis

The Financial Crisis

Origins and Implications

Edited by

Philip Arestis

Rogério Sobreira

and

José Luis Oreiro

palgrave
macmillan

First published 2011 by
PALGRAVE MACMILLAN

Palgrave Macmillan in the UK is an imprint of Macmillan Publishers Limited, registered in England, company number 785998, of Houndmills, Basingstoke, Hampshire RG21 6XS.

Palgrave Macmillan in the US is a division of St Martin's Press LLC, 175 Fifth Avenue, New York, NY 10010.

Palgrave Macmillan is the global academic imprint of the above companies and has companies and representatives throughout the world.

Palgrave® and Macmillan® are registered trademarks in the United States, the United Kingdom, Europe and other countries.

ISBN 978–0–230–27159–3   hardback

This book is printed on paper suitable for recycling and made from fully managed and sustained forest sources. Logging, pulping and manufacturing processes are expected to conform to the environmental regulations of the country of origin.

A catalogue record for this book is available from the British Library.

Library of Congress Cataloging-in-Publication Data

The financial crisis: origins and implications/edited by Philip Arestis, Rogério Sobreira and José Luis Oreiro.
        p. cm.
ISBN 978–0–230–27159–3 (alk. paper)
1. Global Financial Crisis, 2008–2009.   2. Financial crises—History.
        3. International finance.   I. Arestis, Philip, 1941–   II. Sobreira,
        Rogério.   III. Oreiro, José Luis.
HB37172008 .F56 2010
330.9'0511—dc22   2010033951

10   9   8   7   6   5   4   3   2   1
20   19   18   17   16   15   14   13   12   11

Printed and bound in Great Britain by
CPI Antony Rowe, Chippenham and Eastbourne

Contents

List of Tables and Figures

Tables

Figures

Notes on the Contributors

Philip Arestis, Cambridge Centre for Economics and Public Policy, Department of Land Economy, University of Cambridge, UK; Professor of Economics, Department of Applied Economics V, Universidad del País Vasco, Spain; Distinguished Adjunct Professor of Economics, Department of Economics, University of Utah, US; Senior Scholar, Levy Economics Institute, New York, US; Visiting Professor, Leeds Business School, University of Leeds, UK; Professorial Research Associate, Department of Finance and Management Studies, School of Oriental and African Studies (SOAS), University of London, UK; and current holder of the British Hispanic Foundation 'Queen Victoria Eugenia' British Hispanic Chair of Doctoral Studies. He is Chief Academic Adviser to the UK Government Economic Service (GES) on Professional Developments in Economics. He has published as sole author or editor, as well as co-author and co-editor, a number of books, contributed in the form of invited chapters to numerous books, produced research reports for research institutes, and has published widely in academic journals.

Emiliano Brancaccio is research fellow and professor of Political Economy and Labour Economics, Department of Analysis of Economic and Social Systems (DASES), University of Sannio (Benevento, Italy). He has published several articles dedicated to the advances in the critique of mainstream economic theory. He is the author of the article 'On the Impossibility of Reducing the Surplus Approach to a Neo-classical Special Case' (*Review of Political Economy* 2010) and co-editor of the book *The Global Economic Crisis: New Perspectives on the Critique of Economic Theory and Policy* (forthcoming). His area of study also encompasses banking systems, financial markets, European economic policy.

Germana Corrado is currently Assistant Professor at the Department of Economics and Institutions, Faculty of Economics, University of Rome 'Tor Vergata' and Lecturer in European Economy and International Economics at the University of Rome 'Tor Vergata'. She has published as sole author, as well as co-author, and several works in academic journals in the following research fields: international monetary economics, housing economics and financial markets and institutions.

Gary Dymski received his doctorate in economics from the University of Massachusetts, Amherst in 1987. He was a fellow in economic studies at the Brookings Institution, and since 1991 has been a member of the economics department at the University of California, Riverside. From 2003 to 2009 he served as founding director of the University of California's academic/policy center in Sacramento. Gary's most recent books are *Capture and Exclude: Developing Nations and the Poor in Global Finance* (co-edited with Amiya Bagchi, 2007) and *Reimagining Growth: Toward a Renewal of the Idea of Development* (co-edited with Silvana DePaula, 2005). His current research interests include: money, space, and inequality; the social and economic aspects of banking and finance; financial regulation and economic policy; financial fragility and financial exclusion; and the subprime and other financial crises.

Fernando Ferrari-Filho is Full Professor of Economics at Universidade Federal do Rio Grande do Sul (Federal University of Rio Grande do Sul) and Researcher at Conselho Nacional de Desenvolvimento Científico e Tecnológico (National Counsel of Technological and Scientific Development), Brazil. He has published, as author and co-editor, some books, and contributed in the form of invited chapters to a number of books. He has also published in academic journals. The focus of his research is on the following subjects: post Keynesian theory, macroeconomics (stabilisation and growth), monetary and exchange rate policies and financial and currency crises.

Giuseppe Fontana is Professor of Monetary Economics at the University of Leeds (UK) and Associate Professor at the Università del Sannio (Italy). He has recently been awarded the first G.L.S. Shackle Prize, St Edmunds' College, Cambridge (UK). He is a Visiting Research Professor at the Centre for Full Employment and Price Stability (University of Missouri Kansas City, USA), and the Cambridge Centre for Economic and Public Policy (University of Cambridge, UK). He has authored and co-authored over twenty book chapters, and over thirty international journal papers including publications in the *Cambridge Journal of Economics*, the *International Review of Applied Economics*, the *Journal of Economic Psychology*, the *Journal of Post Keynesian Economics*, *Metroeconomica*, *Revue Economie Politique*, and the *Scottish Journal of Political Economy*. He has recently co-edited three books with international publishers and has just published *Money, Time, and Uncertainty*.

Elias Karakitsos is Director of Guildhall Asset Management, chairman of Global Economic Research and an Associate Member of the Centre for Economic and Public Policy, University of Cambridge. He was a Professor at Imperial College, Head of Economics for ten years and has acted as an advisor to governments and financial institutions, including Citibank, Oppenheimer, Allianz, Crédit Agricole and Standard Chartered. He is the author of five books/monographs, 90 papers in learned journals and more than 330 reports on financial markets.

Costas Lapavitsas teaches Economics at the School of Oriental and African Studies, University of London. His research interests include political economy and the sociology of money and finance, the Japanese economy, and the history of economic thought. He has been visiting academic at several universities across the world, including the University of Tokyo, the Athens School of Economics, and the Middle Eastern Technical University. He has published widely, including *Political Economy of Money and Finance* (with M. Itoh, Macmillan, 1999), *Development Policy in the Twenty-first Century* (with B. Fine and J. Pincus, 2001), *Social Foundations of Markets, Money and Credit* (2003) and *Beyond Market-Driven Development* (with M. Noguchi, 2005). His most recent book (edited) is *Financialisation in Crisis* (2010). Currently he is researching the financialisation of contemporary capitalism.

Ramona Meyricke is a researcher at the University of Cambridge and a Fellow of the Institute of Actuaries of Australia. She completed her undergraduate degree in Finance and Applied Statistics at the Australian National University, where she was awarded the University Medal. Subsequently she qualified as an actuary, specialising in pension funding. As a consulting actuary, Ramona has advised institutional clients on investment, risk management and regulatory compliance. She has published in academic journals in the area of survival and failure time modeling. Her current research focuses on corporate failure and credit risk.

José Luis Oreiro is Associate Professor of Economics at the University of Brasilia (UnB), Level I Researcher at the National Scientific Council (CNPq/Brazil), Director of the Brazilian Keynesian Association (AKB) and member of the Editorial Board of the *Brazilian Journal of Political Economy* (REP). He has published more than 60 articles in academic journals in Brazil and other countries, three books as editor and contributed in the form of invited chapters to many other books. According to REPEC, he belongs to the top 10 per cent of academic economists in Brazil.

Malcolm Sawyer is Professor of Economics, University of Leeds, UK and formerly Pro-Dean for Learning and Teaching for the Faculty of Business. He is the managing editor of *International Review of Applied*

Economics and the editor of the series *New Directions in Modern Economics.* He is the author of 11 books, has edited 25 books and has published over 100 papers in refereed journals and contributed chapters to over 100 books. His research interests are in macroeconomics, fiscal and monetary policy, the political economy of the European Monetary Union, the nature of money, causes and concepts of unemployment and the economics of Michal Kalecki.

Rogério Sobreira is Associate Professor of Economics and Finance, Brazilian School of Public and Business Administration at the Getulio Vargas Foundation and CNPq Researcher. He has published several articles in academic journals and invited chapters mainly on banking regulation, banking firms, investment financing and public debt management. He has co-edited five books, all in Portuguese: *Financial and Banking Regulation, Development and the Building of a Nation – Economic Policy, Development and the Building of a Nation – Public Policy, Fiscal Adjustment: The Case of Selected Countries* and *Monetary Policy, Central Banks and Inflation Targeting.* He is a member of the Brazilian Keynesian Association.

Engelbert Stockhammer is Senior Lecturer, School of Economics, Faculty of Arts and Social Sciences, Kingston University. He is Research Associate at the Political Economy Research Institute of the University of Massachusetts at Amherst and member of the coordination group of the Research Network Macroeconomics and Macroeconomic Policy. He has published numerous academic articles. In 2004 he published *The Rise of Unemployment in Europe* and in 2009 he co-edited *Macroeconomic Policy on Shaky Foundations: Whither Mainstream Economics?*

Gennaro Zezza is Associate Professor in Economics, Department of Economics, University of Cassino, Italy and Research Scholar, Levy Economics Institute, New York, US. He has contributed consistently to the development of the Levy Model for medium-term projections of the US and world economy. He has contributed in the form of invited chapters to a few books, produced research reports for research institutes, and has published regularly in academic journals.

1
Introduction

Philip Arestis, Rogério Sobreira and José Luis Oreiro

The recent financial crisis was the biggest economic crisis of capitalism since the Great Depression of 1929. Starting in the United States after the collapse of a speculative bubble in the housing market fuelled by a massive credit expansion caused by the utilisation of new financial instruments (the subprime loans, securitisation, derivatives and so on), the financial crisis spread all over the world in just a few months. The triggering event of the crisis was the bankruptcy of Lehman Brothers on 15 September 2008 after the Federal Reserve (Fed) refused to bail it out. This decision had a tremendous impact over the state of expectations in financial markets, since there had been a general belief that the Fed would continue to bail out financial institutions affected by the collapse of the speculative bubble in the housing market. After that, it was no longer possible to believe that the Fed would always rescue financial institutions that are considered 'too big to fail'. The result of this change in the state of expectations was the emergence of panic between financial institutions that resulted in a huge increase in their liquidity preference, mainly by commercial banks, producing a sharp decline in asset prices and in the supply of credit for almost every type of commercial and industrial transaction. The 'credit evaporation' resulted in a very rapid and deep decrease in industrial production and in the international trade all over the world (see Table 1.1). In the last quarter of 2008, industrial production and GDP of developed countries experienced a huge fall, in some cases the annualised rate of GDP contraction was greater than 10 per cent. Even developing countries that do not have problems with their financial system, such as Brazil, had observed a tremendous reduction in industrial production and GDP. In Brazil, for instance, industrial production fell by almost 30 per cent in the last quarter of 2008 and GDP had fallen at an annualised rate of 11 per cent during this period (Table 1.2).

Table 1.1   Industrial production: percentage change over previous year (monthly data)

Industrial Production – percentage change from same period prev. year

Country	2008 M10	2008 M11	2008 M12	2009 M01
Brazil	0.2	−5.4	−16.4	−15.3
Canada	−6.1	−8.2	−7.8	−11.3
France	−7	−8.8	−10.4	−15.1
Germany	−3.5	−7.5	−12.3	−20.2
Italy	−8.5	−10.5	−13	−17.5
Japan	−8.3	−13.7	−21.2	−28.9
Spain	−14.6	−15.7	−19.7	−20
United Kingdom	−6.3	−8.3	−9.7	−12.2
United States	−4.7	−6.5	−8.9	−10.9

Source: Joint IMF–OECD Statistics, 30 March 2010. M stands for relevant month; *World Economic Outlook*, October 2009.

Table 1.2   Gross Domestic Production: Percentage change over previous quarter (quarterly data)

GDP – A quarterly percent change

Country	2008 Q2	2008 Q3	2009 Q1	2009 Q2
Brazil	1.1	−2.92	−0.88	1.08
Canada	0.1	−0.95	−1.79	−0.87
France	−0.2	−1.5	−1.3	0.3
Germany	−0.32	−2.44	−3.52	0.44
Italy	−0.87	−2.18	−2.71	−0.49
Japan	−1.3	−2.7	−3.6	1.5
Spain	−0.55	−1.08	−1.7	−0.96
United Kingdom	−0.93	−1.8	−2.61	−0.69
United States	−2.7	−5.4	−6.4	−0.7

Source: Reuters Statistics, 30 March 2010. Q stands for relevant quarter.

Governments in developed countries responded to this crisis by means of monetary and fiscal policy expansions. The Fed reduced the short-term interest rate – the Fed funds rate – to almost 0 per cent and increased its balance sheet almost three times in order to provide liquidity to financial markets in the US. Similar policies were adopted by the European Central Bank and the Bank of Japan. In the US, the new president, Barack Obama, managed to approve a fiscal expansion of almost $800 billion to increase aggregate demand and boost the US economy. In the euro area, governments were allowed to increase the fiscal deficit beyond the tight limits of the Maastricht Treaty in order to help an economic recovery. Similar efforts were undertaken in the UK and elsewhere, including in some developing countries. In China the government, for instance, increased expenditure in public investment – mainly infrastructure – by more than $500 billion in order to maintain the economy's high growth path. In Brazil fiscal policy expansion began earlier than monetary policy expansion due to an irrational commitment by the Brazilian government to a very tight inflation-targeting regime. The Lula administration approved a fiscal stimulus package at the end of 2008, comprising increases in public investment, reductions in tax and increases in the value of unemployment benefits and the minimum wage. The reduction in interest rates began only in January 2009 after a huge collapse of industrial production at the end of 2008 and widespread rumours about the replacement of the president of the Central Bank of Brazil. As a consequence of that delay in easing monetary policy, GDP growth fell from 5.1 per cent in 2008 to –0.7 per cent in 2009 (IMF, 2009, p. 85).

The economic consequences of the 2008 crisis will be long-lasting. In 2009 the main industrial economies witnessed huge falls in GDP. In fact, the US had a fall in GDP of 2.7 per cent, the euro area a fall of 4.2 per cent, Japan had a fall of 5.4 per cent and the UK a fall of 4.4 per cent (IMF, 2009, p. 69). For 2010, the IMF projections were for a slow recovery for the US and Japan, and a near stagnation for the euro area and the UK. This means that GDP level pre-crisis will not be reached before the end of 2011 or the beginning of 2012 despite the substantial fiscal and monetary stimuli.

Despite the huge fall in industrial production and GDP in both developed and developing countries, the severity of the 2008 financial crisis was very far from the catastrophic outcomes observed during the 1930s. At the end of 2009, the US economy began to show positive signs of recovery, signalling a modest growth for 2010. France and Germany exited from 'technical recession' in the middle of 2009 and the same occurred for the UK in the last quarter of the same year. During the crisis developing countries had a much better average economic performance than developed countries. GDP growth in China was 8.5 per cent in 2009, showing a very small reduction compared to 2008 when its economy had grown at a rate of 9 per cent (IMF, 2009, p. 74). The economic performance of India was also good. After a GDP growth of 7.3 per cent in 2008, economic growth had fallen to 5.4 per cent in

2009. For 2010, IMF projections show a GDP growth of 5.4 per cent for India. Brazil's economic performance during the crisis was not as good as that observed in China and India. After a robust GDP growth of 5.1 per cent in 2008, GDP fell by 0.7 per cent in 2009. However, growth is expected to resume in 2010 to a rate of 7.0 per cent (Ministry of Finance, 2010). Among the larger developing economies, only Russia showed a substantial decrease in GDP. According to the IMF, GDP in Russia fell by 7.5 per cent in 2009 after experiencing positive growth of 5.6 per cent in 2008. For 2010, the expected growth rate for Russia is about 1.5 per cent.

The intensity of the 2008 financial crisis poses three fundamental questions for economists and policymakers. The first relates to the origins of the crisis; the second is concerned with the consequences of this crisis for the world economy; and the third question is about what did not happen – namely, why did the 2008 financial crisis not cause a catastrophic fall of GDP as witnessed the 1929 crisis?

Regarding the first question there is a widespread opinion that the 2008 financial crisis was solely the result of inadequate financial regulation together with a very loose monetary policy conducted by the Federal Reserve during Greenspan's term. If that is so, there is no need to reform the international monetary system or to worry about the pattern of income distribution in developed economies. A restricted change of financial regulation and a redefinition of inflation targeting in order to include the stabilisation of asset prices as one of the goals of monetary policy will be enough to avoid financial crisis in the future.

In respect of the second question, there is a widespread opinion that this crisis was only a temporary detour from the normal course of events, so that in the near future capitalist economies will resume the high growth path observed before the crisis. Growth could again be led by credit expansion in the US and economic policy can be conducted in a similar way as it had been before the crisis.

In terms of the third question, there is a widespread view that the fundamental reason that explains the avoidance of the harmful experiences of 1929 was the fiscal and monetary policy expansions in developed countries. No important role is assigned to developing countries in terms of the effects of the August 2007 financial crisis.

This book will present a challenge to these views about the origins and the consequences of the August 2007 financial crisis. A common unifying element of the chapters in the book is the view that in order to avoid a new financial crisis in the future what is required is not only a profound change in the financial regulation but also a change in the conduct of economic policy, a reform of the international monetary system and a radical change in the pattern of income distribution. Following the current financial crisis, it is no longer possible to return to 'business as usual'. A profound change in the way the capitalist economies operate is required for a return to a growth path with financial stability.

In the second chapter of this volume, Philip Arestis and Elias Karakitsos argue that from a policy perspective a monetary policy rule based on inflation and the output gap may be insufficient to prevent the ramifications of the credit crisis. They suggest that this drawback is the result not only of the limited nature of the policymakers' objective function, but also of the structure of the relevant paradigm, namely the New Consensus Macroeconomics (NCM). The NCM is the theoretical framework employed by a significant number of central banks and academic economists around the world in their work. They examine the relevance of the NCM models, and the policy implications that emanate from it, in light of the current crisis. The NCM models suffer from a number of deficiencies. The policy implications advocated in NCM models are assumed rather than being derived explicitly from such models. The NCM models are based on the transversality assumption which leads to the conclusion that commercial banks do not exist in the model, nor monetary aggregates or liquidity preference. Interestingly enough, the absence of financial institutions and monetary aggregates may be at the root of the current crisis. The NCM models ignore the role of wealth in affecting the decisions of households to spend and save. It is clear that these deficiencies mean that the NCM theoretical framework does not reflect the situation in the real world. This chapter attempts to rectify some of the drawbacks of the NCM models. In this respect the chapter highlights the potential problems a central bank is likely to face, and in view of the current crisis, when it targets just inflation and the output gap in the fashion of the so-called Taylor's rule.

In chapter 3, Emiliano Brancaccio and Giuseppe Fontana discuss the causes of the August 2007 financial crisis and the related economic recession. Conventionally, it is argued that there are three main causes of the current crisis. First, it is argued that the cause of the crisis is the result of a loose monetary policy, what has also been labelled the 'Greenspan put': central banks – and, in particular, the Fed – came to the rescue of financial markets by lowering the short-run interest rate significantly and consistently. Secondly, it is maintained that the crisis is to the result of world financial imbalances: chronic and persistent trade deficit in the US (but also in the UK, Ireland and Spain) are mirrored by chronic and persistent trade surpluses of oil-exporting countries and, in particular, East Asian countries (e.g. China and Japan). Finally, it is argued that the crisis is due to the misguided under-pricing of risk: financial investors 'played with fire' by being overconfident about the ability of their mathematical models of measuring and managing risk. The chapter assesses the merits and drawbacks of these three conventional causes, looking at the peculiar type of relationship between these explanations and their theoretical frame of reference, namely the New Consensus Macroeconomics (NCM) model. Brancaccio and Fontana show that these different causes are not always consistent with each other, and hence they signal potential problems with the nature of the established theoretical compromise in the NCM model. The chapter also compares these three conventional interpretations of the crisis with an alternative explanation, which identifies the cause of the current financial crisis and related economic recession in the structural changes in income distribution.

In chapter 4, Gary Dymski argues that the current global crisis of banking and finance has highlighted the central role of power in the problem of financial governance. Prior to the crisis the banking/financial systems of the US and Europe were increasingly characterised by widespread securitisation, the offloading of risk to guarantors, and the use of excessive balance-sheet leverage to boost earnings. These systems have been severely weakened by the subprime crisis, the collapse of the asset-backed commercial paper market, the implosion of the market for credit default swaps, and the losses (declared and undeclared) due to structured investment vehicles. Governmental authorities in the US and in Europe have taken equity positions in many leading firms in these nations' financial sectors. Nonetheless, these leading firms have fiercely and effectively resisted efforts to rein in their prerogatives, to reform their core methods of doing business, and to engage in a thorough review of whether fundamental financial reform is needed. This essay considers this puzzle from the viewpoint of the origins, locus, and use of power in finance. The premise is that these institutions, while weakened through losses, have retained power because of their control of key resources and linkages in the modern-day financial system. Many of these linkages are not within the firm, but instead reside in the firms' privileged role within the nexus of financial processes and markets in which the firm participates. It is hypothesised that a regulator interested in reshaping finance so that it is less prone to speculative excess and financial exploitation – and thus more economically and socially functional – must have the authority and will to oversee and control not just depository institutions but the entire financial nexus within which these firms operate.

Genaro Zezza, in chapter 5, is concerned with modelling that relates to the origins of the crisis. The main results of the chapter's modelling approach enables the author to track down the origins of the global recession, which started in 2007, by resorting to the behaviour of the private sector in the US economy. The mainstream interpretation of the crisis is that it originated from a low-probability shock to financial markets, and more specifically to the shadow banking sector, and especially the subprime mortgage market, which was not properly regulated. Contrary to the mainstream approach, the author claims instead that the crisis has its roots in the shift in income distribution towards the top quintile – a trend which is stronger in the US, but common to several developed economies since the 1980s, especially within the European Union, combined with an increasing role of relative consumption in households' decisions. Financial markets allowed the private sector to finance expenditure beyond real disposable income, and provided a powerful channel for the globalisation of the crisis. In this view, therefore, financial markets multiplied the crisis at the global scale. More regulation will be needed, but a sustainable growth path will not be achieved unless action is taken to revert to an income distribution, which allows for sustainable growth in the living standards of the median household. The approach of this chapter is grounded in the stock-flow model, which is at the heart of the Levy Institute macroeconomic framework based on the US economy. This model is used to compare his results with the original 'New Cambridge' approach, and the current debate on the 'twin deficits' along with the impact of fiscal policy.

In chapter 6, Malcom Sawyer argues that the past three decades have witnessed a rapid growth and globalisation of the financial sector in an essentially neoliberal framework. This period has been characterised by frequent financial crises around the world, culminating in the present global financial crisis. This chapter begins by considering whether the developments in the financial sector and the resources, which it uses, have contributed to economic welfare. This is followed by a discussion of the appropriate role of the financial sector (e.g. provision of payments system, allocation of funds). It is argued that the financial sector has become too large in terms of the resources, which it employs relative to the benefits, which it generates. This leads to a consideration of the implications of a much smaller financial sector, in terms of employment effects and the alternative use of resources, particularly for countries such as the UK and the US, which have become dependent on financial services as a source of income generation. With regard to a re-structuring of the financial sector, the chapter's arguments for the separation of the banks from the financial system, with a focus on the regulation of the banking system. The chapter notes the general trend away from the involvement of state and mutual organisations in the provision of banking and other financial services. The case for the reversal of that trend is made, and proposals made for a 'People's Bank', the more general development of state-owned banks (at say the regional level) and the active encouragement of mutual organisations, particularly in the area of housing finance and credit unions.

Costas Lapavitsas argues in chapter 7 that the current global crisis has cast a new light on the issue of financial regulation. Since the early 1970s financial regulation has exhibited two distinct but related tendencies. On the one hand, there has been systematic deregulation of prices, quantities, and functional specialisation within the financial system. This can be understood as systemic deregulation of finance, consonant with the gradual ascendancy of neoliberalism within economic theory and policymaking. The state has gradually withdrawn from controls over interest rates and quantities of credit, while allowing financial institutions to enter fields that were previously barred to them. The underlying logic was that the free operation of financial markets is beneficial to growth, employment and income. On the other hand, there has been a systematic extension of prudential regulation of financial institutions. This has focused primarily on banks and has amounted essentially to a shift of regulatory attention away from the asset and towards the liability side of the balance. Thus, regulation of liquidity through reserves has declined, while the regulation of solvency through capital has been on the ascendant. Meanwhile, the state has also implicitly or explicitly guaranteed the deposits of commercial banks. This can be thought of as individual regulation that does not go against systemic deregulation. The crisis of August 2007 has shown that individual regulation has been ineffectual, while systemic deregulation has been disastrous. Furthermore, individual regulation has had the perverse effect of exacerbating systemic instability. The crisis calls for a rethinking of the relationship between individual and systemic regulation. In that context, it also poses the question of the balance between private and public property in finance.

In chapter 8 Ramona Meyricke argues that institutional investors are now important actors in the financial markets of most developed economies and some developing economies. This chapter examines whether countries with higher levels of institutional investment were more resilient to the current crisis. Institutional investors, as well as their portfolio policies, can promote stock market development and liquidity, and lower stock market volatility. For example, pension funds and life insurers can make longer-term investments because of the nature of their liabilities and because members cannot withdraw their funds from these institutions. Higher demand for equity and long-term assets has been associated with a decrease in leverage and an increase in the maturity of debt. In addition, contractual savings may increase firms' resilience to shocks because lower leverage reduces a firm's exposure, and because these savings are a source of funds that firms can draw upon in an economic downturn. Institutional investors exhibit a range of different financial structures and investment behaviors, however, some of which increase volatility. Their behaviour is influenced by the structure of the financial system and the regulatory framework within which they operate. It is argued that the net effect of institutional investment depends crucially on the structure and the regulation of the financial system. To investigate whether institutional investment increases financial stability, the impact of the current crisis is compared across countries with different levels of institutional investment, allowing for differences in national financial systems and regulations. Particular attention is paid to Australia, one of the few developed countries where banks emerged from the current crisis almost unscathed.

The lending of last resort function is re-examined by Germana Corrado in chapter 9. The panic of 2008, originating from the subprime crisis of 2007, has shown clearly that rethinking the international monetary and financial architecture is a very urgent need. Undoubtedly, progress has been considerable after the 1990s Asian crisis in setting international financial standards. On the other hand, much less progress has been made with respect to strengthening the measures against financial crisis such as the provision of emergency liquidity support facilities. In this work, Germana Corrado analyses the lending of last resort (LOLR) function from both a historical and a contemporary perspective. It is possible to summarise the different views on the LOLR function in the following way: (i) the classical position embodied in the well-known Bagehot statement; (ii) the case for open-market operations; (iii) the case of a LOLR facility for helping both illiquid and insolvent banks; and (iv) the free-banking view that refuses the notion of emergency liquidity support, assessing that a competitive market should guarantee a panic-proof banking system. The author agrees with the more recent strand of literature that although it is appropriate to dismiss Bagehot's view as obsolete, there is not a well-defined set of rules to replace it or a theory of the LOLR interventions. The more recent lesson from the first global crisis of the twenty-first century is that the role of lender of last resort role has been profoundly reshaped. In this work Germana Corrado attempts to analyse rigorously the following issues: how to extend and properly design such emergency liquidity lending facilities in a domestic and international context.

In chapter 10, Fernando Ferrari-Filho argues that since the collapse of the Bretton Woods system in the early 1970s, the increased international mobility of capital and trade and financial liberalizations – i.e. the financial globalisation process – has substantially altered the dynamic process of the international economy. In other words, the financial globalisation process, in the absence of government macroeconomic policies to stimulate economic growth and to limit the movements of capital flows, has been responsible for serious monetary and exchange rate problems. Examples include the European monetary crisis in 1992–93, the Mexican peso crisis in 1994–95, the Asian crisis in 1997, the Russian crisis in 1998, the Brazilian *real* crisis in 1998–99, the Argentina crisis in 2001–2 and, most recently, the August 2007 subprime crisis and, as a consequence, the international financial crisis. According to post Keynesian theory, currency and financial crises result from an unprecedented volatility of financial and exchange rate markets that increase the liquidity preference of economic agents. In this context, the chapter aims to answer a specific question: what can be done to avoid the financial and exchange rate instabilities and, as a consequence, the effective demand crisis in global economy? In doing so, it returns to Keynes's revolutionary ideas and proposals about the international monetary system presented at the Bretton Woods Conference in 1946. It presents a post Keynesian proposal to reform the international monetary system in order to alter the current logic of financial globalisation process and to prevent international financial and exchange rate crises. The prerequisite in all of this is the reduction of the economic agents' uncertainties, which is necessary to secure an expansion in global effective demand.

Finally, in chapter 11, Engelbert Stockhammer highlights the polarisation of income distribution (in particular, the decline of the wage share) in OECD countries as an underlying cause of the present crisis. In particular, the often-quoted 'international imbalances' are intrinsically linked to the issue of income distribution. The author highlights two stylised facts: First, the neoliberal mode of regulation came with a decisive shift in power relations at the expense of labour, which is clearly reflected in the fall of wage shares across OECD economies. This has resulted in potential shortfall of domestic effective demand. Second, financial globalisation has relaxed balance of payment constraints and thereby allowed the build-up of large international imbalances. Changes in income distribution have interacted in a complex way with the accumulation dynamics in the finance-dominated accumulation regime. The combination of real wage moderation and financial liberalisation has led to different strategies (or at least outcomes) in different countries. While some countries (such as the US) have 'compensated' wage growth with credit-fuelled consumption growth that comes with large current account deficits, others (like Germany and Japan) have accepted stagnant domestic demand and relied on an export-driven growth model with large current account surpluses. Real wage depression has thus resulted in quite different macroeconomic outcomes and played a crucial role in the building up of the international imbalances that are frequently regarded as an important cause for the crisis.

We would like to thank the authors for their contributions. We would also wish to thank Taiba Batool and Gemma Papageorgiou at Palgrave Macmillan, and their staff, who have been extremely supportive throughout the life of this project.

References

International Monetary Fund (IMF) (2009), *World Economic Outlook*, October, Washington DC: International Monetary Fund.
Ministry of Finance (2010). *Economia Brasileira em Perspectiva*. June/July 2010. www.fazenda.gov.br/portugues/docs/perspectiva-economia-brasileira/edicoes/ BrazilianEconomicOutlook-ENG-JunANDJul-10.pdf. Accessed on 5 September 2010.

2
The Lessons from the Current Crisis for Macro-theory and Policy

Philip Arestis and Elias Karakitsos

1 Introduction[1]

We examine the relevance of the New Consensus Macroeconomics (NCM) models in light of the current crisis. The NCM models suffer from a number of deficiencies. The policy implications advocated in NCM models are assumed rather than being derived explicitly from such models. The NCM models are based on the transversality assumption, which leads to the conclusion that commercial banks do not exist in the model, nor monetary aggregates or liquidity preference. Interestingly enough, the absence of monetary aggregates and liquidity preference may be at the root of the current crisis. The NCM models ignore the role of wealth in affecting the decisions of households to spend and save. This chapter attempts to rectify some of these drawbacks of the NCM models. In this respect the chapter highlights the potential problems a central bank is likely to face, and in view of the current crisis, when it targets just inflation and output gap to a lesser extent.

This chapter goes on to argue that from a policy perspective a monetary policy rule based on inflation and the output gap may be insufficient to prevent the ramifications of the credit crisis (see, also, Arestis and Karakitsos, 2009). This drawback is due not only to the limited nature of the policymakers' objective function, but also to the structure of the NCM paradigm. A number of studies have demonstrated the problematic nature of this paradigm (see, for example, Arestis, 2007, 2009a, 2009b; Arestis and Karakitsos, 2007; Goodhart, 2004; Weber et al., 2008). In particular, the NCM models suffer from a number of deficiencies. First, there is an internal inconsistency in that the policy implications advocated in NCM models are assumed rather than being derived explicitly from such models (Karakitsos, 2008). The propositions that inflation is under the direct control of the central bank, while output and unemployment in the long run are not, are imposed on the model rather than demonstrated theoretically in a convincing manner (Arestis, 2009; Karakitsos, 2008). Second, the NCM models are based on the transversality assumption, which leads to the conclusion that commercial banks do not exist in the model, nor monetary aggregates or liquidity preference. Interestingly enough, the absence of monetary aggregates may be at the root of the current crisis (Arestis, 2009a, 2009b; Goodhart, 2007, 2008). Financial innovation in the last ten years or so has made traditional monetary aggregates obsolete as measures of overall liquidity. Hence, the NCM models cannot detect and monitor the liquidity in the economy that has been responsible for the finance of three major bubbles in the last ten years (internet, housing and commodities) and other minor ones, such as private equity and shipping. Fourth, the NCM models ignore the role of wealth in affecting the decisions of households to spend and save, which is likely to drive the effects of the ongoing credit crisis on the economy in the next two years (Arestis and Karakitsos, 2009). In a recent paper, Arestis (2009a) has also critically raised a number of issues with both the NCM's theoretical foundations, as well as with its monetary policy, which is of course the inflation-targeting framework. The discussion and assessment of the NCM in the Arestis (op. cit.) contribution is in the context of an open economy (see, also, Arestis, 2007b). This means that attention is given to the exchange rate channel of the transmission mechanism of monetary policy in addition to the aggregate demand channel and the inflation expectations channel. Problems summarised or identified therein, in addition to the ones mentioned above, include: low inflation and price stability do not always lead to macroeconomic stability; insufficient attention is paid to the exchange rate; there is insufficient evidence for a long-run vertical Phillips curve; there is insufficient evidence that NAIRU is unaffected by aggregate demand and economic policy; countries that do not pursue IT policies have done as well as the IT countries in terms of the impact of IT on inflation and 'locking-in' inflation expectations at low levels of inflation; insufficient evidence to downgrade fiscal policy; insufficient evidence that the NCM theoretical propositions are validated by the available empirical evidence; the IT policy framework can only pretend to tackle demand-pull inflation but not cost-push inflation. It is the case, then, that NCM is based on inconsistencies and a great deal of *ad hocery*. This suggests that a great deal more research is necessary to tackle all these issues. This chapter is an attempt on this front.

This chapter utilises a model that does not suffer from the drawbacks just alluded to in the case of the NCM model in an attempt to study the origins and implications of economic policy of the current economic experience, which we label as the 'Great Recession'. We organise the chapter as follows. Section 2 discusses the origins of the current crisis. Section 3 assesses empirically the likely impact of the credit crisis on the US economy. Section 4 analyses the dynamic adjustment of the model to the credit crisis and shows that the model is capable of explaining the stylised facts of asset-led business cycles; not only the current crisis but also other crises, such as the 1930s and Japan in the 1990s. Section 5 analyses the credit crisis for a leveraged economy and highlights the potential problems a central bank is likely to face when it targets just inflation and the output gap. Section 6 reviews the role of central banks and suggests a new policymakers' objective function that is more appropriate for the current economic environment. Section 7 analyses the merits and perils of wealth targeting. Section 8 summarises the arguments and concludes.

2   The emergence of the 'Great Recession'

We suggest that a main reason behind the US housing market being the main cause of the credit crisis, and the current economic problems of the global economy, is liquidity. It was actually the huge liquidity that was put in place by 'bad' financial engineering and some mistakes in the conduct of monetary policy, especially in the US (Arestis and Karakitsos, 2009). This liquidity has financed a number of bubbles in the last ten years with a major impact on the economy (internet, housing, and commodities) and a few more (shipping and private equity) with a minor impact on the economy. From a European perspective microeconomic fundamentals and country-specific factors have differentiated the countries in the euro-zone area with housing bubbles emerging in some countries, like Spain, but not in others, like Germany. Thus, what is needed is both a macro- and micro-perspective to understand the full story.

From a macro-perspective liquidity is the real culprit. Without this excessive liquidity there would have been no bubbles – no credit, no bubble. Although one might point to some errors on the part of the Federal Reserve System (the Fed) in the US, and central banks in other countries, in removing the accommodation bias on a number of occasions in the last ten years, financial engineering has played a much more important role in creating this prodigious liquidity. Financial engineering is deemed in the press to be synonymous with fraud – finding loopholes in the law and the regulatory environment to make money – and it is accordingly condemned. 'Bad' financial engineering has resulted in a 'shadow banking' that developed and worked in parallel with regulated banking. The 'shadow banking' operated outside the regulation and control of the authorities. So, whatever was not allowed in regulated banking was developed in the 'shadow banking'.

The backlash to the greed of financial institutions is likely to result in increasing calls for strict regulation of the industry. As the taxpayer is called to clean up the mess of the banks tougher regulation of the industry is very likely to ensue. But from a policy perspective it should be recognised that regulation is backward rather than forward looking. Smart people will always take advantage of any given legislation by finding loopholes. Regulators will always react with a long lag to close the loopholes and on some occasions, as in the current crisis, too late to prevent a calamity. A better approach than over-regulation is for the central bank to have a target on asset prices in a way that does not impede the functioning of free markets and does not prevent 'good' financial innovation. Since securitisation implies the transfer of assets and risk to the personal sector the ideal target variable for a central bank is the net wealth of the personal sector as a percentage of disposable income, which is a stationary variable and therefore a target range can be set. In the US, for example, this can be a range around five times the net wealth of the personal sector. In this way the central bank will monitor the implications of financial innovations as they impact net wealth, even if it is ignorant of these innovations as in the case of SIVs.[2] With a wealth target the central bank will act pre-emptively to curb an asset upswing cycle from becoming a bubble. Information on the constituent components of net wealth is available in the US with a one-quarter lag, a month after the release of the NIPA accounts, thus making it useful for policy analysis and targeting. In the euro zone there are huge efforts to compile such data, a prerequisite for targeting.

Asset-led business cycles, such as the current one, and those experienced in Japan in the 1990s and in a number of countries in the 1930s, produce a larger variability in output than inflation. In the upswing of the cycle output growth surpasses historical norms giving the impression that potential output growth has increased, and thereby creating a general feeling of euphoria and prosperity, as it did in the US in the second half of the 1990s. But in the downswing the recession is deeper than normal, and, even more importantly, it lasts for a long time with many false dawns, as in the case of Japan. As asset prices fall the past accumulation of debt becomes unsustainable and households and businesses engage in a debt reduction process by retrenching. This depresses demand, putting a new downward pressure on asset prices and thereby creating a vicious circle. The policy implication is that in asset-led business cycles guiding monetary policy by developments in inflation alone will not prevent the bubble from becoming bigger than otherwise. Mild, but not excessive, wealth targeting may be necessary.

This, however, is a policy for the future, and as such it is not helpful in getting the economy out of the current problems. The burst of a bubble in the last five hundred years has entailed asset and debt deflation that has triggered retrenchment on the part of households and firms with severe consequences for profits, the incomes of households and jobs. The deflation process is usually long and painful and the evidence of the last three episodes (1870s, 1930s and Japan in the 1990s) is that it usually lasts for ten years. The policymakers' efforts so far have concentrated on unfreezing the credit markets and restoring confidence in banks by pumping liquidity and guaranteeing bank loans so that the interbank market can start to function again. They have also assigned public funds to recapitalise banks by buying mostly preferred shares and increased the guarantee limit on deposits to deflect runs on depository institutions. In the US the Fed has, in addition, extended credit facilities to non-depository institutions and has lowered the quality of assets that it accepts as collateral for lending. Although these measures may be adequate to ease the panic phase of the burst of a bubble, they are inadequate to deal with the crisis in the long run, as they deal with the supply side of credit, but not with the demand for it.

The challenge for the policymakers is to break the vicious circle between falls in house prices and bank losses if they are to shorten the asset and debt deflation process to less than ten years. This requires preventing households from falling into negative equity; otherwise, delinquencies rise and bank losses mount; mortgage lenders repossess the properties and dump them onto the market that only causes lower house prices and even higher bank losses. Spending public money to cover the losses of the banks without supporting households to keep their homes and encourage others to obtain new mortgages is like throwing money into a black hole. Hence, the policies that should be pursued are on both sides of the credit market: demand and supply. Unless demand for credit and demand for the general products of the banks are boosted in the months ahead, no amount of money can salvage the financial system. Dealing just with the supply side of credit by ignoring its dependence on demand will be a waste of resources. Hoarding of cash by banks, mutual funds, hedge funds, businesses and individuals will be a terrible blow to demand that will trigger new losses for the financial institutions in the new year, thus creating a vicious circle. We are now in what Keynes called a 'liquidity trap'. Monetary policy does not work in this environment and neither does fiscal policy in the form of tax cuts; people will hoard the extra money – they will not spend it. What is needed is public works. A new Fannie Mae should be created, along the lines of the original model of the 'New Deal', as the current one does not inspire confidence. The new Fannie should take from the banks the loans to all those who are threatened with foreclosure or business bankruptcy and offer them affordable loans to boost demand.

Although the measures adopted so far are dealing with the panic, the policymakers are inconsistent in their long-term objectives in that they want both deleverage and high asset prices. They should either engineer an orderly deleverage, while at the same time accepting that in the new long-run equilibrium asset prices would be substantially lower; or they should flood the system with liquidity to prevent the erosion of asset prices, but knowing that deleverage would not materialise. In other words, the policymakers are not clear as to whether they target in the long-run deflation or inflation. It is a hard fact of life, however, that from a long-term perspective the first target is what makes sense; otherwise, the excess liquidity that financed so many bubbles in the last ten years will not be drained and will carry on financing new bubbles. Irrespective of whether the policymakers target deflation or inflation, the forces of deflation are more powerful. So, even if the policymakers wished to reflate asset prices, they might find it extremely hard to achieve their objectives.

3   The consequences of the credit crisis – an empirical assessment

The credit crisis is the outcome of financial distress, which in the refined Minsky (1982, 1986) model is the third stage of a bubble cycle: displacement, euphoria, distress, panic and crash. The credit crisis can be seen as unfolding in three stages. In the first stage credit spreads are widening as banks become unwilling to lend to each other for fear of contagion from potential losses on the collateral assets of the borrowing banks. In the second stage the losses of the financial institutions are unravelling, while in the third stage the ramifications to the economy are felt. Credit spreads have widened since the summer of 2007, although coordinated central bank efforts have succeeded at times in suppressing them (see Figure 2.1). In spite of central bank action the credit crisis deepened with credit spreads widening yet again culminating to the pinnacle and the panic in September and October 2008. In February 2009 the Obama Administration made a U-turn in its anti-Wall Street strategy. It abandoned its polemics and adopted the 'business-as-usual' model for the 'big-banks'; it shelved the 90 per cent tax on bank bonuses that the House had passed; it allowed banks to use their discretion in valuing their distressed assets by suspending the standard accounting practice of mark-to-market fair value method. This U-turn enabled banks to report overall profits for the remainder of 2009, as they stopped writing losses on their distressed assets, while continuing to make profits from current operations. This, along with the added liquidity in the form of emergency lending to financial institutions by the Fed, managed to narrow the credit spreads to the pre-crisis normal levels (see Figure 2.1).

The losses of financial institutions are likely to reach $3.4 trillion by the end of 2010 according to the latest estimate of the IMF in September 2009, as asset-backed securities have lost around three-quarters of their value. Since the outbreak of the crisis the systemic risk has fluctuated but mainly it has remained elevated. It subsided with the bailout of Bear Stearns, but surged again in the autumn of 2008, as Fannie Mae and Freddie Mac that hold or guarantee nearly half of mortgage-backed securities ($5.4 trillion) came to a bankruptcy point and had to be

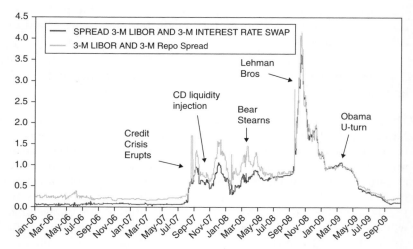

Figure 2.1   Liquidity and credit risk vs credit risk (Libor OIS vs Libor Repo)

bailed out by the US Treasury. In spite of the bailout of the two giants in the US mortgage market, the systemic risk hit new highs with the bankruptcy of Lehman Brothers in mid-September and finally with the near collapse and subsequent bailout of the insurance company AIG. The crisis has brought the demise of the investment-bank model and the remaining institutions (Morgan Stanley and Goldman Sachs) have run for cover behind the façade of commercial banks.

The ramifications to the economy are likely to stem from the response of the banks to these losses – tightening of lending standards, higher cost of lending, lower availability of credit, hoarding of money balances. The only certain way that banks will get out of this mess in the long run is through a very steep yield curve in government bonds. The Fed moved to a zero interest rate policy at the end of 2008, which is likely to be maintained for a long period until the recovery becomes sustainable, while the 10-year yield has hovered around 3.5 per cent offering more than 3 per cent gain in the banking system. The credit crunch will impair GDP growth and trim the rate of growth of potential output, as even companies with good ideas and profitable new products will be denied credit. On the positive side, the credit crunch will enable households and companies to curb their debt through time, thus rebuilding their impaired balance sheets. But as asset prices (houses, shares, commodities, commercial real estate, vessel prices and corporate bonds) fell the net wealth of the personal sector was further eroded, thus forcing the savings ratio up and consumer expenditure down. With consumption falling companies responded by shedding their labour force, cutting production and curtailing investment expenditure, thus further harming the incomes of households. This is the asset and debt deflation process!

The US economy bottomed in mid-2009, as the U-turn of policy against Wall Street put an artificial end to the losses of financial institutions, thereby fuelling a rally in equities that more than offset the continuous losses in housing wealth. A huge fiscal package of the order of $786 billion spread over two years (2009–10) boosted the level of demand in the economy, while easy monetary policy triggered dollar depreciation that buoyed exports. The recovery was further boosted by re-stocking, as companies embarked on the process of replenishing their depleted stock of inventories of goods and services following the collapse of domestic demand in the second half of 2008. Hence, the Great Recession is over, as the economy expanded at a solid pace in the second half of 2009. Nonetheless, the prospects for a new long and robust cycle are not so rosy and despite the end of the recession there is still

6.5 per cent spare capacity of potential GDP. The major threat to the sustainability of the recovery stems, firstly, from the exit strategy from the extraordinary measures, both fiscal and monetary, that were adopted in the course of the crisis; secondly, from the continuous deleverage of the personal and banking sectors; and, thirdly, from the sovereign risk crisis in the euro area that has forced tight fiscal policy in the Southern countries. This is now threatening to halt the recovery in the entire euro area with a feedback effect on the US, China and the global economy. The prodigious fiscal package has resulted in a soaring budget deficit to double-digit figures and federal debt is mounting. This would require tight fiscal policy for a number of years that would thwart the economy from generating jobs.

Under current law, the federal fiscal outlook beyond this year is daunting; projected deficits average about $600 billion per year over the 2011–20 period. As a share of GDP, deficits drop markedly in the next few years but remain high – at 6.6 per cent of GDP in 2011 and 4.1 per cent in 2012, the first full fiscal year after certain tax provisions originally enacted in 2001, 2003, and 2009 are scheduled to expire. Thereafter, deficits are projected to range between 2.6 per cent and 3.2 per cent of GDP through 2020.

Those accumulating deficits will push federal debt held by the public to significantly higher levels. At the end of 2009, debt held by the public was $7.5 trillion, or 53 per cent of GDP; by the end of 2020, debt is projected to climb to $15 trillion, or 67 per cent of GDP. With such a large increase in debt, plus an expected increase in interest rates as the economic recovery strengthens, interest payments on the debt are poised to skyrocket. CBO projects that the government's annual spending on net interest will more than triple between 2010 and 2020 in nominal terms (from $207 billion to $723 billion) and will more than double as a share of GDP (from 1.4 per cent to 3.2 per cent).

These projections assume that major provisions of the tax cuts enacted in 2001, 2003, and 2009 will expire as scheduled and that temporary changes that have kept the alternative minimum tax (AMT) from affecting many more taxpayers will not be extended. The baseline projections also assume that annual appropriations rise only with inflation, which would leave discretionary spending very low relative to GDP by historical standards. If the tax cuts were made permanent, the AMT was indexed for inflation, and annual appropriations kept pace with GDP, the deficit in 2020 would be nearly the same, historically large, share of GDP that it is today. The President's budget for 2011 has turned easy once more of the order of 1.5 per cent of GDP for fear that without a further stimulus the economy would lose its momentum. But the President's budget, if enacted, has long-term implications. The federal budget is expected to remain more than 5 per cent on average for the entire decade 2011–20, while the federal debt is expected to hit 100 per cent of GDP. Hence, the US has the choice of postponing the inevitable fiscal tightening for a few more years, but at the cost of harsher measures later on. The luxury of this choice, however, depends on the appetite of markets for risk. It assumes that investors would be willing to lend the US at the low interest rates that have done so far.

A similar threat to the sustainability of the recovery arises from the exit strategy of the Fed. The Fed has pumped more than $1 trillion of liquidity to help the financial system. This liquidity does not pose a threat of inflation at the moment, as it does not circulate in the economy. It appears in the form of excess reserves of the commercial banks with the Fed. This liquidity is at the moment helping banks to repair their impaired balance sheets. However, as the economy recovers with growth near potential the Fed would have to drain that liquidity, as markets are spooked by the potential inflation threat. The withdrawal of this liquidity will adversely affect growth in the long run.

Another threat to the new business cycle stems from the continuing deleveraging of the personal and banking sectors. Credit to households and companies is being cut, although it is not clear whether this is prompted by a credit crunch by the banks or whether households and companies are curbing their debt levels. So far the personal sector has reduced its debt level from 130 to 124 as a percentage of disposable income. But in spite of it, the net wealth has tumbled from peak-to-trough by 30 per cent of disposable income, as there has been a marked fall in asset prices. The equity market rally of 2009 has pared this loss in net wealth to 24 per cent of disposable income. Nonetheless, the gains in net wealth will be significantly lower in the next few years, while the effort to curb debt is likely to intensify. Accordingly, the savings ratio of the personal sector is likely to remain elevated, thereby depriving the economy from a robust growth that would generate sufficient number of jobs to dent unemployment that has doubled in the last few years.

The final threat to the new business cycle stems from the Greek crisis that spread swiftly to Spain, Portugal and Ireland. European policymakers with the help of the IMF responded with a huge package of the order of €750 billion in order to avert the break-up of the 11-year-old monetary union. This pool of money will make sure that the countries on the periphery would not have to resort to capital markets for rolling over their sovereign debt. Accordingly, credit spreads will abate.

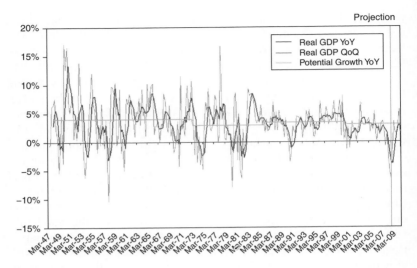

Figure 2.2   Real GDP

However, in exchange for the lending facilities the periphery countries would have to adopt severe austerity measures in the form of very tight fiscal policy. The sovereign debt crisis in the euro area has forced countries such as Germany to postpone indefinitely the planned tax cuts, which nonetheless are imperative for rebalancing the tight fiscal policy in the periphery countries. As a result, growth in the euro area will be impaired, dragging down global growth and in particular that of the US and China. Moreover, the euro area sovereign debt crisis acts as a harbinger of what might happen to the US as a result of fiscal profligacy.

A US macroeconomic model utilised elsewhere (Arestis and Karakitsos, 2010), the K-Model, provides an assessment of the short-term effects of this asset-debt deflation process. According to the K-Model growth is likely to be around 3 per cent in 2010 and 2011 as a result of the easy fiscal policy (see Figure 2.2), while inflation is expected to remain muted at between 1 per cent and 2 per cent (see Figure 2.3).

4   The dynamic effects of a credit crisis

The micro-foundations of the NCM or Neo-Wicksellian model are established in Rottemberg and Woodford (1995, 1997). The similarities of the NCM with Wicksell (1898) are pointed out in Woodford (2003)

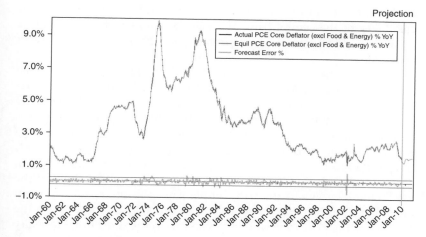

Figure 2.3 PCE core deflator

and Fontana (2006). A critical review of the NCM model can be found in Arestis (2007) and Goodhart (2004).

Following Karakitsos (2008), we suggest that the natural rate of interest has played a key role in theories of output and inflation determination in dynamic general equilibrium New Consensus Macroeconomic models (see, for example, Rottemberg and Woodford, 1995; Arestis, 2007). These models combine intertemporally optimising agents from the real-business-cycle school with imperfect competition and nominal rigidities from traditional Keynesian models. These nominal rigidities, i.e. stickiness in prices and/or wages, imply that changes in the nominal short-term interest rate affect short-term *real* rates and, thus in turn, aggregate real activity and inflation. Woodford (1997) has described these models as 'Neo-Wicksellian', and, to repeat, we follow this tradition in this contribution. In these models the natural interest rate is defined as the equilibrium real interest rate that would prevail in a fictitious economy where there are no nominal rigidities, i.e. in an economy in which nominal adjustment is complete.

As the Neo-Wicksellian models are derived from intertemporal optimisation, the emphasis is on the interdependency between current economic variables and expectations about their future realisations. Thus, current output and inflation depend on the entire path of expected future interest rates. This feature has immensely affected the theory and practice of monetary policy, as it assigns a major role to the management of private sector expectations and consequently to the credibility of the central bank as an important element in anchoring inflation expectations (see, for example, King, 2005; Arestis, 207; Weber et al., 2008).

Neo-Wicksellian models adopt all the principles of the original Wicksellian theory. Money is neutral in the long run, not because money is a 'veil', but because inflation is influenced by the interest rate gap, and not by the forces of demand for and supply of money. Say's Law does not hold in the short run; it does, however, hold in the long run. Consequently, disequilibrium in one market (money or goods) is transmitted to the other in the short run; but not so in the long run. The central bank controls the rate of inflation through changes in the rate of interest, which affects the output gap – the discrepancy between an endogenous demand for goods and an exogenous supply – with the latter affecting prices and price expectations in the short run. Monetary policy can influence the rate of inflation, but not output (or the growth rate of the economy) and unemployment in the long run, i.e. the Philips curve is vertical. The rate of growth is determined in the long run by supply considerations, such as multi-factor productivity, the rate of growth of the labour force, market flexibility, especially labour market etc., all of which are beyond the control of the monetary and fiscal authorities.[3] With output converging to its exogenously given supply unemployment will always converge to its exogenously given NAIRU.

What is stunning is that the original insight of the natural rate of interest as the reward of capital (the real profit rate) has been lost. In modern models it is simply a long-run equilibrium real interest rate. The attraction, therefore, has shifted from the original role of the real profit rate in determining inflation to a real interest rate that can define neutral monetary policy. The 'Wicksellian muddle' may have contributed significantly to this diversion. Wicksell's (1898) insight is that as long as there is a positive divergence between the real profit rate and the loan rate, inflation will continue to rise. This may be self-evident, as any divergence between the two rates will affect demand in the economy, which, with a fixed supply, will lead to rising inflation. The natural interest rate should not be defined as the rate consistent with stable inflation and, therefore, the rate that equates demand and supply in the goods market.

In Neo-Wicksellian models the natural rate of interest is a constant. The real profit rate that plays such an important role in microeconomics is simply a constant in macroeconomics. It is about time to remove this anomaly and endogenise the profit rate. In doing so, other anomalies in macro, such as the counter-cyclical behaviour of the real wage rate, may also be remedied.

The reduced form of the model in Karakitsos (2008) consists of six equations:

$$Y_t = a_o(G-T) + a_1 Y_t + a_2 Y_{t-1} + a_3 E_t Y_{t+1}$$
$$+ a_4[R_t - E_t(P_{t+1}) - RR_t] + a_5 NW_t + u_{1t} \qquad (1)$$

$$Y_t^g = a_0(G-T) - q + (a_1 - b_1)Y_t + a_2 Y_{t-1} + a_3 E_t(Y_{t+1})$$
$$+ a_4[R_t - E_t(P_{t+1})] - (a_4 + b_2)RR_t + a_5 NW_t + u_{2t} \qquad (2)$$

$$P_t = d_0 + d_1 E_t(P_{t+1}) + d_3 P_{t-1} + (d_4)Y_t^g + u_{3t} \qquad (3)$$

$$RR_t = q + f_1[P_t - E_t(P_{t+1})] + f_2 Y_t + f_3 R_t + f_4 Y_t^g + u_{4t} \qquad (4)$$

$$R_t = (1 - \gamma_0)[R_t + E_t(P_{t+1}) + \gamma_1 Y_{t-1}^g + \gamma_2(P_{t-1} - P^T) + \gamma_0 R_{t-1} + u_{5t} \qquad (5)$$

$$NW_t = \Omega_1 R_t + \Omega_2 RR_t + \Omega_3 RC + u_{6t}$$
$$\Omega_1, \Omega_3 < 0, \quad \Omega_2 > 0 \qquad (6)$$

All variables are expressed as rates of growth (log-differences): Y is (the rate of growth of) output, which is equal to the rate of aggregate demand; Y^s is (the rate of growth of) the supply of output (potential-output); Y^g is the output gap, the difference between the growth rates of current output and potential output; R is the nominal short-term interest rate; RR is the natural interest rate or real profit rate; P is the inflation rate; P^T is the central bank target inflation rate; NW is net household wealth; RC is credit risk; and $E_t(X_{t+1})$ is the expectation of variable X in period $t+1$, as with information at time t.

The system of equations (1)–(6) determines the six endogenous variables: Y_t^g, Y_t, P_t, R_t, RR_t, and NW_t.

The similarities and differences with the NCM (or Neo-Wicksellian) model are the following. The NCM model is simply equations (2), (3) and (5) with the last two terms in (2) being omitted. In the reformulated model there are three more equations: equation (1), which determines the equilibrium level of output from the level of demand in the economy; equation (4), which determines the rate of profit, which is treated as a constant in NCM models; equation (6), which determines net wealth. The reformulated model through the last two terms in equation (2) emphasise: (i) the influence of the profit rate in determining the output gap; and (ii) the wealth effect on consumption.

The dynamic effects of the credit crisis are analysed by simulating a numerical analogue of the theoretical model put forward in Karakitsos (2008), where a number of problems enumerated in section 1 are tackled. The equation-coefficients are calibrated to fit the stylised facts and satisfy the stability conditions; they are given in Table 2.1.

The credit crisis is portrayed in the model by a widening of credit spreads – corporate bond yields increase over government bond yields and money market rates over central bank rates. In the calibrations it is assumed that for four years credit spreads widen by 450 bps, consistent with the stylised facts of the current crisis. As a result, net wealth falls from its steady-state value of 3 per cent to –10 per cent in the next three years, as both equities and house prices plunge, but then gradually recover. Net wealth overshoots its initial steady state by 1.5 per cent and then converges to it. The whole dynamic adjustment lasts for ten years, which is consistent with the experience of the 1930s and Japan in the 1990s.

The fall in net wealth creates a recession with a negative output gap, which reaches a trough at nearly –3 per cent in three years. But then the economy recovers and converges to its initial steady state in ten years, while overshooting it for a short period of time. Potential output growth also diminishes during the credit crisis by a maximum of 1 per cent, but

Table 2.1   Numerical model

Y – EQUATION

a(1)	a(2)	a(3)	a(4)	a(5)
0.3	0.25	0.25	–0.4	0.13

P – EQUATION

d(1)	d(3)	d(4)
0.3	0.3	0.16

RR – EQUATION

f(1)	f(2)	f(3)	f(4)
0.2	0.85	–0.25	–0.04

R – EQUATION

G(0)	G(1)	G(2)	G(3)
0.5	0.75	1.5	0.3

NW – EQUATION

Z(1)	Z(2)	Z(3)
–0.1	1	–1.2

YS – EQUATION

b(1)	b(2)
0.2	0.2

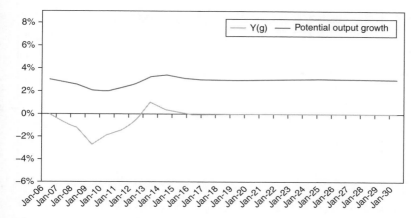

Figure 2.4 Output gap and potential output

ultimately returns to its initial steady state (see Figure 2.4). The fall in potential output mitigates the negative output gap and therefore it has a stabilising effect on the deflationary impact of the credit crisis. The decrease in potential output is due to lower growth and the impact of declining profitability on the capital accumulation process.

As a result of the negative output gap inflation falls by less than 1 per cent in three years and then converges to its initial steady state, largely following the path of the output gap. The central bank has two targets – inflation and the output gap. As inflation falls below the central bank target and the economy falters with a negative output gap, the central bank responds by cutting interest rates aggressively from 4.5 per cent to less than 0.5 per cent in four years, consistent with the stylised facts of Japan in the 1990s and the US in 2000s. A year after the economy begins to recover the central bank gradually removes the accommodation bias. During the overshooting it lifts the interest rate above the target level, but then it takes it back to its initial steady state. The profit rate (the natural interest rate of the Wicksellian model) plays an equally important, if not greater, role than interest rates in weathering the credit crisis and restoring the initial steady state. It falls initially, in response to the negative output gap, but it is the first to recover, as the central bank cuts interest rates and company pricing power returns early in the cycle (see Figure 2.5).

The calibrations show that the model captures the stylised facts of asset and debt deflation, caused by bank losses during the burst of an asset bubble that trigger widening of credit spreads. The credit crisis

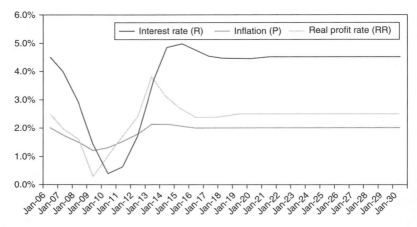

Figure 2.5   Interest rate, inflation and real profit rate

causes larger swings in the output gap than in inflation, a characteristic of all asset and debt deflations and shows the importance of the output gap as a target of central bank policy. Reliance on inflation alone is likely to exacerbate and prolong the deflationary impact of the credit crisis.

5   Sensitivity analysis – leveraged economies

The central role of wealth in an asset and debt deflation process reveals the drawback of NCM models to detect the roots of the current crisis and deal with its consequences. Net wealth depends on interest rates, as they affect house prices and equities. The other major determinant of net wealth is profitability that influences aggregate demand and equities. Both the interest rate and profit sensitivity of net wealth are related to the degree of leverage of the economy. In a highly leveraged economy both sensitivities are elevated; in fact, the more leveraged the economy, the higher these sensitivities are. As an example, consider the implications of SIVs that created a parallel banking outside the control and regulation of the authorities, which have contributed significantly to the expansion of liquidity. SIVs used to finance their activities through the London money market. Their profitability depended on the yield curve (the relationship between short-term and long-term interest rates). In fact, they went bust as the yield curve became slightly inverted, thus making them very sensitive to changes in interest rates. A small rise in money market rates above mortgage rates was sufficient to cause the collapse of the SIVs. Since the asset-backed securities issued by SIVs are held by the personal sector, the net wealth of households becomes very sensitive to changes in interest rates.

As an example of the high sensitivity of net wealth to profitability consider the investment banks that are highly leveraged; they operate with 30–40 times leverage. Because of the high degree of leverage they are also very sensitive to short- and long-term interest rates. A small fall in their assets is sufficient to wipe out their capital base and make them insolvent. No wonder, therefore, that the most significant victims of the credit crisis were Bear Stearns, Lehman Brothers and Merrill Lynch. In the upswing of the asset cycle investment banks made huge profits that boosted the net wealth of households, but in the downswing they made huge losses that dragged down equities and, hence, the net wealth of households. Banks have operated with a smaller degree of leverage than investment banks – around 20 times their capital. Their profitability is also very sensitive to interest rates, which again contributes to fluctuations in personal sector wealth through equities. Leveraged buy-outs (LBOs) were another frequently used method throughout the upswing of the asset-cycle to acquire companies and boost the net wealth of households through enhanced equity profitability. They are also very sensitive to changes in interest rates.

Thus, it is important to explore the sensitivity of the dynamic path of the economy to interest rates and profitability, as this enables the study of leveraged economies, a characteristic of the current credit crisis. The results of these calibrations show that the economy oscillates around the initial steady state for a quarter of a century, instead of converging in ten years; moreover, interest rates and profitability tend to move away through time from their initial steady state; in other words, the system tends to instability. The results also show that with a high net wealth response to profitability the output gap remains negative for 25 years, while improvement in net wealth from profitability is offset by the higher interest rates engineered by the central bank.

Therefore, in a leveraged economy the central banks face a much more difficult problem in stabilising the economy. A high response of net wealth to interest rates and profitability would prolong the credit crisis, as the central bank is forced to move interest rates up and down the target rate. An ever-increasing response of net wealth to interest rates and profitability makes the system unstable and the economy never converges to its initial steady state, following a temporary credit crisis. The oscillatory central bank behaviour, which ultimately causes instability, is due to the cyclical pattern of profitability. Given the differential speed of the economy to a change in interest rates and profitability with the former impacting slowly, while the latter does so rapidly, central bank action would delay, if not cause instability, to a credit crisis. This differential speed of adjustment is not just a feature of this model, but a stylised fact of the real world. Given that the real profit rate plays an important role in stabilising the economy, as it moves faster than interest rates and, given the influence of the interest rate on the real profit rate, which is responding to economic developments, it is not unreasonable that the central bank may destabilise a highly leveraged economy.

6   The merits and perils of wealth targeting

So far, we have shown that if monetary policy is guided solely by inflation, then the central bank is unlikely to deal adequately with a credit crisis. The reason for this important conclusion is that in an asset-led business cycle the volatility in the output gap is greater than the volatility of inflation. In the upswing of the cycle when credit expands and asset prices soar, inflation remains subdued for two reasons. First, potential output increases in the upswing, thus dampening the positive output gap and containing inflationary pressures. Second, cyclical productivity improvements, which appear as structural as they did in the late 1990s in the US, reduce unit labour costs, thereby putting a lid on inflation. On the other hand, the expansion of credit and the soaring asset prices increase output disproportionately compared to a standard demand-led business cycle. Therefore, a central bank is well advised to have two targets in an asset-led business cycle – inflation and the output gap. With these two targets and despite the fact that the central bank is using only one instrument – interest rates – it is more likely to be successful in dealing with a credit crisis and the consequences of the burst of the asset bubble. However, in a highly leveraged economy, like the US, even the two targets of inflation and the output gap are likely to prove inadequate to deal with the crisis. As the degree of leverage increases guidance of monetary policy by these two targets is likely to lead to a prolonged crisis and possibly to instability because of the differential speed of the economy to changes in interest rates and profitability. In this section we explore the merits of complementing the traditional targets of economic policy by wealth targeting. In the calibrations reported in this section the priority on the wealth target in the central bank objective function (8) now becomes operative with $\gamma_3 = 0.3$.

The widening of credit spreads leads to a smaller reduction in net wealth and therefore to a milder recession. The negative output gap is just –0.9 per cent with wealth targeting and –2.7 per cent without (see Figure 2.6). The milder recession results in smaller deflation, less negative inflation (see Figure 2.7). The milder recession also leads to a smaller profit fall under wealth targeting and this necessitates smaller rate cuts

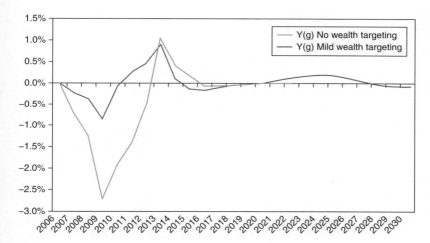

Figure 2.6 Output gap

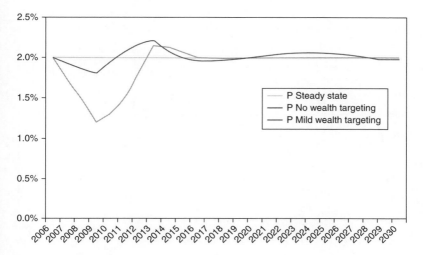

Figure 2.7 Inflation

by the central bank (see Figures 2.8 and 2.9). The swings in interest rates are thus smaller under wealth targeting and this enables the economy to weather the burst of the bubble with smaller costs in terms of output lost. Therefore, a mild wealth targeting is beneficial in the central bank task of stabilising the economy in an asset-led business cycle.

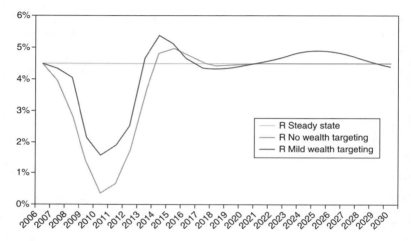

Figure 2.8   Interest rate

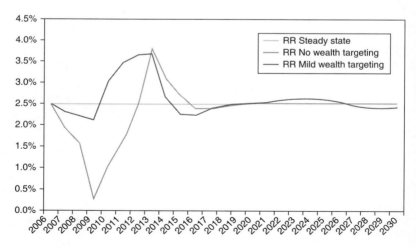

Figure 2.9   Real profit rate

This makes it necessary to examine what would happen to the dynamic adjustment of the economy if the central bank went wild with enthusiasm about wealth targeting. This situation is examined by simulating the model with $\gamma_3 = 0.5$. The results are summarised in Figures 2.10, 2.11 and 2.12. The central bank achieves in arresting

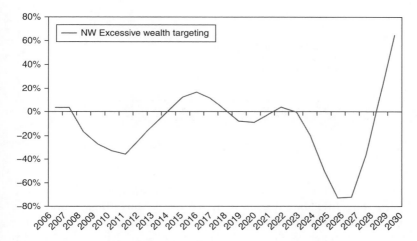

Figure 2.10   Net wealth with excessive wealth targeting

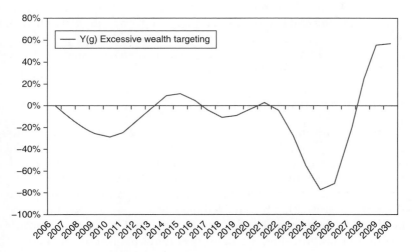

Figure 2.11   Output gap with excessive wealth targeting

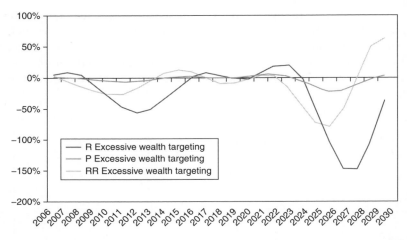

Figure 2.12   Interest rate, real profit rate and inflation with excessive wealth targeting

initially the fall in net wealth and the recession is milder than without wealth targeting, but deeper than with mild targeting. However, in time the swings in interest rates are too large and, given the lags in the effects of monetary policy and the fast response of demand and wealth to profitability, this volatility destabilises the economy. Hence, excessive wealth targeting leads to a prolonged recession and risk destabilising the economy. Therefore, a mild wealth targeting is preferable to both no wealth targeting and excessive wealth targeting. The simple rationale of this conclusion stems from the fact that in the real world profitability adjusts faster than interest rates and the economy responds faster to changes in profitability than to interest rates.

8   Summary and conclusions

Financial innovations, along with very accommodating monetary policy in the US and Japan in the last ten years or so, have combined to create huge liquidity in the US and the global economy. This liquidity has financed three consecutive major bubbles (internet, housing and commodities) and other minor ones, such as private equity and shipping. Securitisation has enabled the sale of complex securities, such as CDOs, to the personal sector and the financial institutions of other countries, thus providing the transmission mechanism of contagion of the US housing market to the global economy. The losses of banks have so far amounted to $700 billion and the crisis has cost the life of the most eminent financial institutions.

Central banks have not been able to detect and monitor this liquidity, which has taken place in a parallel banking system outside regulation and, therefore, not reflected in traditional monetary aggregates. The approach initiated by Alan Greenspan and adopted by other central banks is to deal with the consequences of the burst of the bubble and not with their causes. They have not attempted to prevent the ballooning of these bubbles. Every time a bubble has burst central banks have injected liquidity to avoid the systemic risk from threatening the financial system. Moreover, they have cut interest rates to deflect the asset and debt deflation that follows the burst of a bubble, thus making the temporary injection of liquidity permanent. These practices have maintained, if not fuelled, the excessive liquidity. The commodity bubble, however, promises to be the last one, as it feeds directly CPI-inflation, which central bankers are not willing to tolerate, although there is increasing resistance amongst politicians and financial markets alike for a delay of this tightening, as the major economies are in the middle of a slowdown that may develop into a deep and protracted recession. Evidence now suggests that even the commodity bubble has burst as the de-coupling theory, namely that the BRIC countries (Brazil, Russia, India and China) would be able to sustain their growth momentum even as growth in the western world wanes, which has given rise to the last phase of exaggeration in this bubble in the first half of 2008, has collapsed. Since the summer of 2008, the prevalent view is that growth in the BRIC countries would be adversely affected by the downturn in the US, Europe and Japan. Moreover, the very fast deleverage that is now taking place in the financial system suggests that the commodities bubble would be unable to recover.

To some extent these mistakes in the conduct of monetary policy are due to the wrong specification of the policy objective function and the underlying theoretical NCM model, which forms the intellectual basis as a constraint in the optimisation of economic policy. This chapter has argued that the policy objective function should be augmented to include mild, but not excessive, wealth targeting in addition to the traditional targets of inflation and the output gap. Such an addition will make sure that asset price booms do not grow to become bubbles, while it sidesteps the undesirable task of killing financial innovations and enforcing old regimes, such as forcing banks to be responsible for the portfolio of loans they originate, simply for the sake of avoiding bubbles. But, whereas mild wealth targeting may be beneficial to the central bank task of stabilising the economy, excessive wealth targeting is likely to prove harmful in terms of output loss and is also likely to lead to instability. This important conclusion stems from the fact that profitability responds faster than interest rates and the economy reacts faster to changes in profitability than to interest rates. In terms of policy two more conclusions can be drawn. First, in an asset-led business cycle reliance on inflation alone in guiding monetary policy is likely to prove inadequate in dealing with the problems of the burst of a bubble. This is due to the higher volatility of output than inflation in an asset-led cycle. Thus, reliance on inflation as well as on the output gap is more likely to prove more efficient in dealing with the consequences of the burst of the bubble. Second, in a leveraged economy, like the US, reliance on even the two traditional targets of inflation and the output gap is likely to prove problematic. The more leveraged the economy is, the longer the crisis and the higher the risk of instability.

According to the K-Model, US relative house prices, which have already fallen by more than 25 per cent since their peak in July 2006, are likely to fall by another 15 per cent by the end of 2009. Even nominal house prices, which have already fallen 17 per cent in the same time period, are likely to fall by another 12 per cent by the end of 2009. This fall in house prices, followed by further losses in financial wealth with the benchmark S&P 500 bottoming at around 700, will probably drag the US economy into recession through a weakness in consumption. Inflation will dissipate to 1.5 per cent in the next 12 months, while the Fed is likely to pursue a zero interest rate policy. However, the risks are on the downside as house prices are likely to overshoot their long-run equilibrium, thus triggering second-round effects in bank losses and the wealth of the personal sector. The precise forecast will depend on the final estimate of the bank losses, which are now estimated at $1 trillion.

Notes

1. We are grateful to the participants at the EFMA Annual Conference (Athens, June 2008), the 5th International Conference on Developments in Economic Theory and Policy, (Bilbao, July 2008) and the Conference on Housing Market Challenges in Europe and the US: Any Solutions Available? Central Bank of Austria (Vienna, September 2008) for helpful comments. The usual disclaimer applies.
2. SIVs stands for Structural Investment Vehicles. The unprecedented growth of the subprime market (loans to borrowers with poor credit history or with questionable ability to service their loans in adverse economic conditions) enabled banks to set up SIVs with a simple legal structure (trust or just a limited liability company) that required a very small capital base. This created the 'shadow banking', referred to in the text, working in parallel to banking

but outside the regulatory umbrella and sowed the seeds for the current credit crisis (see, for example, Arestis and Karakitsos, 2009).
3. Clearly fiscal policy is ineffective within the NCM analysis. It may have temporary short-run effects but none in the long run.

References

Arestis, P. (2007) 'What is the New Consensus in Macroeconomics?', in P. Arestis (ed.), *Is There a New Consensus in Macroeconomics?* Houndmills, Basingstoke: Palgrave Macmillan.

Arestis, P. (2009a) 'New Consensus Macroeconomics and Keynesian Critique', in E. Hein, T. Niechoj and E. Stockhammer (eds), *Macroeconomic Policies on Shaky Foundations: Wither Mainstream Macroeconomics?* Marburg, Germany: Metropolis-Verlag.

Arestis, P. (2009b) 'The New Consensus in Macroeconomics: A Critical Appraisal', in G. Fontana and M. Setterfield (eds), *Macroeconomic Theory and Macroeconomic Pedagogy* Houndmills, Basingstoke: Palgrave Macmillan.

Arestis, P. and Karakitsos, E. (2007) 'Unemployment and the Natural Interest Rate in a Neo-Wicksellian Model', in P. Arestis and J. McCombie (eds), *Unemployment: Past and Present*. Houndmills, Basingstoke: Palgrave Macmillan.

Arestis, P. and Karakitsos, E. (2009) 'Subprime Mortgage Market and Current Financial Crisis', in P. Arestis, P. Mooslechner and K. Wagner (eds), *Housing Market Challenges in Europe and the United States*. Basingstoke: Palgrave Macmillan.

Arestis, P. and Karakitsos, E. (2010) *The Post 'Great Recession' US Economy: Implications for Financial Markets and the Economy*. Houndmills, Basingstoke: Palgrave Macmillan.

Fontana, G. (2006) 'The "New Consensus" View of Monetary Policy: A New Wickselian Connection?', *Levy Economics Institute Working Paper No. 476*, New York: Levy Economics Institute of Bard College.

Goodhart, C.A.E. (2004) 'Review of *Interest and Prices* by M. Woodford', *Journal of Economics*, 82(2), 195–200.

Goodhart, C.A.E. (2007) 'Whatever Became of the Monetary Aggregates?', The Peston Lecture delivered in honour of Maurice, Lord Peston, Queen Mary, University of London, 28 February.

Goodhart, C.A.E. (2008) 'The Continuing Muddles of Monetary Theory: A Steadfast Refusal to Face Facts'. Paper presented to the 12th Conference 'Macroeconomic Policies on Shaky Foundations – Wither Mainstream Economics' of the Research Network, *Macroeconomics and Macroeconomic Policies* (RMM), 31 October–1 November, 2008.

Karakitsos, E. (2008) 'The "New Consensus Macroeconomics" in the Light of the Current Crisis", *Ekonomia*, 11(2), Winter.

Minsky, H.P. (1982) *Can 'It' Happen Again? Essays on Instability and Finance*. Armonk, NY: M.E. Sharpe.

Minsky, H.P. (1986) *Stabilizing an Unstable Economy*. New Haven, CT: Yale University Press.

Rottemberg, J.J. and Woodford, M. (1995) 'Dynamic General Equilibrium Models with Imperfectly Competitive Product Markets', in T.J. Cooley (ed.), *Frontiers of Business Cycle Research* Princeton, NJ: Princeton University Press, pp. 243–93.

Rottemberg, J.J. and Woodford, M. (1997) 'An Optimization-Based Econometric Framework for the Evaluation of Monetary Policy', *NBER Macroeconomics Annual 1997*. Cambridge, MA: National Bureau of Economic Research, pp. 297–346.

Weber, A.A., Wolfgang, L., and Worms, A. (2008) 'How Useful is the Concept of the Natural Real Rate of Interest for Monetary Policy?', *Cambridge Journal of Economics*, 32(1), 49–64.

Wicksell, K. (1898) *Geldzins und Güterpreise*, Verlag Gustav Fischer: Frankfurt. English translation in R.F. Kahn (1965), *Interest and Prices*. New York: Kelley.

Woodford, M. (2003) *Interest and Prices*. Princeton, NJ: Princeton University Press.

3
The Conventional Views of the Global Crisis: A Critical Assessment

Emiliano Brancaccio and Giuseppe Fontana

1 Introduction

Since the summer of 2007, the world has faced – and will continue to face at least for the next few years – what in retrospect is likely to be judged the most virulent global financial crisis ever recorded together with a recession, which seems comparable to the Great Depression of 1929 (Eichengreen and O'Rourke 2009). Among the conventional interpretations of the current crisis which can be found in the growing literature on the nature and cause of the crisis, much attention has been paid to the following two. First, it is argued that the crisis is due to the misguided under-pricing of risk: financial investors 'played with fire' by being over-confident about the ability of their mathematical models of measuring and managing risk. Secondly, it is argued that the cause of the crisis is the loose monetary policy of the early 2000s, what has also been labelled the 'Greenspan put': central banks – and in particular the Fed – came to the rescue of financial markets by lowering the short-run interest rate significantly and on a consistent basis. This chapter assesses the merits and drawbacks of these two conventional causes, looking at the peculiar type of relationship between these explanations and their theoretical frame of reference, namely the New Consensus Macroeconomics (NCM) model. The structure of the chapter is as follows. Section 2 presents a brief chronology of the financial crisis, with a particular focus on the key stages of the crisis. Section 3 reviews the main features of the modern securitization process, and it highlights the most problematic aspects of it. Then, Section 4 assesses the argument that an accommodative monetary policy in early 2000s has fuelled the housing and credit bubbles, which have led to the financial crisis and related recession. Section 5 provides a summary of the main arguments and then concludes.

2   A brief chronology of the financial crisis

There are several important dates marking key stages of the crisis. Originating primarily in the United States, the first sign of the crisis appeared with rising defaults in its subprime market, i.e. the market for borrowers with high default rates, excessive debt experience as well as a history of missed payments, or recorded bankruptcies (Temkin et al., 2002). In May 2007, the credit agency Moody's indicated that it was going to reduce the assessment of creditworthiness of 62 tranches of mortgage-backed securities (MBS), namely debt obligations representing a claim on the cash flows generated from mortgage loans. In June and July 2007 further tranches were downgraded. On 9 August 2007 the large French bank BNP Paribas temporarily halted redemptions on three of its funds because it could not reliably assess the value of the US subprime mortgage securitisations held by the funds. As a result, across the world a number of financial institutions started to reassess the value of the collateral accepted against their lending. Suddenly, trust and confidence in the system was shaken. Many institutions raised doubts about the evaluation of securitised assets and started to hoard large amounts of cash in order to cover potential losses in their portfolios. The market for securitisation came under stress and overnight there was a sharp increase in the level of interest rates.

Figure 3.1 shows the daily spread between the 3-month London Inter-Bank Offered Rate (LIBOR) and the 3-month expected Federal Funds rate between January 2007 and May 2008 (Cecchetti, 2009). The LIBOR is the benchmark rate for interbank lending, which is the basic rate used for determining other interest rates in the economy, including consumers and business loan rates. Normally, the difference between the LIBOR and the 3-month expected Federal funds rate, the so-called LIBOR spread, is less than 10 basis points. However, on 9 August the spread jumped to 40 basis points, and it then fluctuated between 25 and 106 basis points.

Within just a few weeks, the interbank lending market had dried up. Banks suddenly realised that they could not be certain of the value of their balance sheets, and that therefore they could not properly assess the risk attached to their lending. For the sake of avoiding any confusion, it may be worthwhile recalling one of the main propositions of the endogenous money theory (Fontana, 2009), namely that banks do not need monetary reserves in order to make loans. Banks first make loans and then look for reserves in order to preserve the smooth functioning of their economic activities. However, loans represent risky assets on the

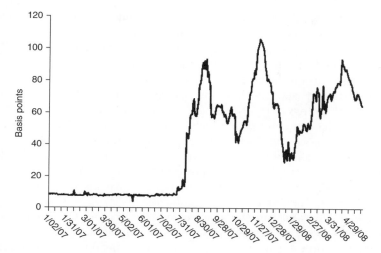

Figure 3.1 Spread between 3-month LIBOR and 3-month expected Federal funds rate, from January 2007 to May 2008, Daily
Source: Cecchetti, 2009.

balance sheets of banks. Therefore, when making loans banks assess their impact on the balance sheets. Starting in August 2007, banks realised that they could not assess the impact of further lending activities on their balance sheets. As a result they kept a tight rein on new lending. Many financial institutions began to experience severe liquidity problems.

Liquidity problems were amplified by the increasing reliance on the 'liquidity through marketability' approach, namely the practice of many financial firms to hold long-term maturity assets funded by short-term liabilities on the grounds that these assets could be easily and readily sold in markets when circumstances required. As explained in the Turner Review (2009, p. 21: see also House of Lords, 2009) 'this assumption was valid at the level of firms individually in non-crisis conditions, but became rapidly invalid in mid 2007, as many firms attempted simultaneous liquidation of positions'. One of the major casualties of this new situation was the failure of the British bank Northern Rock in September 2007. Interestingly, US total commercial bank credit extended rose by $575 billion in the last five months of 2007, before coming to a sharp decline in the first quarter of 2008 (Cecchetti, 2008; see, for a similar situation in the UK, Bank of England, 2008). This rise in commercial bank credit is consistent with the view that during the same period the interbank lending market dried up. The credit extension in the USA and the UK is in fact explained by the involuntary lending of banks: as financial institutions were unable to get liquidity from the market, as long as their contract allowed it, they relied for their liquidity needs on the credit lines with banks.

As the crisis progressed, rating agencies increasingly downgraded their credit ratings of securitised assets. On 30 January 2008 in one single report Standard and Poor's downgraded more than 8,000 securities. This steady process of downgrading credit ratings added further uncertainty to the value of the balance sheets of financial institutions. Banks responded by changing the composition and the size of their balance sheet, namely they replaced risky assets with safer assets, while at the same time contracting their balance sheets.

In part, this situation was exacerbated by the pro-cyclical nature of some aspects of the regulatory framework. In the face of the downgrading of the value of their assets and more generally of the liquidity problems described above, financial institutions tried to dispose of their assets in order to meet accounting rules and capital requirements. In order to do this, they were required to value assets according to mark-to-market principles. Unfortunately, these principles are inherently pro-cyclical. They push up profits and reserves when asset prices increase, but when prices decrease they imply significant writing down of assets, which leads to a vicious cycle. A financial institution makes 'fire sales' in order to maintain capital requirements. However, these sales further reduce asset prices and hence force other institutions to 'fire sales' in order to maintain capital requirements. This action in turn affects the mark-to-market value of the assets for the original institution, which then triggers further 'fire sales' and so on.

The liquidity problems in the financial sector worsened throughout the summer of 2008, and soon turned into solvency problems for major financial players. The housing market problems had intensified from the start of the year, and they were now recognised as widespread in US but also the UK, Spain, and other countries. On 7 September, the two publicly traded but government-chartered institutions Fannie Mae and Freddie Mac were taken into federal conservatorship. Fannie Mae and Freddie Mac held a large proportion of US mortgages. Their failure raised further concerns about the value of mortgage-backed securities, and the solvency of the institutions that were exposed to them. On 15 September Lehman Brothers went into administration after a late attempt by Timothy Geithner, the president of the Federal Reserve Bank of New York, to secure a future for the investment bank with Barclays and Bank of America. The day after, the stock price of AIG, a large international insurance company, fell by more than 90 per cent. Worried about the situation in relation to credit derivatives, the US Federal Reserve quickly organised a bailout of $85 billion in exchange for an 80 per cent equity stake. What the US Treasury and Federal Reserve officials failed to realise were the full effects of letting Lehman Brothers go into administration. In this respect, it is worth remembering that the deal with Barclays and Bank of America was unsuccessful because the US authorities refused to offer a government guarantee. The bankruptcy of Lehman Brothers led to a massive loss of confidence in the financial system: at a stroke it destroyed the market preconception that no large financial institution would be allowed to fail. The remaining financial institutions responded by attempting to diminish their exposure to each other. Therefore, in mid-2008 not only did the liquidity problems described above become worse, but solvency problems appeared, and soon they became widespread. At the same time, the crisis which started and developed in the financial market spread to the real economy, with dramatic consequences on the level of output and unemployment in many developed and developing countries. There are several mechanisms that explain the contagion to the real economy. First, in the face of growing liquidity problems and solvency risks many banks tried to replenish their capital by maintaining a liquid portfolio, and hence they refused or severely curtailed new lending. Secondly, with the collapse of the price of financial assets prices and of houses, households suffered negative wealth effects which constrained their demand of goods and services. Finally, in the face of an uncertain future, firms postponed their investment, preferring to use their cash flow for restoring more prudent debt to capital ratios. The overall effect of all of these contagion mechanisms was a general decrease in the level of aggregate demand with deleterious effects on the levels of output and employment. For instance, the unemployment rate in US rose from 4.7 per cent in the fourth quarter of 2007 to 9.2 per cent in the second quarter of 2009. Similar types of increases of the unemployment rate were recorded for the same period by many countries: UK moved from 5.1 per cent to 7.76 per cent, France from 7.54 per cent to 9.11 per cent, Spain from 8.61 per cent to 17.9 per cent, and Ireland from 4.64 per cent to 12.02 per cent (OECD, 2010). This led to huge interventions on the part of the monetary and fiscal authorities around the world in order to attempt to contain the effects of the financial crisis and related recession. The generalised weakness of aggregate demand continued throughout 2009 and into the first months of 2010.

3   The modern securitisation process

There is no doubt that at the heart of the evolution of the financial events described above there is the replacement of the 'originate and hold' banking model with the 'originate and distribute' banking model together with the securitisation process of structured finance products, which – in different shapes and forms – has interested the most advanced countries in the world either directly, as in the case of the US and the UK, or indirectly, as in the case of Germany. In the traditional 'originate and hold' model, the issuing bank will hold loans until they are repaid, whereas in the current 'originate and distribute' model the issuing bank sells loans to other banks and financial intermediaries, via the securitisation process. There are two major problems with this change. First, the incentive for the loan officer of the bank to collect information and properly assess the loan application of the borrower is diluted in the 'originate and distribute' model. Since the loan will not be on the books of the issuing bank for a very long time, the main concern of the officer is likely to be how many loans will be approved rather than whether or not the loan will be repaid. Secondly, as a result of the complexity of the modern securitisation process, even if information is collected it is not necessarily passed on to other banks and financial intermediaries. A description of the modern securitisation process may help to explain this second problem.

The process of the securitisation of finance products has been known and practised for several decades although only recently has it become an important source of funds for banks. In its modern form, it consists of two steps. First, a diversified portfolio is formed by pooling together corporate bonds, mortgages, loans (such as car loans or student loans) and any other type of credit-sensitive assets. Secondly, the newly formed diversified portfolio is sliced into different tranches, which are sold to investors with different risk appetites. Pooling and tranching are the two key features of the modern securitisation process of the so-called structured finance products, often referred to as collateralised debt obligations (CDO). When a package of credit-sensitive assets is securitised, they are transferred to a special subsidiary company of the originating bank, namely a Special Purpose Vehicle (SPV). In turn, the SPV uses these credit-sensitive assets to support the issuance of a prioritised capital structure of claims, namely bonds, with different levels of risk and maturities profiles attached to them. These bonds are known as tranches. The prioritisation scheme used in structuring claims is essential in making some of these manufactured bonds safer than the average asset in the newly formed diversified portfolio, with the so-called senior tranches absorbing the default losses of the portfolio only after the capital of the junior claims has been exhausted. The advantages of pooling and tranching in the securitisation process of structured finance products can be illustrated with some examples.

Let's assume that a bank has two identical securities which pay 0£ on default and 1£ otherwise, and both have a default probability (p_D) equal to 10 per cent. The bank then decides to pool these securities into the portfolio of an appositely created SPV. The nominal value of the portfolio will be equal to 2£. The SPV can then issue two tranches against this portfolio, namely a 'junior' tranche and a 'senior' tranche, the main difference being that the latter will bear losses only after the capital of the former has been exhausted. For instance, the tranches could be written such that the junior tranche will pay 0£ if either bonds default and 1£ otherwise, while the senior tranche will pay 1£ if no bonds default, or only one of the bonds defaults, and 0£ otherwise. Coval et al. (2009a, 2009b) explains that if the defaults of the two bonds are uncorrelated, in this case the senior tranche will only have a 1 per cent probability of default, against 19 per cent for the junior tranche. In other words, as a result of the pooling and tranching of the securitisation process described above, the senior tranche will pay either 1£ or 0£ as in the case of the original securities. Yet the senior tranche is much less likely to default than either of the underlying securities, namely 1 per cent against the original 10 per cent.

Importantly, by including more securities in the portfolio of the SPV, a greater component of the capital can be repackaged into tranches that are less likely to default than either of the underlying securities. For instance, let us assume that the portfolio of the appositely created SPV now contains three identical securities, which as in the previous case pay 0£ on default and 1£ otherwise, and all have a default probability (p_D) equal to 10 per cent. The tranches could be written now such that the junior tranche will pay 0£ if any of the three bonds default and 1£ otherwise, the 'mezzanine' tranche will pay 0£ if two or more bonds default and 1£ otherwise, while the senior tranche will pay 1£ if no bonds default, or only one or two out of three bonds defaults, and 0£ otherwise. In this case, assuming again that the defaults of the three bonds are uncorrelated, the senior and the mezzanine tranches will only have 0.1 per cent and 2.8 per cent probability of default, respectively. In other words, as a result of the securitisation process the senior and mezzanine tranches, which represent two-thirds of the capital of the portfolio, will pay either 1£ or 0£ like in the case of the original three securities. However, the senior and mezzanine tranches are much less likely to default than the underlying securities, namely 0.1 per cent and 2.8 per cent against the original 10 per cent. Furthermore, the securitisation process could be applied again to junior tranches achieving a further credit enhancement. For instance, in the case above of the two securities making the portfolio of the SPV, the probability of default for the junior tranche is 19 per cent. If the SPV pools together two 1£ junior tranches the resulting capital of this new portfolio is 2£. The tranches from this second round of the securitisation process, what are usually called CDO-squared, or CDO^2 for short, could now be written such that the resulting senior tranche will pay 0£ if at least one bond defaults in each of the two underlying portfolios, and 1£ otherwise. In this case, assuming again that the defaults of the bonds are uncorrelated, the senior tranches will only have 3.6 per cent probability of default against the original 19 per cent.

It should now be clear that the modern securitisation process is an extraordinary mechanism for the credit enhancement of credit-sensitive assets. But at the same time as the result of its inherent complexity, the credit information of these assets becomes increasingly opaque through the different stages of the securitisation process. As Buiter (2007, pp. 3–4) explains

> whatever information is collected by the loan originator about the collateral value of the underlying assets and the credit worthiness of the ultimate borrower, remains with the originator and is not effectively transmitted to the SPV, let alone to the subsequent buyers of the securities issued by the SPV that are backed by these assets. By the time a hedge fund owned by a French commercial bank sells ABSs (asset backed securities) backed by US sub-prime residential mortgages to a conduit owned by a small German Bank specialising in lending to small and medium-sized German firms, neither the buyer nor the seller of the ABS has any idea as to what is really backing the securities that are being traded.

There are two further significant problems with the modern securitisation process. First, the ratings of structured finance products are very sensitive to modest changes in the evaluation of the underlying default risks of the securities, and how likely these default risks are correlated. Secondly, structured finance products are inherently exposed to systematic risks. The first issue is related closely to the novelty of structured finance securities. Single-name securities, like corporate bonds, have been traded for several decades. This means that long and reliable historical data are available in order to assess these products. Furthermore, by its own nature the default rate of a single-name security depends on the misfortune of a specific firm. Therefore, the default risks of single-name securities are not correlated. By contrast, structured finance securities are not only new products, but they have also been introduced during a period of economic boom. As a result of these two features, there was very little historical data and, more importantly, the data were biased because of the strong economic growth and very low default rates, typical of an economic boom period. The combination of scarce and biased data should have called for a cautious approach from investors, rating agencies, and regulators. Unfortunately, this was not the case. In less than a decade, the issuance of structured finance products in the US grew more than tenfold, reaching $100 billion in each of the first two quarters of 2007. Investors, ratings agencies, and regulators equated structured finance products to single-name securities. By doing it, they not only under-priced the underlying default risks of the securities backing the structured finance products, but also ignored that these default risks were highly correlated.

The second issue is an inherent feature of modern securitisation, and it reinforces the problem described above. The process of pooling and tranching credit-sensitive assets in actual fact transforms idiosyncratic and largely diversifiable risks into systematic risks. Structured finance products are what Coval et al. (2010) appropriately call 'economic' catastrophe bonds. Catastrophe bonds, also known as cat bonds, are securities whose default likelihood is dependent upon the occurrence of natural disasters, such as earthquakes or hurricanes. They command a relatively high price, because their default risks are unrelated to the behaviour of any set of economic indicators, e.g. whether the economy is in boom or recession or the Fed rate is going up or down. Therefore, the default risks of cat bonds can be easily eliminated through diversification. Furthermore, given their own features, cat bonds are usually rated below investment grade, i.e. below the grade representing low to moderate levels of default risks (Derivative Fitch, 2006). Structured finance products are catastrophe bonds, in the sense that their default likelihood is unrelated to the idiosyncratic default risks of the underlying assets. However, the trigger event causing the loss of principal is not an earthquake or hurricane; rather, it is the state of the economy. This means that as the economy experiences a severe downturn, investors in structured finance products are increasingly likely to experience significant losses. As a result, structured finance products should be expected to earn a higher rate of return compared to single-name products, whose default likelihood is only affected by the misfortunes of a specific firm. Unfortunately this was not the case. Investors, rating agencies, and regulators equated structured finance products with single-name securities. Structured finance products were priced and rated like standard corporate bonds. In this way, not only did investors, rating agencies, and regulators under-price the underlying default risks of the structured finance products, but they also ignored that these default risks were all highly correlated to a downturn in the economy.

Finally, there is another important lesson to be learned from the modern securitisation process described above. The current financial crisis was a triple-A crisis, in the sense that it was triggered and sustained by the high default rates on triple-A-rated financial products, which represent the scale of products with the broadest usage and the highest profile within the international capital markets. From this perspective, as is increasingly recognised, rating agencies played a key role in creating the conditions for the collapse of the financial markets around the world. They were instrumental in lulling both investors and regulators into a false sense of security by rating many structured finance products triple-A. This in turn led to a large demand from global investors of structured finance products, which were often institutionally restricted in their purchase of securities to triple-A rated products. Rating agencies such as Moody's, Standard and Poor's and Fitch therefore bear considerable responsibility for the success of the securitisation process that has led to the financial crisis. As explained above, the triple-A rating of structured finance products created the illusion of comparability with single-name securities, i.e. liabilities of single companies or institutions. Figures 3.2(a) and 3.2(b) show the rating distributions of Fitch for single-name products and structured finance products in the summer of 2007, respectively.

Figures 3.2(a) and 3.2(b) show that just as the first signs of the financial crisis became evident, triple-A ratings represented only 1 per cent of Fitch ratings of corporate finance products in contrast to roughly 60 per cent of global structured finance products. It is likely that the same applied to the assessments of the other rating agencies, namely Moody's and Standard and Poor's. The main factor contributing to this surge in demand for structured finance products was the above-average yield on these securities, together with the false sense of security offered by the triple-A rating of the agencies. This false sense of security was enhanced further by the purchase of credit default swaps (CDS), namely credit derivative contracts insuring against the default of a particular bond or tranche: in return for the payment of a periodic fixed fee, the buyer of a CDS receives a payoff if the underlying financial instrument defaults. This meant that an

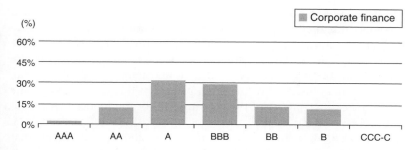

Figure 3.2(a) The global distribution of corporate finance issuer ratings at Fitch as at 30 June 2007
Source: Fitch ratings, 2007.

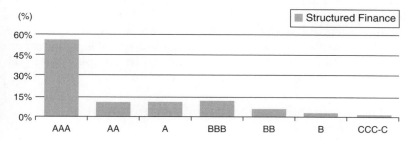

Figure 3.2(b) The global distribution of structured finance instruments ratings at Fitch as at 30 June 2007
Source: Fitch ratings, 2007.

investor holding a triple-A rated tranche of a CDO combined to a CDS could reasonably believe that the investment had a very low risk attached to it, and yet an above-average yield compared to single-name securities (Brunnermeier, 2009). The high demand for structured finance products led to a sharp rise in the demand of the underlying assets, namely mortgages, car loans and all sort of credit-sensitive assets. This led, in turn, to a huge reduction in the borrowing costs for households and firms, which fuelled the credit and house bubbles. In a vicious circle, the sharp increase in the price of houses and other assets gave further support to the creation of new structured finance products, which triggered again the same sequence of high demand of credit-sensitive assets, a reduction in the costs of borrowing, and increases in the price of houses and other assets. Importantly, the entire process could not have started and prospered without the triple-A rating of the agencies. In short, the success of the modern securitisation process, together with its deleterious effects, is in no small part due to the role of rating agencies which have helped to favour structured finance products over traditional corporate finance products. But were investors simply genuine victims of ignorance and the greedy behaviour of rating agencies? Interestingly, Alan Greenspan, the chairman of the Federal Reserve of the United States from 1987 to 2006, maintains that almost all of the main players in financial markets were in fact increasingly aware of the growing risks of the modern securitisation process and the related under-pricing of risk in financial markets. Greenspan (2010, p. 8; see also Brunnermeier, 2009, p. 82) argues that financial firms were aware of the existence of a credit bubble, but they were reluctant to bet against the bubble, because they feared that had they withdrawn too soon from the markets they would have surely lost their market share, and possibly irretrievably. Citigroup former chief executive officer Chuck Prince explained the situation by referring to Keynes's analogy between financial bubbles and the game of musical chairs (Nakamoto and Wighton, 2007): 'when the music stops, in terms of liquidity, things will be complicated. But as long as the music is playing, you've got to get up and dance. We're still dancing.'

4   The favourable macroeconomic environment of low interest rates

The modern securitisation process described above is an essential component for the explanation of the current financial crisis and related recession. Yet it is only part of the story. Financial market developments and innovations did not appear suddenly. They had actually started in the early 1970s as major features of the campaign for financial deregulation. These developments and innovations accelerated dramatically in the past two decades in parts as a result of a favourable culture which favoured market solutions to any form of government interventions. For instance, Greenspan (2010, Table 5) laments that one major factor explaining the surge in the demand for subprime securities was the substantial purchases by the major US Government Sponsored Enterprises (GSE), namely Fannie Mae and Freddie Mac, which responded to the pressure of US authorities to expand affordable housing by investing heavily in subprime mortgage securities: between 2002 and 2006 the purchases by Fannie Mae and Freddie Mac accounted for 25 per cent of all subprime securities outstanding. Greenspan maintains that tighter regulations and controls on mortgage lending would possibly have contained the evolution of the securitisation process described above. However, these regulations and controls would also have dampened down enthusiasm for homeownership from low- and moderate-income groups, and hence defeated the affordable housing goals of the US authorities, 'unless [Greenspan acknowledges] low and moderate income ownership were fully subsidized by government' (Greenspan, 2010, p. 44, note 72). In other words, according to Greenspan the securitisation process which led to the financial crisis is in no small part to the result of the affordable housing goals of the US authorities, and their determination to achieve those goals via market solutions rather than direct government interventions.

In addition to the securitisation process, in the opinion of most academics and practioners there is one major feature of the macroeconomic environment of the past few years that is the main culprit for the financial crisis and related recession, namely the accommodative monetary policy strategies followed by the monetary authorities of the US and most other advanced countries. Accommodative monetary policy strategies, facilitated by growing international macroeconomic imbalances, are blamed for having created the low interest rate environment that has fuelled the recent housing and credit bubbles. The following quote from Jacques de Larosière, the chairman of the high-level group on financial supervision in the EU, giving evidence to the Select Committee on Economic Affairs of the House of Lords in UK is typical of this view.

> The main fundamental cause of what happened was the piling up over 10 or 15 years of easy – too easy – monetary policies, very large current account imbalances in the United States in particular, matched by large structural surpluses in a number of emerging countries which pegged their currencies to the dollar more or less and therefore injected very large amounts of liquidity into the system. This easy money, easy credit condition propagated a search for higher yields than those that were offered by very low interest rates which were associated with this easy monetary policy; financial institutions' investors engaged in search of higher yields, therefore paying less attention to the quality of credits, accepting relatively low spreads for high risks, therefore undermining the fundamental prudence of the banking system. This was the basic set of circumstances that led to the present crisis. So it is an accumulation of international balances and what I would call loose monetary policies. (de Larosière, House of Lords Report, 2009, p. 100)

De Larosière refers explicitly to a long decade of accommodative monetary policies followed by many central banks around the world as one the main factors behind the recent financial crisis. He also mentions the modern features of the securitisation process described above and growing international macroeconomic imbalances. Since the latter factor is often presented as an additional mechanism of transmissions of the deleterious effects of monetary policies, the focus in the rest of this chapter is on the effects of the favourable macroeconomic environment created by low interest rates (see, for a discussion of the international macroeconomic imbalances, Obstfeld and Rogoff, 2009; Caballero, 2008, 2009, and Whelan, 2010).

The standard argument against the long decade of accommodative monetary policies usually proceeds as follows: when a crisis arose many central banks around the world came to the rescue of financial markets by significantly and consistently lowering the short-run nominal interest rate, which in turn affected a variety of interest rates in the economy, and by doing it, it fuelled housing and credit bubbles in many countries. This explanation also goes under the name of the 'Greenspan put', in recognition of the role played by Greenspan's Fed in setting the pace for accommodative interest rate policy decisions by many central banks around the world. Figure 3.3 gives support to the first part of the so-called Greenspan put. It shows the target nominal federal funds rate from August 2000 to August 2009: in response to the 2001 recession the Fed rate felt from 6.5 per cent in December 2000 to 1.75 per cent in December 2001 and then to 1 per cent in June 2003, the latter being the lowest rate since the 1950s.

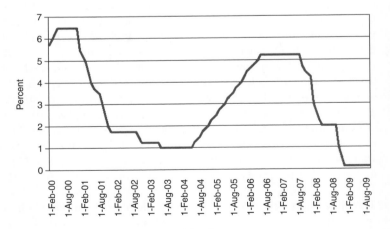

Figure 3.3   The target nominal federal funds rate
Source: Federal Reserve Board, USA.

Figure 3.4 supports the second part of the so-called Greenspan put. It presents the time series for the share of nominal residential investment in GDP: residential investment averaged 4.5 per cent of nominal gross domestic product over the period from 1974 to 2001; after 2002, the share rose substantially and reached 6.25 per cent of nominal GDP in late 2005. This represents the highest share in fifty years.

One of the most strenuous defenders of the causal link between accommodative monetary policies and the housing and credit bubble has been John Taylor. In a long succession of papers (e.g. 2007, 2008, 2009a, 2009b) and a recent book (2009c) he explains the argument in terms of the divergence between the actual Fed funds rate and the Taylor rule rate. According to Taylor during the period 2002–2005 the Fed maintained the target rate at too low a level, in the sense that a Taylor rule predicts a substantially higher target Fed funds rate in this period than actually occurred. Unsurprisingly, this argument has attracted the criticism of Greenspan.

> Mr. Taylor unequivocally claimed that had the Federal Reserve from 2003–2005 kept short-term interest rates at the levels implied by his 'Taylor rule,' 'it would have prevented this housing boom and bust.' This notion has been cited and repeated so often that it has taken on the aura of conventional wisdom. ... while I believe the 'Taylor rule' is a useful first approximation to the path of monetary policy,

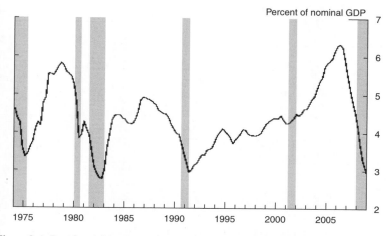

Figure 3.4 Residential investment as a share of nominal GDP
Source: Bureau of Economic Analysis, USA.

its parameters and predictions derive from model structures that have been consistently unable to anticipate the onset of recessions or financial crises. (Greenspan, 2009)

By keeping the target rate too low, the Fed indirectly contributed to the housing and credit bubbles, which then led to the financial crisis and the related recession. Figure 3.5 shows the target Fed funds rate and two policy rates which are calculated according to the following Taylor rule (Taylor, 1993):

$$i_t = i^* + \pi_t + \alpha \left(\pi_t - \pi^* \right) + \beta \left(Y_t - Y_t^* \right)$$ (Equation 1)

where i_t is the target Fed funds rate, i^* is the equilibrium real rate, which is assumed to be 2 per cent, π_t is the current inflation rate, π^* is the target inflation rate, which is again assumed to be 2 per cent, Y_t and Y_t^* are the current and potential level of output. The difference between current and target inflation rates, and the current and potential levels of output are usually called the inflation gap and the output gap,

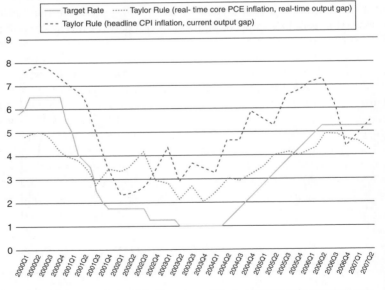

Figure 3.5   The target federal funds rate and Taylor (1993) rule interest rates
Source: Dokko et al., 2009.

respectively. Finally, α and β are the weight for the inflation gap and the output gap, respectively. They are assumed to be equal to 0.5.

Figure 3.5 shows the evolution of three short-term nominal interest rates in the US from the early 2000s. The solid line represents the actual target Fed funds rate, where the dashed line shows the Taylor rule rate when inflation is measured with the headline consumer price index (CPI), and the output gap is calculated with current data using the FRB/US model. Finally, the dotted line presents the Taylor rule rate when inflation is measured using real-time data on core personal consumption expenditures (PCE), which is the favourite Fed measure of inflation, and real-time estimates of the output gap from the FRB/US model. Both Taylor rule rates are calculated by assuming that the weights for the inflation gap and the output gap, namely α and β are equal to 0.5. Looking at the evolution of three short-term nominal interest rates from the early 2000s, it is immediately evident that a comparison between the solid line and the dashed line offers plenty of support to the argument that between 2002 and 2005 the monetary policy of the Fed was too accommodative: on average over this period the Fed rate is about 200 basis point below the Taylor rule rate calculated by using headline CPI inflation and current output gap. However, the same conclusions do not hold when the solid line is compared with the dotted line: from 2003 the latter is only marginally above the Fed rate. More generally, several authors have shown that the magnitude of the deviations of the Fed rate from simple policy rules like the Taylor rule hinges on the choice of the appropriate measures of inflation, output gap and the weights α and β assigned to such factors, as well as on the preference for real-time data or current data (see, for example, Kohn, 2007; Orphanides and Wieland, 2008, and Dokko et al., 2009). Once all of these factors are taken into account, there is little evidence that monetary policy in the US was too accommodative in the 2002–05 period. Furthermore, looking at longer historical periods, there is even less evidence that the magnitude of the deviations of the Fed rate from simple policy rules is higher in the 2000s than in previous decades: if any these deviations were highly significant in the pre-1987 period, but they have since become modest, especially for the controversial 2002–05 period.

Another way of assessing the argument linking accommodative monetary policy to the housing and credit bubbles is to consider the international evidence. Figure 3.6 shows the actual interest policy rates (policy rates for short) along with Taylor rule policy interest rates (policy rules for short) for several countries, including France, Germany, the UK, Switzerland, and the US. The Taylor rule policy interest rates

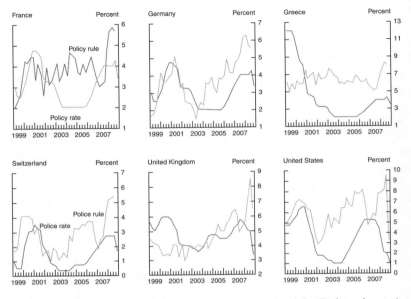

Figure 3.6   Comparison between the actual policy rate and the Taylor rule rate in France, Germany, Greece, Switzerland, United Kingdom and United States
Sources: IMF 2009; Dokko et al. 2009.

are computed by the International Monetary Fund (IMF) for the fall 2009 *World Economic Outlook* (WEO) according to equation (1) above. It is worthy to note that the inflation rates used in Figure 3.6 are the PCE index for US and the CPI for all remaining countries, while the target inflation rate is assumed to be 1.9 per cent, and the output gap is estimated using the Hodrick–Prescott filter.

Overall, the international evidence presented in Figure 3.6 does not seem to support the argument that between 2002 and 2005 the monetary policies followed by many central banks around the world were too accommodative. For instance, while France and Greece seem to experience a significant difference between the Taylor rule rate and the actual policy rate, this experience is not replicated in other countries. More interestingly, the United Kingdom had a housing bubble that was even bigger than the US, but for most of the period the Taylor rule policy rate is often below rather than above the actual interest rate. At the same time, a little like the case in the USA, Germany and especially Switzerland did record a positive divergence between the Taylor rule policy rate and the actual interest rate between 2002 and 2005. However, Germany and Switzerland did not experience any housing bubble.

In conclusion, there is little evidence that the monetary policies followed by many central banks around the world are the cause of the credit and housing bubbles which have led to the financial crisis and the related recession. Of course, whether or not monetary policies were too accommodative, it does not preclude that monetary policies could be questioned for not preventing or limiting the effects of the financial crisis. But this criticism calls into question the role of monetary policy in modern economies rather than if monetary policy followed or not a simple policy rule à la Taylor. In this case, there are different questions to be asked: What is the role of a central bank in modern economies? What is the transmission mechanism of monetary policy? Are low interest rates a problem, how and when? The answers to these questions have been provided by the so-called New Consensus Macroeconomics model (Arestis, 2007; Fontana, 2010). Therefore, if any, the critiques of central banks must be directed to the NCM model and the way in which according to the NCM the central bank is supposed to affect the working of modern economies.

As a matter of fact, as late as August 2008, Olivier Blanchard, the current chief economist of the International Monetary Fund, claimed that the state of macroeconomics was good. 'Macroeconomics is going through a period of great progress and excitement, and that there has been, over the past two decades, convergence in both vision and methodology' (Blanchard, 2008, p. 26). This was a view shared by many academics and practioners: the degree of consensus achieved in macroeconomics has been unprecedented since the 'Golden Age' of the 1950s and 1960s. It is no coincidence that this view was labelled the New 'Consensus' Macroeconomics (NCM). This view is usually represented with the help of a 3-equation model comprising an *IS*-type curve, a Phillips curve and a Taylor rule representing the conduct of the central bank. All three equations can be derived from explicit optimising behaviour of individual agents in the presence of market failures, including imperfect competition, incomplete markets, and asymmetric information. These market failures generate transitory price and wage stickiness, which play an important role in relating the monetary policy rule to the *IS*-type curve: as a result of these nominal rigidities, by changing the short-run nominal interest rate, the central bank is actually able to control the short-run real interest rate. In terms of the mechanics of the model, the central bank plays a key role in adjusting the aggregate demand to the aggregate supply. It affects the consumption component of aggregate demand, and hence the current level of output. This is an important theoretical result, because it goes well with another important tenet of the NCM model, namely that low and stable inflation is conducive to growth, stability and the efficient functioning of market. When the economy is hit by shocks, taking it away from its natural path, the central bank is responsible for achieving the desired rate of inflation in the long run, and, subject to that, also for bringing output and employment to their equilibrium levels in the short run. However, in pursuit of its objectives the central bank faces a short-run trade-off between inflation and output. This trade-off is captured by the Phillips curve, which can be thought of as the aggregate supply component of the NCM model. In summary, the NCM model maintains a rigid separation between the aggregate demand, which is indirectly controlled by the central bank via changes in the short-run nominal interest rate, and the aggregate supply side, which depends only on exogenous changes in labour, capital and technology. This is what has been labelled the principle of independence of aggregate demand and aggregate supply, the trademark of the neoclassical economic paradigm (Fontana, 2010). Putting it slightly differently, the NCM view subscribes to the neoclassical principle that money and monetary policy is neutral in the long run. This view still provides the shared benchmark for the current work of a great majority of academics and practioners. Despite all dramatic events of the financial crisis and related recession very little work has been done to challenge the long-run neutrality of monetary policy (for a critique of the neoclassical foundations of the NCM model, and an alternative interpretation of the role of central bank, see Brancaccio (2009) and Brancaccio and Fontana (2010)).

5 Summary and conclusions

Economies around the world are still suffering from what in retrospect is likely to be judged the most virulent global financial crisis ever recorded together with a recession, which is second only to the Great Depression of 1929: the unemployment rate in US has risen from 4.7 per cent in the fourth quarter of 2007 to 9.2 per cent in the second quarter of 2009. Over the same period there have been similar increases in the unemployment rate in many other countries: the UK has moved from 5.1 per cent to 7.76 per cent, France from 7.54 per cent to 9.11 per cent, Spain from 8.61 per cent to 17.9 per cent, and Ireland from 4.64 per cent to 12.02 per cent (OECD, 2010). Huge interventions on the part of the world's monetary and fiscal authorities have been undertaken in order to contain the most deleterious effects of the financial crisis and the related recession. This generalised weakness of aggregate demand has continued throughout 2009, and it is unlikely to disappear soon.

The main purpose of this chapter has been to assess the conventional view that there are two main causes of the current crisis, namely the modern securitisation process and the accommodative monetary policy of the early 2000s. Certainly, there are several problems with the modern securitisation process. The incentive for the loan officer of a bank to collect information and properly assess the loan application of the borrower is diluted in the 'originate and distribute' model that has now replaced the traditional 'originate and hold' model. Furthermore, even if the information is collected, there is very little chance that will be passed on to other banks and financial intermediaries due to the sheer complexity and opacity of the modern securitisation process. This is not to deny that securitisation is an extraordinary mechanism for the credit enhancement of credit-sensitive assets. However, its future now hangs in the balance. There are two critical issues that are in urgent need of a solution before another wave of triple-A rated products is allowed to flood modern economies. First, the ratings of structured finance products are very sensitive to relatively modest changes in the evaluation of the underlying default risks of the securities, and these default risks are likely to be heavily correlated. Secondly, structured finance products are inherently exposed to systematic risks. Certainly, there are also many problems with the accommodative monetary policy of the early 2000s. It is true that as a result of the 2001 recession many countries around the world had slashed their policy rates to very low levels. For instance, in June 2003 the Fed rate felt to 1 per cent – that is, the lowest rate since the 1950s. However, overall there is little evidence that the monetary policies in the early 2000s are the cause of the credit and house bubbles, which have then led to the financial crisis and related recession. In different ways Germany, and especially Switzerland, did experience a favourable macroeconomic environment of low interest rates. Yet they never experienced a housing bubble. By contrast, the United Kingdom had an even bigger housing bubble than the US, but the Bank of England has never been criticised for maintaining a policy rate too low and too long. As for the US, looking at the historical evidence, changes in the Fed rate were highly significant in the pre-1987 period, but they have since become modest, especially for the controversial 2002–05 period. Of course, whether or not monetary policies were too loose, this does not exclude that monetary policies could be questioned for not preventing the financial crisis. But this criticism calls into question the role of monetary policy in modern economies rather than if monetary policy were too accommodative or not. Overall, the chapter draws two main lessons from the financial crisis. First, financial innovations and developments did not appear suddenly. They had actually begun in the early 1970s as major features of the campaign for financial deregulation. These developments and innovations have accelerated dramatically in the past two decades in part as a result of a culture which favoured market solutions over any form of government intervention. The events of the last few years cannot but call into question this extreme form of pro-market thinking. Secondly, any critique of the role of the central bank in creating the favourable macroeconomic environment of low interest rates, which has allegedly led to the housing and credit bubbles, and hence to the financial crisis in the USA and then across the world, must be directed to the NCM model and the way in which, according to the NCM view, the central bank is supposed to affect the working of modern economies.

References

Arestis, P. (2007) 'What is the New Consensus in Macroeconomics?', in P. Arestis (Ed.) *Is There a New Consensus in Macroeconomics?* London: Palgrave Macmillan, pp. 22–42.

Bank of England (2008) 'Markets and Operations', *Quarterly Bulletin*, 28(1), 6–24.

Blanchard, O.J. (2008) *The State of Macro*, NBER Working Paper, no. 14259, August.

Brancaccio E. (2009) 'The Central Banker as Regulator of Distributive Conflict', in G. Fontana and M. Setterfield (eds), *Macroeconomic Theory and Macroeconomic Pedagogy*. London: Macmillan.

Brancaccio, E. and Fontana, G. (2010) 'A Critique of the Interpretations of the Crisis Based on the Taylor Rule'. Paper presented at the international conference 'The Global Crisis: Contributions to the Critique of Economic Theory and Policy', University of Siena (Italy), 26 January.

Brunnermeier, Markus K. (2009) 'Deciphering the Liquidity and Credit Crunch 2007–2008', *Journal of Economic Perspectives*, 23(1), 77–100.

Buiter, Willem H. (2007) 'Lessons from the 2007 Financial Crisis'; paper submitted in evidence to the UK Treasury Select Committee on Tuesday, 13 November 2007; published as *CEPR Policy Insight No. 18*, December 2007.

Caballero, R.J., Fahri, E. and Gourinchas, P.O. (2008) *Financial Crash, Commodity Prices, and Global Imbalances,* http://socrates.berkeley.edu/~pog/academic/bpea_08.pdf.

Caballero, R.J. (2009) 'Discussion of "Global Imbalances and the Financial Crisis: Products of Common Causes, by M. Obstfeld and K. Rogoff"', Massachusetts Institute of Technology.

Cecchetti, S.G. (2008) 'Monetary Policy and the Financial Crisis of 2007–2008', Centre for Economic Policy Research (CEPR), *Policy Insight*, No. 21, April.

Cecchetti, S. G. (2009) 'Crisis and Responses: The Federal Reserve in the Early Stages of the Financial Crisis', *Journal of Economic Perspectives*, 23(1), 51–75.

Coval, J., Jurek, J. and Stafford, E. (2009a) 'The Economics of Structured Finance', *Journal of Economic Perspectives*, 23(1), 3–25.

Coval, J.D., Jurek J., and Stafford, E. (2009b) 'Economic Catastrophe Bonds', *American Economic Review*, 99(3), 628–66.

De Larosière, J. (2009), Chairman of the EU High Level Group on Financial Supervision, Q352 in House of Lords.

Derivative Fitch (2006) 'Global Criteria for Collateralized Debt Obligations'. London; Fitch Ratings.

Dokko, J., Doyle, B., Kiley, M.T., Kim, J., Sherlund, S., Sim, J. and Van den Heuvel, S. (2009) *Monetary Policy and the Housing Bubble*, Finance and Economics Discussion Series, Federal Reserve Board, Washington, DC.

Eichengreen, B. and O'Rourke K.H. (2009) 'A Tale of Two Depressions', April. Available from: www.voxeu.org. Accessed 4 May 2009.

Fitch Ratings (2007) 'Inside the Ratings: What Credit Ratings Mean', http://bankwatchratings.com/descargas/ratings.pdf.

Fontana, G. (2009) *Money, Uncertainty and Time*. London: Routledge.

Fontana, G. (2010) 'The Return of Keynesian Economics: A Contribution in the Spirit of John Cornwall's Work', *Review of Political Economy*, forthcoming.

Fontana, G. and Palacio-Vera, A. (2007) 'Are Long-run Price Stability and Short-run Output Stabilization All That Monetary Policy Can Aim For?', *Metroeconomica*, 58(2), 269–98.

Greenspan, A. (2009) 'The Fed Didn't Cause the Housing Bubble: Any New Regulations should Help Direct Savings Toward Productive Investments', *Wall Street Journal*, 11 March.

Greenspan, A. (2010) 'The Crisis', mMimeo, March.

House of Lords (2009) *Banking Supervision and Regulation*, Select Committee on Economic Affairs, 2nd Report of Session 2008–09, Volumes I and II: Report, Evidence, London: The Stationery Office Limited, June.

International Monetary Fund (2008) *World Economic Outlook: Financial Stress, Downturns, and Recoveries*. Washington, DC: IMF.

International Monetary Fund (2009) *World Economic Outlook*, Fall. Washington, DC: IMF.

Keynes, J.M. (1936) *The General Theory of Employment, Interest and Money*. London: Macmillan.

Kohn, D.L. (2007) 'John Taylor Rules', speech delivered at the Conference on John Taylor's Contributions to Monetary Theory and Policy, Federal Reserve Bank of Dallas, Dallas, TX, 12 October, www.federalreserve.gov/newsevents/speech/kohn20071012a.

Nakamoto, M. and Wighton, D. (2007) 'Citigroup Chief Stays Bullish on Buyouts', *Financial Times*, 9 July. http://www.ft.com/cms/s/0/80e2987a-2e50-11dc-821c-0000779fd2ac.html.

Obstfeld, M. and Rogoff, K.S. (2009) 'Global Imbalances and the Financial Crisis: Products of Common Causes', paper prepared for the Federal Reserve Bank of San Francisco Asia Policy Conference, Santa Barbara, CA, 18–20 October, http://elsa.berkeley.edu/~obstfeld/santabarbara.pdf.October.

OECD (2010) *Economic Outlook, No 86: Annual and Quarterly Data*, Database accessed on 03/05/10, http://stats.oecd.org/.

Orphanides, A. and Wieland, V. (2008) 'Economic Projections and Rules of Thumb for Monetary Policy', Federal Reserve Bank of St. Louis Review, July/August, 90, 307–24.

Taylor, J.B. (1993) 'Discretion versus Policy Rules in Practice', Carnegie-Rochester Conference Series on Public Policy, December, 39, 195–214.

Taylor, J.B. (2007) 'Housing and Monetary Policy', NBER Working Paper Series 13682, Cambridge, MA: National Bureau of Economic Research, December, www.nber.org/papers/w13682.pdf.

Taylor, J.B. (2008) 'The Financial Crisis and the Policy Responses: An Empirical Analysis of What Went Wrong', speech delivered at a Festschrift in Honour of David Dodge's Contributions on Canadian Public Policy at the Bank of Canada, November, www.bankofcanada.ca/en/conference/2008/taylor.pdf.

Taylor, J.B. (2009a) 'The Financial Crisis and the Policy Responses: An Empirical Analysis of What Went Wrong', NBER Working Paper Series 14631. Cambridge, MA: National Bureau of Economic Research, January. www.nber.org/papers/w14631.

Taylor, J.B. (2009b) 'How Government Created the Financial Crisis', *Wall Street Journal*, 9 February.

Taylor, J.B. (2009c) *Getting Off Track: How Government Actions and Interventions Caused, Prolonged, and Worsened the Financial Crisis*. Stanford, CA: Hoover Institution Press.

Temkin, K., Johnson, J.E.H. and Levy, D. (2002) *Subprime Markets, the Role of GSEs, and Risk-based Pricing*, US Department of Housing and Urban Development, Office of Policy Development and Research.

Turner Review Report (2009) *A Regulatory Response to the Global Crisis*, March. London: Financial Services Authority.

Whelan, K. (2010) *Global Imbalances and the Financial Crisis*, Directorate General for Internal Policies, European Parliament, March.

4
The Global Crisis and the Governance of Power in Finance

Gary A. Dymski

1 Introduction

This chapter argues that resolving the nearly global crisis of financial systems – and, by extension, of macroeconomic stagnation – depends on recognising and responding to the considerable, multidimensional power accumulated by the very financial firms whose dysfunctionality helped create that crisis in the first place. The power of finance, and especially that of the mega-institutions at the heart of the modern financial system, has grown steadily in the past 45 years. Much of the celebrated innovation of these institutions has involved capturing more operational leverage by accessing more liquidity. In the end, the success of these strategies, via competitive global deregulation and the creation of new methods of risk-shifting and risk-taking, ended by compromising global liquidity just when it was most needed.

The economic and financial crisis that has arisen nearly worldwide in the 2007–10 period has posed such a profound challenge for policymakers precisely because it is rooted in the systemic failure of this brave new world of intermediation. Initiating concrete steps toward re-imagining and re-creating a socially efficient and economically productive financial sector requires, first of all, acknowledging the current financial system's inordinate, multidimensional power. The links between this accretion of power and the excessive risk-taking and increased financial exploitation that triggered the crisis must be better understood. This will permit a re-engineering of the financial system that eliminates the destructive tendencies linked to the accumulation of power in finance.

Undertaking this reshaping will not be easy. The existing rhetoric of financial regulation among academic experts and policy insiders evaluates the 'efficiency' and 'stability' of the financial system in narrow terms, and focuses attention on problems of mechanism design. It is blind to the presence and implications of systemic power in this system. But unless the debate over financial regulation is broadened, decades of sub-par growth and excessive financial exploitation lie ahead.

Section 2 describes why this crisis has intensified policy debate and brought about the end of polite discourse in economics. Section 3 summarises received views on financial regulation, which interpret power in finance as stabilising and an indication of competitive fitness. Section 4 explores why the current crisis necessitates a reframing of debate about the governance – not simply the regulation – of finance.[1] Section 5 lists some critical elements for understanding real-world financial systems, including power. Section 6 discusses how the locus of power in finance has shifted with the rise of the 'originate and distribute' model in the 2000s. Section 7 examines the implications of the subprime crisis for the governance of power in finance; and, finally, section 8 contains some ideas on restoring effective financial regulation.

2   The end of polite discourse in economics

Many, if not most, economists prefer debates which are clearly bounded, so that discussion is invariably polite. In particular, this means respecting the authority of those with pre-existing claims to expertise in given subject-matter areas. But the current crisis has engendered a deep discontent with status quo thinking in economics. Prior to this crisis, different theoretical schools developed their own explanations for core questions about the economy: Why do banks exist? Is regulation needed? Does active fiscal policy raise welfare? Each school developed its own answers; the more influential and well-funded the school of thought, the more settled the views.

So while differences of view about core economic questions have persisted over time, in the past three decades, most economists called to positions of economic-policy leadership have portrayed their own views as reflective of a sensible consensus. This suggested that economists' views vary within a narrow band, from slightly-critical-of-unregulated-markets to suspicious-of-government-regulation. Regarding financial regulation, economists have routinely celebrated the importance of free markets and of reducing burdensome regulation. The financial-system flaws most frequently mentioned were the moral-hazard traps that arise due to bad regulatory design, about which pro-market and pro-mild-regulation could readily agree. An example here is the 'consensus view' orchestrated among macroeconomists about whether they subscribed to the new Keynesian or new Classical schools of thought. Maintaining this consensus required that debate be polite: limited to empirical questions and to queries about equilibrium models with pre-agreed analytical features. Economists were certainly free to challenge the premises of this new-Classical/new-Keynesian consensus in favour of alternative ideas derived from overlooked thinkers such as Minsky and Keynes. But to challenge basic premises was disagree impolitely; and such challenges could only be freely exercised outside the inner circles of policy influence.

Nonetheless, as structural cracks and tensions began to emerge in the economy, several leading academics and policy veterans expressed their unease. Geanakoplos (1996, 2009), drawing on his Wall Street experience, began writing papers about 'broken promises' (1996) and 'leverage cycles' (2009) in financial markets – topics which had gone virtually unmentioned since the efficient market hypothesis became a super-orthodoxy in the 1970s.[2] In April 2005, Paul Volcker wrote an op-ed piece in the *Washington Post*, 'Economy on Thin Ice', which foresaw the demise of Wall Street.

Then, after innumerable crises in the global South, a mega-crisis hit the global North. And the truce among economists proved fragile. Suddenly the rules of discourse wavered. The consensus that certain things were not to be spoken of was abandoned. Some economists continued to work from 'first principles', urging caution in response to the crisis. Others set aside theoretical niceties and jumped toward pragmatic responses based on looking hard at the numbers.

The US Treasury's huge bailout proposal in the heart of a national election season added to the drama, and the gloves came off. Stiglitz (2008) wrote an article in *Forbes* entitled 'Capitalist Fools'; Krugman (2009) publicly disparaged the failure of macroeconomics, and was savaged in a weblog by Cochrane (2009). Barbera (2010) responded to Cochrane (2009) in kind, in an article entitled 'If There Were a Fight, They Would Have Stopped It in November 2008'.

This shift from polite to impolite exchanges that challenge established experts has been repeated in other substantive areas. The next two sections discuss and then challenge the expert consensus regarding financial governance, which has overlooked the problematic of megabanks' power.

3 The consensus view of financial regulation: power hiding in plain sight

Expert and academic views on financial regulation have co-evolved over the last 30 years. Banking deregulation was already on the table when the Reagan Administration came to power. Soon, close regulation by examiners was replaced by deregulation with the self-monitoring of risks (Dymski 1999). However, by 1982, amidst skyrocketing interest rates and an oil-price collapse, the US savings-and-loan system and commercial banks in 'oil patch' states systematically defaulted. Savings-and-loans' undue risk-taking after deregulation, including investments in speculative real-estate ventures, and the failure to account for recourse risk, added to the magnitude of system failure.[3]

The question then was implicitly posed – was the 1980s crisis of the US financial system due to inadequate prudential supervision or to ill-advised incentive mechanisms within banking firms? A set of self-appointed experts termed the 'Shadow Financial Regulatory Committee' (Benston et al. 1986) dominated discussion about the causes of these depository-institution crises and what to do about them. This 'Committee' attributed the thrift crisis to moral hazard in lending (Kane 1989; Kaufman and Benston 1990)): deposit insurance removes depositors' incentives to discipline intermediaries whose managers or boards take undue risks. The prescription was continued deregulation, including more limited bank regulation; but the key was to get incentives right so that the financial system could be self-policing.[4] Government intervention would only lead to mismanagement. As Kaufman put it:

> The major source of the instability in the U.S. banking system in the 1980s … was not the private sector but the public or government sector. The government first created many of the underlying causes of the problem by forcing S&Ls to assume excessive interest rate risk exposure and preventing both S&Ls and banks from minimising their credit risk exposure through optimal product and geographic diversification and then delayed in applying solutions to the problem by granting for-bearance to economically insolvent or near-insolvent institutions. That is, the banking debacle was primarily an example of government failure rather than market failure. (Kaufman, 1995, p. 259)

The perspective of the Committee has two intellectual underpinnings. One, noted above, is the efficient-markets approach in financial economics; the second is the public-choice approach to public economics. Some members of this committee (especially Benston, Kane, and Kaufman) see regulators not as neutral purveyors of well-intentioned policies, but as advocates for their own interests. Thus, empowering regulators while reducing the scope for market forces can lead to dysfunctional outcomes (such as the savings and loan crisis itself) and huge inefficiencies. At the same time, financial market forces are viewed through a pragmatic Chicago School lens more than through an efficient-markets hypothesis lens. Committee members would not agree with the conclusion of Fama (1980), based on strict efficient-markets logic, that banks have no effect on resource allocation. But while admitting that markets may misbehave and generate rents for firms capturing monopolistic power, their core belief is that market forces should be given maximum sway and government intrusion minimised. Benston (2000) asks the question that motivates much Shadow Committee research and policy discussion: 'is government regulation of banks necessary?' The author answers in the negative. In his view, only deposit insurance, which leads banks to hold insufficient capital, constitutes a valid rationale for bank regulation. 'Otherwise, banks should be regulated only as are other corporations' (Benston, 2000 p. 185).

For the Shadow Committee, then, the financial industry is threatened by an aggressive and bullying government. One would never imagine that this besieged industry spends millions annually to win friends and influence people in Congress and the Administration. This manifestation of power is not discussed, though Committee members do worry about government regulators are influenced by the prospect of 'golden parachutes'. The Committee's focus is on getting government policy right, and this means maximum scope for market forces: leave owners free to control their firms, and firms freer to enter markets.

This experts' panel continues to function to this day; it is currently sponsored by the American Enterprise Institute. Its members have founded a new academic journal, the *Journal of Financial Services Research*, helping to shape a generation of research. More than half its members have been members of this Committee from its foundation; several have served in appointed governmental positions. The Committee has met several times in 2010 and sponsored press conferences on proposed taxes on big banks, SEC regulation of equity markets, and so on.

Leaving aside the Shadow Committee itself, the literature on bank structure and regulation has centred in recent years on the relationship between concentration and competition in banking. Berger et al. (2004), in their summary of this research, argue for tolerance regarding monopoly power in banking, for several reasons. First, older structural tests for market power are prone to estimation error, especially selection bias. Second, they argue that markets can be both competitive and concentrated. The presence of a monopoly or oligopoly in itself does not imply that rents are being unfairly taken from customers, in these authors' view; markets are competitive as long as they are contestable; Third, more concentrated banking markets can be more stable and less crisis-prone. Here again, financial power is hiding in plain sight.[5]

In the past decade, studies exploring the links between market structures, stability/crisis, and regulation have used three quite separate methodologies. One involves building formal banking models. Repullo (2004) shows that when banks must compete for funds, they will earn fewer revenues per loan, and hence be more likely to make loans to risky customers. In this event, capital requirements can be effective; conversely, when banks face less competition for funds, they will choose safer loans, and capital requirements will be either unneeded or impose deadweight losses. In a similar result, Boyd, De Nicolo and Smith (2004) find the probability of a costly bank crisis is higher under competition than under monopoly.

The second approach involves intensive empirical studies of individual markets. Some recent studies using this approach have come to less comforting conclusions regarding the treatment of bank customers in concentrated markets. Carow et al. (2006) show that borrowers have lost out in bank megamergers. Further, Hale and Santos (2009) examine bank loan data for borrower firms that eventually floated IPOs (initial public offerings). They find that banks do charge higher loan rates for firms that have not gone public; as the authors put it, banks do 'price in' their informational monopoly on firm creditworthiness as long as they maintain it.

Such 'traditional' empirical studies have been joined by a new empirical approach established during the Asian financial crisis. Hoping to better understand the determinants of financial crises, the IMF and the World Bank developed extensive databases on financial crises, macroeconomic conditions, and banking structure and regulation in a large sample of nations, over a wide swathe of historical time. This made it possible to utilise econometric methods to assess the macroeconomic, microeconomic (structural), and regulatory conditions that accompanied or preceded (and thus may have caused) financial crises. So in the same panel, 1981 Mexican GDP growth might be evaluated as a determinant of the 1982 Mexican debt crisis, while 1996 Korean GDP growth would be evaluated vis-à-vis the 1997 Korean meltdown (and so on). Demirgüc-Kunt and Detragiache (1998) conclude that financial liberalisation increases the probability of banking crisis.

It soon became clear that data structures drawing on global experiences over broad time periods could be used to consider other questions, including the links between regulation and banks' market structure and behaviour. In consequence, the large-scale dataset approach is now widely used in the broader literature on bank market structure and regulation. This approach assumes that developing and developed nations are part of one finance–development continuum, and that the experience of any one country (Latvia) should be given equal weight with any other (the United Kingdom).

This approach, while it often leads to complex results, has yielded a coherent set of policy implications. Demirgüc-Kunt and Levine (2004) conclude – based on 150 countries' experience with financial crisis, financial structure, and development – that maintaining outside investors' legal rights and efficient contract enforcement will insure effective financial-sector development. Beck et al. (2004) argue, using this database, that financial-sector development reduces poverty. Barth et al. (2004) used a 107-country study to show that direct government regulation of banking markets is not effective, and leads often to fragility. Financial development and stability is better fostered by empowering and properly incentivising private-sector corporate control of banks. Beck et al. (2006) use data from 69 countries from 1980 to 1997 to show – after controlling for regulatory and macroeconomic policies, and nation-specific shocks – that systematic banking crises are less likely in countries with more concentrated banking systems. Further, regulatory policies that thwart competition are associated with greater bank fragility. A new study of 250 banks in 48 countries by Laeven and Levine (2009) shows that bank risk-taking increases as bank shareholders' power rises in corporate governance.

Taken together, these multi-country, multi-year studies suggest that permitting bank concentration to increase by easing regulations, permitting freer entry into banking markets, and relying on private-market guidance will lead to continuous, stable financial-system development – and thus contribute per the expectations of the finance–development literature to higher rates of economic growth. But insofar as market concentration embodies the accumulation of power in financial markets, this means that the price of stability in financial markets is megabanks' acquisition of market power therein. And potential entry should discipline megabanks and limit their abuse of customers. Power is there, but it is principally a marker of some financial firms' competitive success; and those firms' incentives are for a 'quiet life' in financial markets that are well organised and tranquil.

The peculiarity of this empirical approach is that it does not evaluate the lessons learned in more advanced financial systems for less-developed systems; it establishes a meta-outcome that encompasses simultaneously the experience of the most humble and the most advanced markets. Giving sway to market forces and restricting government intervention into financial systems will not create the panacea envisioned in the efficient-financial-markets hypothesis; indeed, the consolidation that has gradually occurred will hurt some borrowers – as is shown by a study co-authored by a Shadow Committee member (Kane). But insofar as this approach assures a stable and competitive system of finance, such losses count only as collateral damage.

This builds in the presumption that systemic behaviour consists simply in an aggregation of individual markets, and that all markets are created equal for purposes of empirical testing. There is also thus one-dimensionalising of banking – a reduction of banking and financial behaviour to a 'lowest-common-denominator' activity. The distinction that the Congressional investigation of Goldman Sachs' role in the subprime crisis has raised, between megabanks' 'fiduciary responsibility' to their depositors and their autonomous role as 'market makers' operating on their own behalf (Guerrera 2010), does not arise. For what is common in the Turkish and Bangladeshi and US banking systems is the lender–bank–depositor relation, the 'fiduciary' role. Only at the centre of financial power can one find the outsized 'market maker' role – a role replete with remarkable power to make and break entire markets – that Goldman Sachs and other megabanks took on in the 'originate and distribute' model of credit creation. But any investigation of *that* role cannot be undertaken with an empirical tool designed to explain what financial crises around the world all have in common.

4 Moving from settled theory to a rethinking of the critical elements of finance

The agenda championed by the Shadow Committee held sway in the 1990s, opening the way for the deregulated 2000s. Deposit insurance was not eliminated, but restrictions on banking and financial activity were. The notion of self-policing finance was embedded in the proposed shift for global banking guidance, from Basle I to Basle II. Since the mid-1980s, Basle I had imposed uniform asset-based capital requirements on large multinational banks. Under the proposed Basle II rules, ratio tests would be replaced by a requirement that all large banks run their own stress tests about whether their individual mixtures of derivatives and futures-market commitments, would survive various worst-case scenarios.

Even while Basle II was being fine-tuned, the shift to a more deregulated regime continued. Indeed, in the 2000s, megabanks were able to create large volumes of collateralised debt obligations in part because they were not counted in calculating required capital. The Financial Services Modernization (Gramm–Leach–Bliley) Act of 1999 also served to blur the lines between commercial and investment banking, and between various lines of financial business. Subprime-loan and securitisation volumes exploded as secondary-market outlets for credit expanded. Most subprime loans were made by non-bank lenders, sold to megabanks, and then bundled into securities, many of which were insured through credit default swaps (CDS). The CDS itself was invented so that its primary issuer, AIG, could avoid the regulatory oversight that would arise were these underwriting arrangements classified as insurance contracts.

Prudential oversight was clearly lacking in this asset-price build-up and crash – in some sense, by design. The 1999 Act encouraged institutional innovation and line-blurring; Basle II put prudential responsibility in the hands of the megabanks themselves; and megabanks' increasing use of non-bank lenders and funds boosted their earnings. Most megabanks created structured investment vehicles (SIVs), consisting of bundled loans financed by asset-backed commercial paper. They both sold SIVs to generate fees and held them off-balance sheet to boost their revenue flows. That these funds could be regarded as independent of their issuing banks' balance sheets – as having been made without recourse – shows how completely the lessons of the 1980s thrift crisis had been forgotten.

The step-by-step offloading of default risk onto entities outside of the regulatory scope of the banking authorities came back to haunt US regulators in the subprime crisis; so too did the 1999 elimination of the line between commercial banking and other financial activities. In the Long Term Capital Management (LTCM) crisis of 1999, the Federal Reserve was able to call on Wall Street megabanks – especially the then-investment banks – to help restore order. These megabanks had been recruited – strong-armed – into providing the liquidity that permitted LTCM to unwind its oversold position. This was not possible in the subprime crisis since many of these same megabanks were now themselves overexposed in the subprime market (and consequently undercapitalised).

So what was missing? Why did the Shadow Commission's belief – reinforced by both theoretical models and empirical results – that deregulated financial firms would be more stable and more efficient than rigidly controlled markets go so badly wrong? In essence, the mistake the Commission and the research cited here made was to assume that the financial system, once liberated, would behave as financial theory (and specifically, efficient-market theory) expected it to behave. The competition-versus-concentration debate relies on efficient financial-market theory very heavily, if in a veiled way. It is assumed that banking and finance consists of a set of well-defined activities – in particular, the provision of credit (or of insurance) for a set of economic agents that requires this credit to conduct their normal economic activities. Permitting entry by new suppliers and the creation of new instruments adapted to borrowers' unique risk characteristics should simply enhance efficiency. Market power may exist, but it has no affectivity.

So economists could rely on their settled views about what banking is, what the motives of bankers are, and the benefits of competition to understand how regulatory policy should adjust. The reference point of economic equilibrium provided a benchmark for understanding what distortions may have arisen. In academic settings, such distortions could be neatly parsed and discussed one at a time.

But this approach – born of nearly 30 years of heavily influencing both debate about the regulatory agenda and the trajectory of applied research – went badly wrong. The 'one-size-fits-all' approach to evaluating banking-system behaviour which developed amidst the Asian crisis desensitised researchers to the remarkable shift in the size-ordering and scale of the most gigantic financial firms.

Figure 4.1 illustrates this shift by depicting the asset size of the 25 largest bank holding companies (BHCs) in a variety of years, ranging from December 1997 to June 2008. That is, the 25 largest BHCs are shown for each year; the population of banks shifts from year to year because of mergers, failures, etc. This graph shows that from the eighth position downward, bank size has remained remarkably constant. But from one to seven, it's clear that a 'super-sizing' has occurred. Figure 4.2 demonstrates another dimension of difference between large and small banks: small banks' derivatives positions have atrophied to nearly nothing; by contrast, large banks' positions in these instruments have exploded in size. Note that large banks have been approaching derivatives positions of 2000 per cent; small banks, 2 per cent.

As Bookstaber (2007) and Sorkin (2009) demonstrated in very different ways, this difference in the scale of some financial firms implied explosive growth in these firms' activities: in the position-taking that linked these activities, in the derivatives positions that hedged or bet on these activities, in the challenge of understanding (much less controlling) their exposures to risk, and ultimately in the challenge of defining whether their interest lay more fundamentally in serving or in exploiting their customers.

Unsurprisingly, then, when the dizzyingly complex firms at the top of Wall Street's pyramid began to fail in 2007, followed by many of the

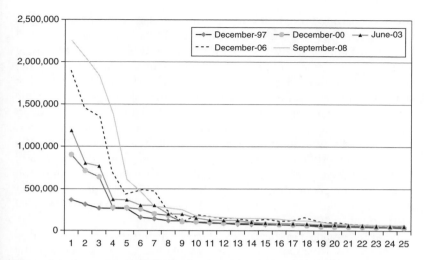

Figure 4.1 Asset size of 25 largest bank holding companies, December 1997 to September 2008 (Figures in US$1,000)
Source: Federal Financial Institutions Examination Council, various quarters.

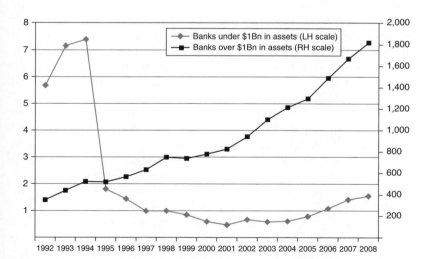

Figure 4.2 Derivatives as percentage of assets, 1992–2008: Banks over and under $1 billion in assets

smaller firms and funds enmeshed in (or created by) these firms' octopus arms, settled theory seemed inadequate to the task. The size and speed of system failure perceived by Treasury and Fed policy insiders, along with the size and speed of the TARP bailout they orchestrated, left the academic literature on how banks fail far behind. The weak results of that bailout have resulted in a sustained reform effort, about which the finance-and-development literature's simple linear distinction between the absence and presence of adequate financial intermediation has nothing to say. Should over-the-counter trading be reined in? Should a 'Volcker rule' forbid 'banks' from trading on their own account? Should banks fund their own bailout fund? Not only have these issues not been researched; no economist imagined that the debate about such reforms would occur only after $700 billion had been channeled to financial institutions, half to the largest megabanks.

What has emerged in this crisis is an entire architecture of financial dysfunctionalities, which range from the exploitation of the vulnerable to the extraction of rents from the unwary to the ability of well-positioned players to pass risks off onto other parties – ultimately, onto the public. There are so many moral-hazard and adverse-selection dimensions to this crisis that economists prepared to analyze second-best Nash equilibria can easily identify one or another incomplete-market problem whose malfunctioning can readily be seen. What is not so easy is to identify the ways in which the dysfunctionalities and second-best equilibria interact – the broader architecture of system failure. The problem is that fixing any one malady without paying attention to this architecture ensures that the process of flying blind will continue. For example, TBTF ('too-big-to-fail') is certainly one flawed dimension of the US financial system. But 'ending' TBTF on the assumption that market forces can handle the fallout from the crash of any financial institution – from the smallest to the biggest – makes assumptions about the resilience, stability, and scale of the requisite money, bond, derivatives, and equity markets that must be evaluated. The structured complexity of the financial system includes not just spot, futures, and state-contingent transactions markets, but also multiple layers of spatial interaction (global (cross-border) markets, regional/common-zone markets, national markets, and local markets). There are agents playing the markets in each 'location', and authorities at each nexus.

Economists, confronted with this situation, have a choice. They can regard this crisis of finance as continuous with those preceding it, and continue to rely on insights and empirical results derived from settled approaches – that is, they can rely on the sort of theoretical and empirical results set out in section 2 to inform their reactions to the current situation. Alternatively, they can see this crisis as requiring that theoretical understandings and policy responses based on the analytics of imagined equilibrium states be set aside or, at the very least, supplemented. The latter seems the only coherent path. The Shadow Committee has painted itself into a corner. The market-equilibrium view that constitutes its foundation has been knocked asunder, as has the notion that private ownership is a sufficiently strong interest to look after the long-term welfare of large financial firms. Indeed, the very definition of the term 'competitive financial market' is unclear, after it was systematically weakened in defence of megafirms' right to take larger shares in ever more markets.

Challenging the implicitly efficient-market view of most settled research on financial regulation and structure risks a plunge into an intellectual abyss: for what can replace the efficient-markets view? At this stage of events, there is no new imagined ideal system that can serve as an alternate system-design reference point. The idea instead is to confront the real-world system of finance as it is, to understand its real-world impacts on diverse firms and individuals, and to examine how to turn it to socially efficient and economically productive purposes.

5   Core elements of finance for re-establishing coherent governance

Four analytical elements that are missing in efficient-market-based thinking about financial governance are readily identified.[6] The first is system complexity and structural interaction. A second dimension, invariably overlooked in analyses that focus on mechanism design and breakdown, is power. It's clear that some players in this matrix of financial interactions have the ability to force action by others, or to extract rents from others, or to rely on the inability of system logics to find alternative outcomes. In this case, power has payoffs. Again, power operates in different ways and at different levels of the financial system. The way in which the exercise of power has created systemic dysfunctionalities, distorted incentives, and affected crisis-resolution pathways deserves careful study.

The very complexity of interactions – the structural displacement of the borrower–lender–depositor relationship from the centre of the financial circuit to its periphery – means that information and its control or absence becomes a key feature of the crisis scenario. Information problems here involve more than the problem of asymmetric information within pair-wise transactions in the credit market: the inability of one party in this transaction to know the true 'state' of the other party's condition. Instead, information problems involve opacity, secrecy and private arrangements, privileged technical information (that often runs ahead of regulators' oversight capability), and so on. Indeed, the very lack of opacity in the emerging set of securitised financial relations was interpreted by some as equivalent to the creation of a new type of banking (see Dymski 2010). But opacity defeats oversight. In the current efforts at financial reform, the debate over whether derivatives should be exchange-traded involves, in part, the issue of whether a set of regulators or overseers (the 'exchange') will have real-time information on open derivatives positions and evolving terms and conditions in markets.

A final core element of the real-world financial system consists of the beliefs, confidence, and credibility – that is, what Akerlof and Shiller (2009) term the 'animal spirits' – of the agents interacting in financial markets. These authors argue that market outcomes are systematically affected by the fact that the agents interacting in markets often misinterpret information, have distorted perceptions, or even react emotionally rather than rationally. So these elements matter, as gaps can readily emerge between what system architects and players intend others to understand and do, and how those others actually see things and react. These problems can be interpreted as arising in one of two ways: they could be rooted in perceptual errors linked to psychological processes (as Tversky and Kahnemann 1981 see it); or they could represent reactions to fundamental uncertainty about the true state of the world (as Minsky, 1986 sees it).

Only an analytical approach that takes into account, then, system complexity and structural interaction, power, problems of information, and the problems created by agents' reactions to uncertainty, can comprehend how the financial system is structured, and how it has broken down and malfunctioned.

We leave as an open question whether a subset of these four elements, or only all four together, can suffice for a coherent post-efficient-markets understanding. Two recent volumes have largely focused on the fourth element – the fragility of agents' beliefs and confidence. Akerlof and Shiller (2009) make this the centrepiece of their defence of the role of government in the economy: they argue that central banks' power resides in their ability to stabilise 'animal spirits' in financial markets, thus occasionally – and crucially – stabilising market forces that would otherwise sometimes cascade out of control. They argue that the current crisis requires stronger intervention – direct credit injections, as per TARP. Reinhart and Rogoff (2009) are more circumspect; they straddle the choice posited in section 4. They argue that the present crisis is continuous with previous crises. However, they omit any reference to efficient financial-market theory, and affirm – without elaboration – the 'concept of financial fragility in economies with massive indebtedness' (p. 292). They largely concur with Akerlof and Shiller that breakdowns in beliefs and confidence are at the root of the crisis. But they do not mention, as Akerlof and Shiller do,[7] that this already places them at some distance from equilibrium theorising.

6   The nature of power in finance

We elaborate in the remainder of this chapter on the second of the four elements identified above, one that is often overlooked in discussions of financial regulation: the problem of power in finance. As seen above, power is invisibly present in analyses of banking concentration, its possible impact frequently discounted. But how does power enter into systems of finance? Is it limited to market concentration, without taking other forms?

The literature reviewed in section 3 presumes that the answer to the second question is 'yes'; and because financial markets are assumed to be contestable, power is not important in financial dynamics. Here we attempt to differentiate the loci and forms of power that arise in finance, and develop a wider view of how power can affect financial processes and outcomes.[8]

One locus of power occurs in some relations within a time-using economic process, such as a borrower–creditor contract. Another locus of power is transactional, involving only the moment of exchange. A third locus of power is structural. It arises when the outcomes of agents' interactions, whether transactional or time-using, are forced or predetermined by a set of determining parameters.

There are, in turn, several forms of power. Hirschman (1970) suggested one: exit-power. This arises when one agent in a relationship (a credit contract, for example) can leave it without damaging one's net revenue streams, but the other agent in the relationship will indeed suffer an expected loss from such a break. A second form of power arises when one agent in a transaction has private knowledge relevant to the terms and conditions of that transaction, but the other agent does not. A third form of power arises when one agent in a relationship is more – or more powerfully – networked or interconnected with external partners or activities that are economically valuable. In this event, the less powerful agent cannot dissolve his/her relationship with the more networked agent without suffering from reduced access, directly or indirectly, to other valued contacts. Finally, there is asymmetric resilience, which arises when one agent in a relationship has a greater ability to suffer losses or to renew resources. This agent can then 'outlast' the other in any war of attrition.

The loci and forms of power interact. In a time-using locus, positional power can arise, as one agent can bargain harder (extract more rent) than the other, knowing the latter has no exit option. In a purely transactional frame, arbitrage power can arise, due to the fact that one agent is interconnected with a network that has the capacity to exploit a price differential, while another, less-networked agent lacks that capacity. Further, the forms of power can often offset one another. For example, in a subprime loan contract, the borrower may have informational power vis-à-vis her own creditworthiness; but the lender may have exit-power in that the borrower is socially isolated and can identify no other lender options.

In received versions of financial theory, power is seldom, if ever discussed directly. The power problematic that is discussed involves the borrower–lender relation. Typically, it is hypothesised that both lender and borrower may have exit options, but the borrower implicitly has positional power because of an informational advantage. This advantage may arise due either to borrower intentions (moral hazard) or capacity (adverse selection). Moral hazard may also arise when a bank is willing to take more risks than its depositors would be comfortable with, but deposit insurance has made those depositors risk-indifferent. Much, if not most, discussions of regulatory reform – say, by the Shadow Committee – centre on the need to structure regulations so that owners' interests in maximising the value of their banking firm (its asset price) – and not governmental decrees or imperatives – can guide financial institution to efficient credit and resource allocation. These discussions have led to policy change. Activity deregulation for banks and thrifts in the 1980s and 1990s, for example, should have provided financial firms' owners with the means to discipline their banking firms' activities by subjecting them to competition (the highest-return activities grow most).

But deregulation did not lead to this outcome. One reason is that large banks' links to the borrower–lender relationship underwent a complete transformation. Once this happened, efforts to reduce the adverse impact of moral hazard within the borrower–lender relation per se were superseded and displaced to other loci that were outside the purview of bank regulators. In particular, the rise of the 'originate and distribute' lending model repositioned the megabanks that bundled and sold collateralised debt obligations vis-à-vis the borrower–lender relation. These megabanks were no longer in the position of 'lender'; instead, they were in the position of facilitating the activity of loan networks in which they were not positioned as the ultimate lender to borrowers approved for credit.

Two forms of network-based power arose in this new lending model. One involved positional power within the networks that recruited and then ultimately funded (or denied) borrowers. This positional power occurred at two choke points. One involved the link between the loan brokers, finance-company workers, and loan officers who proposed loan packages to prospective borrowers. Insofar as these borrowers were savvy and well capitalised, they could obtain fair loan offers. But borrowers who lacked capital, and/or were from populations or areas that had been historically denied access to fair-market credit, could be offered exploitative terms and conditions. A second choke point arose because megabanks controlled access to secondary markets for the lenders and loan brokers that offered them loans. This was underlined by megabanks' informational advantages about underwriters' and loan distributors' risk-tolerance levels.

In turn, megabanks' power within the lending network also facilitated two types of transactions-based arbitrage power. First, they could share in the rents that lenders extracted from borrowers by charging high fees for providing securitisation, underwriting, and/or servicing for these loans. Second, they could exploit interest-rate differences in different locales at the same point in time, so as to earn arbitrage-based income. In effect, the creation of structured investment vehicles permitted the exercise of network power involving access to investors and insurers, access to liquidity, and trading capacity. In effect, this arbitrage power resulted from megabanks' positional power within the lending network. Note that this is also a way of characterising the carry trade.

Of course, Goldman Sachs and other investment banks came up with arbitrage- and positional-power strategies for revenue-making that were far more complex than this baseline scenario. Suffice it to say that the impact of the 'originate and distribute' model was, among other things, to create new potential sources of power for megabanks with access to distribution networks and other required networks. This power could generate substantial revenues when asymmetries of information or exit-options were there to be exploited. And it should not be forgotten that at the heart of the subprime lending boom was the systematic financial exploitation of socially excluded individuals and communities (California Reinvestment Coalition, 2010; Dymski, 2010).

7   The governance of power in finance after the subprime crisis: some considerations

Stiglitz (2010) defines the factors that govern regulation in any set of markets: market failure, market irrationality, and distributive justice. The position of the Shadow Committee vis-à-vis reform of financial regulation is that these considerations are largely irrelevant in resolving the crisis of housing finance and banking. The Shadow Committee has been participating in the 2010 Congressional debates on the possible reform of financial regulation; it weighed in against the imposition of further regulatory constraints or fees on financial institutions, especially megabanks.[9] Individual members of the Shadow Committee have gone further and argued that excessive governmental regulations and intrusions into financial markets were the root cause of the subprime crisis (Dymski, 2010).

This view is rejected here, based on an evaluation of the relevance of each of the criteria cited by Stiglitz. The absence of adequate controls over non-bank lending and over the securitisation of credit, for example, clearly permitted a virus-like transmission of market irrationality, resulting both in the housing bubble and in the huge stock of zero-down-payment and negative-cash-flow mortgage loans. Further, distributive justice would have been furthered had the Community Reinvestment Act been used to stem the flow of exploitative subprime loans.[10]

But the criterion that deserves special attention in the wake of the subprime crisis is the first cited by Stiglitz – market failure. Market failure arises, of course, when all the benefits of a good are not captured in a private-market transaction, or when some of the costs of a good's production are not borne by the parties to the transaction. Elinor Ostrom (1990) won the 2009 Nobel Prize in Economics for pointing out that 'tragedy of the commons' situations, wherein agents overuse an unpriced asset until it is depleted, can be overcome through appropriate governance.

Arguably, one of the problems that gave rise to the subprime crisis was the failure of the system of financial governance to adequately regulate the exercise of power in finance, and to prevent a 'tragedy of the commons' abuse of a key public-good resource in the financial sector. The resource in question is liquidity – access to ready, short-term funding at a dependable price in the financial market. The 'originate and distribute' model operates by offloading securitised debt from banks' balance sheets – where this debt is at least partially financed by depositors – to the open financial market, where it is financed by short-term borrowing. As noted above, the asset-backed commercial paper market was a dominant source of finance for securitised mortgage debt (until that market crashed in September 2007).

In principle, if the same volume of loans were financed by depositors in one financial system and by short-term commercial paper in another, there might be little to choose between the two. But the accrual of arbitrage power by megabanks in the network of markets that supported the 'originate and distribute' model – and, in particular, the lack of recourse on the part of borrowers and lenders who wanted access to that model – led to a situation in which all the incentives were to increase fee-based income by generating ever more credit through this mechanism. A housing bubble arose as ever more people were lured into accepting potentially ruinous mortgage loans so as to buy homes. And debt-to-income ratios rose precipitously throughout the economy, as the network servicing the securitisation machine accommodated the inclusion of ever more types of household and business debt. Accompanying the growth of these out-of-control spot-market transactions, of course, was an even greater explosion of off-balance sheet derivatives activities (see Figure 4.2), which further increased the drain on available liquidity. Needless to say, the hyper-leverage of the megabanks – especially the large investment banks and hedge funds – necessitated these firms' excessive reliance on available liquidity.[11]

In effect, the brave new system of finance displaced and multiplied moral hazard problems, while decentring credit creation in a way that put this multiplying moral hazard outside the reach of established – bank-centred – channels of financial regulation. Firms participating in 'originate and distribute' networks engaged in arbitrage-based activities that offloaded substantial amounts of risk. Risk-tolerant megabanks staked out positions in this new system by drawing so heavily on markets with 'commons' characteristics as to abuse their limits. And all this was insured by insurers – notably AIG – that made insurance 'bets' based on the assumption that there was a stable distribution of risk in these evolving and ever-more stressed markets. In effect, the 'originate and distribute' model gave rise to a cascade of interlinked, hierarchically distributed principal–agent problems which largely escaped regulatory notice, much less control. Excessive leverage and greed by the megabanks at the heart of the new credit network eventually eroded the resilience of the liquid markets on which they depended, even while stripping away the tolerance for risk and willingness to 'go long' and 'believe in the borrower' that make credit markets work.

These dynamics pushed people on both sides of the borrower–lender relation, in ways quite different from those anticipated in the simple theory of financial intermediation that is relied upon by most policy analysts and empirical work in this area. The end result is a deterioration of the willingness and ability of the financial system to provide any real functionality to the real economy, even while its activities and its revenues consume ever more of national income.

8   Restoring effective regulation

As was seen in the discussion in section 2, regulators have not regarded either the governance of power in finance or the protection of the public-good character of liquidity as within their areas of responsibility. The language of financial regulation has been formulated very close to the idealised model of efficient financial markets, without taking into consideration the characteristics of the real-world model of finance that came into maturity in the early 2000s and then crashed in the late 2000s. This must now change. The term 'concentration' can no longer stand in for 'power'; and the governance of power in finance has to become an explicit objective of financial regulation. If the megabanks are not forced by Act of Congress to shrink to a manageable size, then the links between individual megabanks' network power and the actual networks that lie at the heart of financial markets will be too tight to unwind. In this event, 'too big to fail' is a reality. The Shadow Committee's unconvincing distinction between concentration and competition in banking markets serves only to illustrate how little stomach its members have for policies that would indeed insure that no banks are too big to fail.

The only thing that will insure a socially efficient and economically productive financial system is dedicated regulation that takes full consideration of the power asymmetries, the 'commons' dimensions of financial markets, and social justice criteria. This is a huge challenge, in particular because the USA's privileged position in the neoliberal order – its steady surplus on capital account combined with the dollar's privileged status as a reserve currency – has dissuaded regulators from insisting on too much prudential behaviour on the part of the banks they were charged with overseeing.[12] The neoliberal era has given rise to many structural imbalances, which, in turn, have been exploited by firms with arbitrage power. Given that structural imbalances cannot be wished away, the arbitrage activity that feeds on these imbalances must be reduced.[13] A further possible complication is that regulatory actions aimed at reining in financial institutions' risk-taking will in many cases have implications for the overall pace of macroeconomic activity, insofar as these actions may slow or quicken the pace of loan-making. But it is one thing to have a dysfunctional financial system, and quite another to have a substitute system ready to do better what was not done well before. This does not mean laying down arms before the executive officers of megabanks who see it as their right to operate as 'principals' on their own behalf, while accepting public subsidies and guarantees reserved for 'intermediaries' operating on behalf of their depositors. It will, however, require a reframing of the terms and conditions of financial regulation. It is high time to displace the efficient-markets ideal as a guide to what it is about the financial system that must be controlled or overseen; it is time to recognise the deep implications of unchecked power in finance, and to restore the terms and conditions of public governance so as to renew the economic functionality and social efficiency of the system of finance. An energetic debate about how to govern finance has been initiated, and must continue. This cannot be a polite conversation: it must be real.

Notes

1. The term 'financial governance' often refers to shareholders' guidance of financial firms. Here this term refers to the public governance of financial institutions and markets.
2. Fox (2009) describes how the efficient-markets hypothesis came to dominate research on financial markets.
3. Recourse risk arises when a lender sells a loan (or other asset) it has made or bought to a third party to whom a minimum rate of return has been promised. If the asset underperforms, the third-party holding it has recourse to the lender to be made whole on its contract. See Wall (1991).
4. Similarly, analyses of the Latin American debt crisis attributed non-payment to inadequate debtor 'effort', that is, to moral hazard factors – not to 'type'. See, for example, Eaton, Gersovitz and Stiglitz (1986).
5. In the 1980s, the latter view won out over the former in the Federal Reserve and other regulatory agencies (Dymski 1999).
6. These four themes have many intellectual forebears in classical political economy, New and post Keynesian economics, and neo-Marxian and post-Walrasian approaches; space constraints preclude a discussion of these lineages here.
7. See footnote 6 to the 'Introduction'.
8. This analysis is indebted to the pioneering work of Greider (2010) and Epstein (1992) on the role of power in finance.
9. One example among many is Shadow Financial Regulatory Committee (2010).

10. Dymski (2010) summarises studies that counter the notion that the Community Reinvestment Act was among the causes of the subprime crisis.
11. To recognise limits to liquidity is not an assertion that liquidity has an absolute bound. Like Minsky (1986), we can consider liquidity as variable, subject to the beliefs and fears throughout the financial system.
12. This argument is made in Dymski (2009).
13. Consider the carry trade. The very presence of an uneven global map of economic crisis – some countries whose low interest rates reflect a desperation for stimulus, and other countries whose crises have forced them to restrict credit and raise rates – encourages the symbiotic growth of arbitrageurs who feed on both sides of this macroeconomic misery.

References

Akerlof, G. and Shiller, R.J. (2009) *Animal Spirits*. Princeton, NJ: Princeton University Press.

Barth, J.R., Caprio Jr., G. and Levine, R. (2004) 'Bank Regulation and Supervision: What Works Best?', *Journal of Financial Intermediation*, 13(2), 205–48.

Beck, T., Demirgüc-Kunt, A. and Levine, R. (2004) 'Finance, Inequality and Poverty: Cross-Country Evidence', *World Bank Policy Research Working Paper 3338*. Washington, DC: The World Bank, June.

Beck, T, A., Demirgüc-Kunt, A. and Levine, R. (2006) 'Bank Concentration, Competition, and Crises: First Results," *Journal of Banking and Finance* 30(5), 1581–603.

Behr, P., Schmidt, R.H. and Xie, R. (2010) 'Market Structure, Capital Regulation and Bank Risk Taking', *Journal of Financial Services Research*, 37(2), 131–58.

Benston, G.J. (2000) 'Is Government Regulation of Banks Necessary?', *Journal of Financial Services Research*, 18(2/3), 185–202.

Benston, G.J., Eisenbeis, R.A., Horvitz, P.M., Kane, E.J. and Kaufman, G.G. (1986) *Perspectives on Safe and Sound Banking: Past, Present, and Future*. Boston, MA: MIT Press.

Berger, A.N., Demirgüc-Kunt, A., Levine, R. and Haubrich, J.G. (2004) 'Bank Concentration and Competition: An Evolution in the Making', *Journal of Money, Credit, and Banking*, 36(3), Part 2, 433–52.

Bookstaber, Richard (2007) *A Demon of Our Own Design: Markets, Hedge Funds, and the Perils of Financial Innovation*. Hoboken, NJ: John Wiley and Sons.

Boyd, J.H., De Nicolo, G. and Smith, B.D. (2004) 'Crises in Competitive Versus Monopolistic Banking Systems', *Journal of Money, Credit, and Banking*, 36(3), Part 2, 487–507.

California Reinvestment Committee (2010) *From Foreclosure to Re-Redlining: How America's Largest Banks Devastated California Communities*. San Francisco: California Reinvestment Coaliation, February. Downloaded at http://calreinvest.org/system/assets/214.pdf.

Carow, K.A., Kane, E.J. and Narayanan, R.P. (2006) 'How Have Borrowers Fared in Banking Megamergers?', *Journal of Money, Credit, and Banking*, 38(3), 821–37.

Cochrane, J.H. (2009) 'How did Paul Krugman get it so Wrong?', mimeo, University of Chicago, 16 September. Web-published at http://faculty.chicagobooth.edu/john.cochrane/research/Papers/#news.

Demirgüç-Kunt, A. and Detragiache, E. (1998) *Financial Liberalization and Financial Fragility*, IMF Working Paper 98/83, Research Department, June. Washington, DC: International Monetary Fund.

Demirgüç-Kunt, A. and Levine, R. (eds) (2004) *Financial Structure and Economic Growth: A Cross-Country Comparison of Banks, Markets, and Development.* Cambridge, MA: MIT Press.

Dymski, G.A. (1999) *The Bank Merger Wave.* Armonk, NY: M.E. Sharpe, Inc.

Dymski, G.A. (2009) 'Financial Risk and Governance in the Neoliberal Era', in G.L. Clark, A.D. Dixon and A.H.B. Monk (eds), *Managing Financial Risks: From Global to Local.* Oxford: Oxford University Press, pp. 48–68.

Dymski, G.A. (2010) 'From Financial Exploitation to Global Instability: Two Overlooked Roots of the Subprime Crisis', in M. Konings (ed.), *Beyond the Subprime Headlines: Critical Perspectives on the Financial Crisis.* London: Verso Press.

Eaton, J., Gersowitz, M. and Stiglitz, J. (1986) 'The Pure Theory of Country Risk', *European Economic Review*, 30(3), 481–515.

Epstein, G. (1992) 'Political Economy and Comparative Central Banking', *Review of Radical Political Economics*, 24(1), 1–30.

Fama, E.F. (1980) 'Banking in the Theory of Finance', *Journal of Monetary Economics*, 6(1), 39–57.

Fox, J. (2009) *The Myth of the Rational Market: A History of Risk, Reward, and Delusion on Wall Street.* New York: HarperBusiness.

Geanakoplos, J. (1996) 'Promises Promises', *Cowles Foundation Discussion Paper No. 1057*, Cowles Foundation for Research in Economics, Yale University.

Geanakoplos, J. (2009) 'The Leverage Cycle', *Cowles Foundation Discussion Paper No. 1715*, Cowles Foundation for Research in Economics, Yale University, July.

Greider, W. (2010) 'Political Fever', *The Nation*, 15 February, 7–8.

Guerrera, F., and T. Braithwaite (2010) 'Goldman Lobbies against Fiduciary Reform', *Financial Times*, 12 May.

Hale, G. and Santos, J.A.C. (2009) 'Do Banks Price Their Informational Monopoly?', *Journal of Financial Economics*, 93(2), 185–206.

Hirschman, A.O. (1970) *Exit, Voice, and Loyalty.* Cambridge, MA: Harvard University Press.

Kane, E.J. (1989) 'The High Cost of Incompletely Funding the FSLIC Shortage of Explicit Capital', *Journal of Economic Perspectives*, 3(4), Fall, 31–48.

Kaufman, G.G. (1995) 'The U.S. Banking Debacle of the 1980s: A Lesson in Government Mismanagement', *The Freeman: Ideas on Liberty*, 45(4), 254–9.

Kaufman, G.G. and Benston, G.J. (eds) (1990) *Restructuring the American Financial System.* Norwell, MA: Kluwer Academic.

Krugman, P. (2009) 'How Did Economists Get It So Wrong?', *New York Times* (Sunday Magazine), 6 September.

Laeven, L. and Levine, R. (2009) 'Bank Governance, Regulation and Risk Taking', *Journal of Financial Economics*, 93(2), 259–75.

Minsky, H.P. (1986) *Stabilizing the Unstable Economy.* New Haven, CT: Yale University Press.

Ostrom, E. (1990) *Governing the Commons: The Evolutions of Institutions for Collective Action.* Cambridge: Cambridge University Press.

Reinhart, C., and Rogoff, K. (2009) *This Time Is Different.* Princeton, NJ: Princeton University Press.

Repullo, R. (2004) 'Capital Requirements, Market Power, and Risk-Taking in Banking', *Journal of Financial Intermediation*, 13(2), 156–82.

Shadow Financial Regulatory Committee (2010) 'The FDIC's Proposal for Setting Insurance Premia of Large Banks', *Shadow Statement No. 291*. Washington, DC: American Enterprise Institute, 26 April.

Sorkin, A.R. (2009) *Too Big to Fail*. New York: Viking Press.

Stiglitz, J.E. (2010) 'Government Failure vs. Market Failure: Principles of Regulation', in E.J. Balleisen and D.A. Moss (eds), *Government and Markets: Toward a New Theory of Regulation*. Cambridge: Cambridge University Press, pp. 13–51.

Tversky, A. and Kahneman, D. (1981) 'The Framing of Decisions and the Psychology of Choice', *Science*, New Series, 211(4481), 30 January, 453–8.

Wall, L.D. (1991) 'Recourse Risk in Asset Sales', *Economic Review*, Federal Reserve Bank of Atlanta, September, 1–13.

5
Income Distribution and Borrowing: Growth and Financial Balances in the US Economy

Gennaro Zezza

1 Introduction[1]

According to the more widespread interpretations of the economic and financial crisis which started in 2007, its origin is either due to an exogenous shock which could occur with low probability, or to some kind of misbehaviour in the conduct of monetary policy, or to the misbehaviour of unregulated financial markets. Accordingly, the problems which generated the crisis can be fixed in the medium term by a more stringent regulation of those segments of financial markets which misbehaved, and by a return to the Taylor rule for managing monetary policy. All measures which have been undertaken to sustain the economy in the short run, such as injections of liquidity in financial markets and fiscal expansion, are seen as potentially harmful in the medium term, requiring – sooner rather than later – a change in policy to eliminate the threat of inflation and to reduce public debt.

As we write (March 2010) a large majority of commentators are arguing that the US economy has now passed the trough of the current recession, and recovery is under way, with a possible return to a positive and large growth rate in GDP by 2010. A growth rate above 5 per cent in US real GDP in the last quarter of 2009, and an increase in employment in the first months of 2010 seem to support this view. Accordingly, political pressure to reverse the course of fiscal policy is increasing.

Most of those adhering to this line of thought do not believe that the economic theories dominant in the pre-recession era need any change. Eugene Fama's theorem on market efficiency is still believed to hold, despite the evidence given by market collapses: the only remedies should pertain to how information on financial assets risk is treated, and economists are also blamed because they did not extend in a timely fashion their models to new features of financial markets for derivatives. Surprisingly, or may be not so, none of the adherents to this line of thought had any perception of the incoming crisis. On the contrary, as late as 4 August 2007,[2] Taylor claimed that the economy was up and running with no perceptible threat.

A research project – pioneered by Wynne Godley at the Levy Institute of Economics – has developed a completely different approach, which we claim to be based on the 'New Cambridge' tradition put forward by Godley and associates at Cambridge in the 1970s. According to this approach, a sustainable growth path can only be achieved if all stocks of assets/debt tend to stable ratios to income (or GDP). A corollary of this result is that whenever the deficit for any macroeconomic sector is larger than a given threshold, an imbalance in the assets/income ratio is bound to arise, drifting the economy into a path which will be unsustainable.

Following this approach, we will discuss an alternative interpretation of the current recession, which was bound to happen – sooner or later – because the debt-led growth path the US economy had embraced in the 1990s could not be sustained. If our interpretation is correct, the US economy – and other countries sharing similar macroeconomic imbalances – will need both short-run policies to sustain aggregate demand and employment in the short run, and more structural changes to switch to a sustainable growth path for the medium term.

We will start our discussion, in section 2, with a brief comparison of the main features of the 'New Consensus' model with other heterodox approaches; we will then discuss, in section 3, the characteristics of the growth path of the US economy before the recession; and section 4 will conclude with policy suggestions for the short and the medium run.

2   The 'New Consensus' model, and 'flow of funds' models

2.1   The 'New Consensus'

Just before the recession started, Blanchard (2008) noted that macroeconomics was in a healthy state, with a large majority of economists converging on what has been labelled a 'New Consensus' (NC) model.[3] Minor divergences remained between the 'freshwater' and the 'saltwater' groups,[4] while heterodox approaches were marginalised and basically ignored.

However, the recession which started in 2007 was unexpected by mainstream macroeconomists, casting doubts on their underlying model, and reviving interest in the ideas of Keynes and Minsky. Many of those who had been claiming that a recession was inevitable[5] were in the neglected, heterodox group, and although they 'saw it coming', their research agenda is not receiving the attention it deserves yet.[6]

Why did mainstream economists fail to foresee the recession? In our view, the flaw lies at the heart of the 'New Consensus' mainstream model. The characteristics of such a model, in its simplest form, have been summarised, among others, by Blanchard:

> First, the aggregate demand equation is derived from the first-order conditions of consumers, which give consumption as a function of the real interest rate and future expected consumption. As there is no other source of demand in the basic model, consumption demand is the same as aggregate demand. And given the assumption that, so long as the marginal cost is less than the price, price setters satisfy demand at existing prices, aggregate demand is equal to output. Putting these three assumptions together, the first relation gives us output as a function of the real interest rate and future expected output.
>
> Second, under the Calvo specification, the Phillips curve-like equation gives inflation as a function of expected future inflation, and of the 'output gap', defined as actual output minus what output would be absent nominal rigidities.
>
> Third, the monetary policy rule is formalised as a 'Taylor rule', a reaction function giving the real interest rate chosen by the central bank as a function of inflation and the output gap. (Nominal money does not explicitly appear in the model: The assumption is that the central bank can adjust the nominal money stock so as to achieve any real interest rate it wants. And, what matters for activity is the real interest rate, not nominal money per se.) (Blanchard 2008, 8–9)

More formally, following Tamborini et al. (2009),

$$x_t = E_t x_{t+1} - \sigma(i_t - E_t \pi_{t+1} - r_t^*) \tag{2.1}$$

$$\pi_t = \beta E_t \pi_{t+1} + \kappa x_t \tag{2.2}$$

$$i_t = i_t^* + \gamma_\pi(\pi_t - \pi^*) + \gamma_x(x_t - x^*) \tag{2.3}$$

where x denotes the gap between the current level of output and the 'natural rate of output', i the nominal interest rate, π the inflation rate, r^* the 'natural rate of interest' and E denotes expectations. Equation 2.1

implies that when the output gap is zero, the market value of the real interest rate equals the 'natural' rate of interest, and any interest rate above the 'natural rate' will decrease output.

Equation 2.2 is the 'New Keynesian Phillips Curve', where actual inflation depends on expected inflation and the output gap.

Finally, equation 2.3 is one form of the 'Taylor rule', where the interest rate is governed by a reaction function to inflation and the output gap.

This approach is behind the empirical work which was carried out in most central banks through Dynamic Stochastic General Equilibrium (DSGE) models,[7] and therefore theoretical model flaws will (and did) imply forecasting failures in central banks.

The model is based on the assumption of forward-looking individuals who maximise utility, together with the New Keynesian assumption of some degree of monopoly, or other assumptions that imply that prices do not move instantaneously to clear all markets. The model also 'solves' the dichotomy between growth models and short-run models, since it is both compatible with long-run equilibrium growth, and as a tool to address short-run deviations from the 'natural' level of output.

Money and credit do not appear explicitly in this model: it is assumed that the stock of money can be adjusted so to get the interest rate to the level required by the Taylor rule, while credit may be (implicitly) provided to households to increase current consumption whenever (rational) expectations of future income increase.

A crisis can occur, in this framework, either because of an unexpected shock (usually modelled as a supply-side or technology shock), or because of policy failure (i.e. failure to adopt the Taylor rule). Accordingly, mainstream interpretation of the recession focused: (1) on the fact that the recession was triggered by an extraordinary shock ('it is not so surprising that models designed to capture the average quarter in the economy's life would not do so well when very unaverage events arise', Altig, 2009); (2) on policy failures ('there is clearly evidence that there were monetary excesses during the period leading up to the housing boom'; Taylor, 2009a, p. 3);[8] or (3) failure of the theoretical and empirical models to capture recent evolution of financial markets.

The NC model sketched above describes a closed economy. An additional mainstream interpretation of the crisis refers to the 'saving glut hypothesis'.[9] According to this theory, high saving in developing countries with under-developed financial markets – notably China – were invested in US financial assets, bringing down interest rates and strengthening the dollar. Easy money was thus not the effect of monetary policy, but the consequence of 'excess' liquidity, with the apparent paradox that developing countries were financing the US housing bubble and excessive consumption.

We will not focus on open economy features in this chapter, but we note that the largest amount of US Treasury bills has been acquired by foreign central banks, not by individuals or private financial firms seeking the highest return in a well-developed financial market. The level of the interest rate was therefore not determined on the saving–investment market, but by monetary and exchange rate policies. Central banks in East Asia were eager to acquire any amount of US financial assets which would balance the net supply of US dollars against their currencies, which remained undervalued, enabling exporters in East Asia to remain competitive on US markets, and generate employment and growth. A fragile equilibrium, since a devaluation of the US dollar would have caused capital losses to Central banks in East Asia, but an equilibrium which could be maintained.

What are the shortcomings of the NC model?

1. The desire to derive a macro model from aggregating the behaviour of representative agents with forward-looking expectations impose implausible constraints, and it is not well suited for a model which aims at tracking the economy in a recession, i.e. out of equilibrium;
2. The incoherence between short-run models (usually with some 'Keynesian' assumptions) and growth models has been solved in favour of growth models, which are assumed to be valid also for the short run. This undermines the ability of such models to deal with shocks which push the economy far from the growth path;
3. The time dimension in the model has no real relevance. Dynamic model solution usually imply a sequence of optimal equilibria where the trajectory of the economy over time is not relevant;
4. Financial markets are not explicitly modelled, since NC results show that credit conditions are not relevant for decisions in real markets;
5. Forward-looking expectations are at odds with the possibility of bubbles.

2.2 Common features of alternative views

Bezemer (2009) has made an attempt to identify common features of research groups who saw the crisis coming, according to a plausible criterion:

In distinguishing the lucky shots from insightful predictions, the randomness of guesses is a feature to be exploited. Random guesses are supported by all sorts of reasoning (if at all), and will have little theory in common. Conversely, for a set of correct predictions to attain ex post credibility, it is additionally required that they are supported by a common theoretical framework. These requirements, applied in this chapter, will help identify the elements of a valid analytical approach to financial stability, and get into focus the contrast with conventional models.

In collecting these cases in an extensive search of the relevant literature, four selection criteria were applied. Only analysts were included who provide some account on how they arrived at their conclusions. Second, the analysts included went beyond predicting a real estate crisis, also making the link to real-sector recessionary implications, including an analytical account of those links. Third, the actual prediction must have been made by the analyst and available in the public domain, rather than being asserted by others. Finally, the prediction had to have some timing attached to it. (Bezemer, 2009, p. 8)

The selection process identified 12 economists, and their research groups, many of which shared a common view.

Surveying these assessments and forecasts, there appears to be a set of interrelated elements central and common to the contrarians' thinking. This comprises a concern with financial assets as distinct from real-sector assets, with the credit flows that finance both forms of wealth, with the debt growth accompanying growth in financial wealth, and with the accounting relation between the financial and real economy. (ibid., p. 9)

Our research group, headed by Wynne Godley, was among those identified by Bezemer (op. cit) as correctly stating what was bound to happen. In addition, it is the only research group to base its analysis on a formal model of how borrowing and debt are affected by decisions taken in real markets, and how they affect in turn the growth trajectory of the economy.

2.3   Models of financial balances

Our analysis of the evolution of the US economy is based on an empirical model developed by Wynne Godley at the Levy Institute of Economics, with its origins in the 'New Cambridge' theories developed in Cambridge (UK) in the 1970s.[10]

This class of models is usually labelled as 'stock-flow-consistent' (SFC), in that one of the main features – with respect to other heterodox approaches – is the emphasis on dynamic stock-flow accounting for the whole economy. However, this requirement should be explicitly or implicitly valid for any consistent model, be it mainstream or heterodox. A better label is needed, but for the time being we will keep using 'stock-flow-consistent post-Keynesian' (SFC-PK) models when referring to this approach. Its crucial features are the following:

1. The model is dynamic, and the position of the system in a given period is crucially affected by its previous historical path;
2. The model is consistent, in that every monetary flow is recorded as a payment for one sector and a receipt for another sector. In addition to flow consistency, every relevant stock – of real or financial assets – is linked to a corresponding flow. For instance, the net stock of assets for the household sector changes its value in a given period through household saving and capital gains;
3. The banking system is explicitly represented;
4. The accounting structure of models adheres to the principles laid down in the System of National Accounts (SNA) for flows, flow of funds and stocks accounting, helping to move from theoretical models to applied models;
5. Prices do not necessarily clear markets. At any moment in time, the stock of an asset may differ from its 'desired' level. Quantity adjustments towards 'desired' or 'equilibrium' levels for model variables require some buffers.

The first four features are based on accounting identities linking sectors in the economy, and therefore should be present, implicitly or explicitly, in any macro model.[11] The last feature, on the contrary, is a hypothesis specific to Godley's approach. Other features of SFC-PK models may and do vary. Generally speaking, authors adopting this approach do not feel the need for micro-foundation of the aggregate behaviour of agents, while they prefer the post Keynesian or Marxian approach of splitting individuals into different groups, say 'rentiers' or 'capitalists' and 'workers'. Other crucial features are easily derived: there is no distinction – in principle – between a SFC-PK model built to evaluate the short-run dynamics of an economy, and one where the long-run growth path of output is obtained through a sequence of short-run adjustment processes.[12] The explicit representation of the financial sector makes it possible to build models à la Minski or – more generally – to investigate the 'financialisation' of the economy.[13]

We will not discuss further the theoretical foundations of SFC-PK models here,[14] since we are more interested in the relevance of this approach for empirical applications and its relative merits in predicting the current recession. We will specifically focus on the financial balances of the major sectors in the economy, which have become a key synthetic indicator of the state of the economy, increasingly adopted for countries other than the US.[15]

Adopting the Social Accounting Matrix (SAM) approach pioneered by Richard Stone, and largely incorporated into the System of National Accounts (UN 2008), a complete set of flow accounting for a simplified economy can be represented as in Table 5.1,[16] where monetary payments are recorded in the columns, and receipts in the rows.

Accounting consistency requires that the sum of saving for all sectors (i.e. our financial balances) be zero, i.e.

$$Sh + Sb + Sf - GD^* - BP = I \qquad (2.1)$$

where Sh is household saving, Sb and Sf are undistributed profits in the business and financial sector, respectively, GD^* is government deficit, net of investment, BP the balance of payments on current account and I gross investment.

Sector saving in row 7 of Table 5.1 are linked to uses and sources of funds, so that, for any sector, saving equals the change in assets less the change in liabilities. Merging together the business and financial sectors, equation (2.1) can also be written as

$$(Sh - Ir) + (P - In) = GD + BP \qquad (2.2)$$

where now Ir is residential investment, In non-residential investment, P profits for all firms, and GD is the government deficit including public investment. The first bracket measures the net acquisition of financial assets (NAFA) by the household sector, which are detailed in the rows 7a to 7e as the net increase in financial assets of this sector less the increase in liabilities. The second bracket measures NAFA for the business sector, showing the sources and uses of funds, and so on.

When the NAFA is positive, the sector is cumulating financial assets, and some other sector is increasing its net liabilities. A negative NAFA is a signal for the increase of liabilities over assets, or – to put it differently – for the increase of the financial fragility of this sector.

Table 5.1 Social accounting matrix and flow of funds for a simplified economy

	Production	Households	Non-financial business	Financial sector	Government	Rest of the World	Capital Account	Total
1. Production		Consumption			Government expenditure	Exports	Investment	Aggregate demand
2. Households	Wages		Dividends	Dividends, Interest payments	Govt. transfers to households, Interest payments	Net income payments		Household income
3. Non-financial business	Profits				Govt. transfers to business			Business s. income
4. Financial sector	Fin. Profits		Interest payments		Interest payments	Interest payments		Financial s.income
5. Government	Net indirect taxes and s.c.	Direct taxes and s.c.	Taxes on profits					Govt. receipts
6. Rest of the world	Imports	Private s. net transfers to RoW		Interest payments	Govt. net transfers to RoW			Payments to RoW

(continued)

Table 5.1 Continued

	Production	Households	Non-financial business	Financial sector	Government	Rest of the World	Capital Account	Total
7. Capital account		Household saving	Undistributed profits	Undistributed profits	Govt. surplus	2(Balance of payments)		Receipts on capital account
7a. Deposits		$+\Delta Deposits$		$-\Delta Deposits$				0
7b. Loans & mortgages		$-\Delta Lh$	$-\Delta Lb$	$+\Delta L$				0
7c. Government liabilities		$+\Delta Bh$		$+\Delta Bb$	$-\Delta B$	$+\Delta Bw$		0
7d. Equities		$+\Delta Eh$	$-\Delta E$	$+\Delta Eb$		$+\Delta Ew$		0
7e. Foreign liabilities				$+\Delta F$		$-\Delta F$		0
7f. Real assets		Residential investment	Non-residential investment	Non-residential investment	Public investment			Investment
Total	Value of output, plus imports	Private s. income	Outlays of non-financial b.	Outlays of the financial s.	Govt. outlays	Receipts from RoW	Payments on capital account	

Having derived the financial balances from the GDP accounting identity it should become clear how such balances are linked to the components of aggregate demand. An increase in domestic investment will have an impact on the NAFA of the business sector only when the increase in demand, spurred by investment, does not generate a sufficient level of profits. In this case, for instance, we would expect higher income to increase household saving, government tax revenues and imports, so that investment-led growth should imply a larger NAFA for the household sector, a smaller government deficit and an improvement in the external balance.

When aggregate demand increases because of a shock to net exports, we would expect an increase in profits and saving of households, and an increase in tax revenues, so that NAFA should increase for both the household and the business sector.

Finally, an increase in aggregate demand generated by additional government spending may improve the balances for the private sector while deteriorating the external balance, through the effects of government expenditure on income, and therefore saving, profits and imports.[17]

Following the 'New Cambridge' approach, the Levy model uses a simplified version of the economy, with no distinction between household and business. Financial balances reduce to

$$NAFA = GD + BP \qquad (2.3)$$

where NAFA is the net acquisition of financial assets for the private sector as a whole. A negative NAFA implies that household saving plus profits are not sufficient to finance investment, so that the private sector is a net borrower.[18]

The analysis of the three balances in equation (2.3) seems to be gaining in popularity. It has been adopted by Martin Wolf (2010, among others) for his analysis of the UK economy; Hatzius, at Goldman Sachs, has modelled financial balances through an error correction approach towards a long-run equilibrium (Hatzius 2005); Taylor and associates (Barbosa-Filho et al. 2007) have also been investigating financial balances, without developing a full model, but analysing the relation of each balance to the business cycle and against each other; Blecker (2009) has analysed the 'twin deficits' theory through a VAR built with financial balances;[19] Brecht and others (2010) discuss the financial balances of Eurozone countries to evaluate the sustainability of the 'Stability and Convergence Programmes'.

3   Our analysis of the current recession

3.1   Seven unsustainable processes

In our view, the current financial and economic crisis is not the consequence of malpractices in some sectors of the financial industry, or a result of policy failure – although both certainly played a role – but rather the inevitable consequence of an unbalanced growth process which started as the end of the 1980s.[20] Godley's first *Strategic Analysis* report pointed to seven unsustainable processes:

> (1) the fall in private saving into ever deeper negative territory, (2) the rise in the flow of net lending to the private sector, (3) the rise in the growth rate of the real money stock, (4) the rise in asset prices at a rate that far exceeds the growth of profits (or of GDP), (5) the rise in the budget surplus, (6) the rise in the current account deficit, (7) the increase in the United States' net foreign indebtedness relative to GDP. (Godley 1999: 2)

Some of these processes – excluding monetary policy (3) and budget policy (5) – characterised both the so-called 'New Economy' growth period, which ended with the 2001 recession (Godley/Izurieta 2002), and the next growth period characterised by a housing bubble, which ended in 2007.

The fall in private sector saving is depicted in Figure 5.1, which shows that saving – the sum of household saving and undistributed profits, or

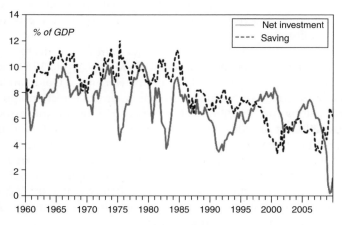

Figure 5.1   Private sector saving and investment
Source: NIPA, FoF.

corporate saving – has declined steadily since the 1980s. In addition, while aggregate saving exceeded investment – including investment in housing – up to 1997, since then saving has been lower than aggregate investment, and therefore the NAFA for the private sector became negative: investment had to be financed, at least in part, by an increase in the net debt of the private sector.[21]

This is confirmed by the analysis of private sector debt and borrowing in Figure 5.2. Private debt has been rising steadily as a share of GDP (Figure 5.2), reaching almost 180 per cent of GDP. Borrowing started to drop in 2008, and it is now negative, implying that, on aggregate, households and firms are paying back their debt, which has started to fall.

In Figure 5.3 we report measures of saving, investment, borrowing and debt for the personal sector. The black line shows the decline of the saving rate for the personal sector, starting from the 1980s. Up to that period, debt was relatively stable relative to disposable income, and aggregate saving was larger than residential investment, so that this sector was financing the purchases of new houses through mortgages, where the increase in mortgages fluctuated around 4 per cent of disposable income, and part of their saving. By the 1990s, saving were no longer sufficient to finance residential investment, and mortgages started to increase, along with the overall stock of debt. In 2001 the net increase in mortgages became larger than residential investment: the housing boom had started, and households were taking new mortgages because the price of *existing* houses was increasing, not because they needed to finance the purchase of a newly built house.

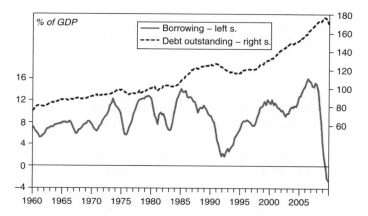

Figure 5.2 Private non-financial sector: debt and borrowing
Source: NIPA, FoF.

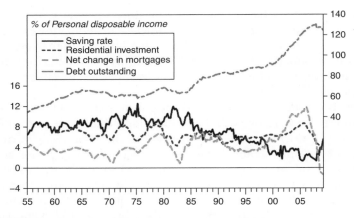

Figure 5.3   Private saving, borrowing, investment and debt
Source: NIPA, FoF.

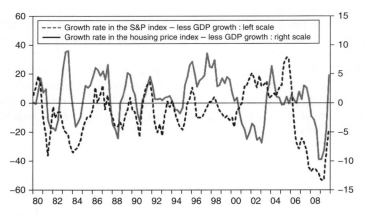

Figure 5.4   Asset prices
Source: BEA, S&P, Realtors.org.

This can be interpreted as the result of speculation getting out of the stock market – after the 2001 crash – and into the housing market.

In Figure 5.4 we report two simple measures of relative growth in asset prices, obtained by subtracting the annual growth rate in nominal GDP from the growth rate in a stock market index and in a price index for the housing market. The picture in Figure 5.4 shows clearly how the stock market bubble played a major role in the 'New Economy' period between 1995 and 2000, and how the housing market bubble started immediately after, with both price indexes now decreasing. The growth rate in stock market prices fluctuated around the growth rate in output until 1995, when it started to exceed it for an unusual period, followed by the stock market crash of 2001. From 2001, the growth rate in house prices started to exceed consistently, for a prolonged period, the growth rate in output, until the crash in 2007.

Capital gains on the stock market first, and on the housing market later, contributed to the acceleration in US consumption. If all agents were rational, perfectly informed and forward-looking, capital gains should not have an impact on consumption at the aggregate level. When the owner of an asset – a house, say – has a capital gain because the market price of her asset increases, she will experience an increase in her wealth which may lead to a smaller saving rate and an increase in consumption. This behaviour implies that at some future period the owner is expecting to sell the asset, and realise the capital gain. There must be somebody else in the economy who is therefore willing to acquire such an asset in the future. When the market price of the asset increases, this 'potential buyer' will have to save more, and reduce consumption, to be able to afford the future purchase of the asset. Capital gains for asset owners always imply a capital loss for somebody else, and when capital gains refer to existing houses traded within the private sector, there should not be any macroeconomic consequences. However, our econometrics show that capital gains on both equities and housing have played a role in increasing private sector demand in the US. This is partly due to asymmetric information, or myopic behaviour, so that asset owners spend more when the market price of their asset increases, while potential buyers do not increase their saving. In addition, innovation on financial markets allowed home owners to refinance their mortgages, or use other financial instruments to transform their future expected capital gains into an immediate source of additional cash, which was used to increase consumption.

The strong increase in domestic demand, financed by credit, was therefore the main source of US growth in the 2000s, resulting in a widening balance of payments deficit, which in turned cumulated into a growing external debt. In Figure 5.5 we report the net asset position of the US, relative to GDP, along with an implicit measure of US debt obtained by cumulating the balance of payments through time, starting from a benchmark value. This latter figure will not depend on fluctuations of either assets market values or the exchange rate, and the figure clearly shows the very specific feature of the US economy: a depreciation of the exchange rate – as the one which started in 2002 – has little

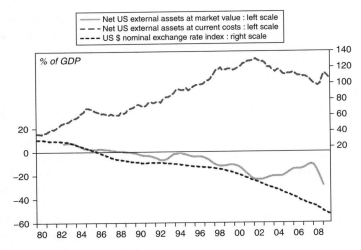

Figure 5.5   US external asset position and $ exchange rate
Source: BEA, Federal Reserve.

effects on US liabilities, which are mainly in US dollars, but increases the market value of US assets abroad, which are mainly in euro, yen and other strong currencies, resulting in an improvement in the net asset position, even against a large and growing current account deficit. The US has the 'exorbitant privilege' of being able to borrow in her own currency, and therefore being able to reach a level of her foreign debt, relative to GDP, which would make other countries default.

It has been suggested (by Bernanke, 2005 among others) that the US external deficit was a cause, rather than a consequence, of US financial imbalances and excessive domestic demand. According to this view, excessive saving in countries where financial markets are not developed, notably China, implied a strong demand for US financial assets, strengthening the US dollar and keeping US interest rates below the level they should have been, so that the growth in domestic demand in the US was overly stimulated. If this was the case, we should observe that the majority of US assets held abroad were held by the private sector, but what happened is that demand for US assets, mainly government liabilities, came from central banks, so that it appears the result of an exchange rate policy, rather than private capitals seeking a safe financial market.

Incidentally, the financial balances approach show that export-led growth implying a surplus in the current account, a strategy pursued in this case by China, can only be achieved if some other country – in this case the United States – is willing to run a current account deficit. This strategy has worked for a long time only because the debtor country is the issuer of a currency commonly accepted as international reserve. Since a devaluation of the US dollar would imply capital losses for those holding US financial assets, with the need to convert them sooner or later in other currencies, this strategy is fragile.[22]

Figures 5.1 to 5.5 show that five of the unsustainable processes outlined in Godley (1999) were still at work in the 2000s, after the 2001 recession and the end of the 'New economy'. Budget policy, however, had changed its stance, moving from a surplus in the Clinton administration to a deficit, a fiscal manoeuvre which was effective in contrasting the fall in private sector demand during the 2001 crisis, so that the recession was shorter than it could have been.

In Figure 5.6 we report three measures of the monetary policy stance, namely the Federal fund rate, and the growth rate in M1 and M2. We subtract the inflation rate to obtain a measure of the *ex post* interest rate, and measures of the growth in the money stock net of inflation. The chart in Figure 5.6 confirms that the stock of M2 was growing rapidly in the second half of the 1990s, although the real interest rate was not low. With the 2001 recession, interest rates were reduced in real terms, and they were gradually raised again in 2004, when the price of oil increased, and inflation seemed to become a threat again.

Some commentators argue that the reason for the current crisis is based on the easing of monetary policy:

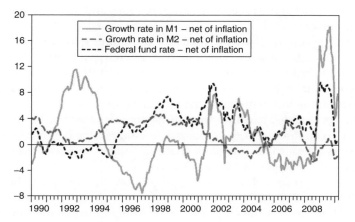

Figure 5.6 Monetary policy
Source: BEA, Federal Reserve.

The classic explanation of financial crises is that they are caused by excesses – frequently monetary excesses – which lead to a boom and an inevitable bust. This crisis was no different: A housing boom followed by a bust led to defaults, the implosion of mortgages and mortgage-related securities at financial institutions, and resulting financial turmoil.

Monetary excesses were the main cause of the boom. The Fed held its target interest rate, especially in 2003–2005, well below known monetary guidelines that say what good policy should be based on historical experience. Keeping interest rates on the track that worked well in the past two decades, rather than keeping rates so low, would have prevented the boom and the bust. (J.B. Taylor 2009b)

This explanation, however, does not take into account that household (and foreign) debt had started to rise well before the monetary easing. The decline in mortgage rates allowed the private sector to increase their debt while keeping interest payments constant as a share of income,[23] and therefore postponed a more severe recession and fuelled a boom. If interest rates had been kept at higher levels, the short growth recession of 2001 would have lasted longer, and would have had more serious consequences on unemployment and output.

In our view, monetary policy was relevant for the *timing* of the crisis. During the housing market boom, households were borrowing at a high rate, while interest rates were declining. On average, interest payments were stable relative to income, since the increase in debt to income roughly matched the decline in the interest rate, and debt was perceived as sustainable.

With the rise in oil prices, monetary authorities started to fear inflation, and raised interest rates, so that interest payments relative to income started to climb, the financial fragility of the household sector became clear, and the mortgage market collapsed, with the familiar impact on the international market for derivatives.

The Levy model, based on the SFC-PK approach described earlier, has proven to be a reliable tool to project a recession scenario, even though it still lacks a detailed description of financial markets, and treats the private sector of the economy as a whole. Our econometrics showed that domestic demand was sustained by capital gains on both the equity and housing markets, and that net borrowing was providing an additional source for expenditure, so that the propensity to save out of income was dropping. Given the fiscal and monetary stance, and a plausible scenario for US trade and growth among US trading partners, the model pointed out that growth required an ever-increasing debt of the private sector relative to income, and therefore increasing financial fragility, which would necessarily imply a turning point. In fact, we expected the turning point to occur earlier.

3.2　Why 'excessive' consumption?

Summing up, the long period of sustained growth in the US was fuelled, in our view, by 'excessive' private domestic expenditure, with a major role played by household expenditure in the 2000s, financed by increasing injections of credit. The mainstream view – before the crisis broke – was that growth in domestic expenditure was not excessive, but rather due to rational expectations on future income growth.

Godley's (1999) seven unsustainable processes show that this growth pattern could not be sustained, and implied a crisis at some point, but does not provide an explanation for why private sector demand increased faster than disposable income for a prolonged time period.

In our view, another unsustainable process was at work, since excessive consumption was – at least in part – determined by two joint factors: a shift in the distribution of income towards the richest quintile, and the struggle of the median household to keep its relative standard of living against the richest quintile.

The plausible impact of the shift in income distribution, and the reasons why income distribution started to change, were discussed as early as 1999:

> There is nothing mysterious about this trend towards greater inequality. Policies are specifically designed to give the already rich more disposable income, particularly through tax cuts and by pushing down wages. The theory and ideological justification for such measures is that higher incomes for the rich and higher profits will lead to more investment, better allocation of resources and therefore more jobs and welfare for everyone. In reality, as was perfectly predictable, moving money up the economic ladder has led to stock market bubbles, untold paper wealth for the few, and the kind of financial crises we shall be hearing a lot about... (George 1999)

The shift in the distribution of income has continued in the 2000s, and is by now well documented,[24] and common to countries other than the US. A simple measure of how the personal distribution of income has changed in the US is reported in Figure 5.7, which draws the income limits of quintiles, and of the top 5 per cent. In 2006, before the recession started, the real income of the top 5 per cent was 35 per cent higher

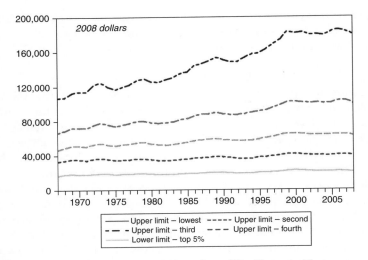

Figure 5.7   Income limits for each fifth and top 5% of households
Source: census.gov.

than in 1985, while the real income of, say, the second quintile had risen by a mere 13 per cent.

The shift in income distribution has taken place both as a change in the *functional* distribution of income, with profits gaining over wages, and as a change in the *personal* distribution of income, in favour of the higher quintile.

The change in the personal distribution of income can be tracked down to different sources. Since the ownership of real and financial assets is concentrated in the highest quintiles of income distribution, an increase in the value of such assets – which has effects on asset returns – would change the distribution of income as well as the distribution of wealth. However, the largest impact on income distribution seems to originate from a shift in relative wages,[25] as well as from the reduction in marginal tax rates.

Such a shift is expected to increase the aggregate saving rate, since richer households have a lower propensity to consume out of income. On the contrary, as we discussed earlier, the saving rate has declined over this period and up to the beginning of the recession, creating a paradox which needs to be addressed.

A possible explanation of why households started to increase their consumption in the face of stagnant real wages refer to theories which emphasise the role of relative consumption, which are gaining ground.[26]

We have discussed these processes elsewhere (Zezza, forthcoming) and, more generally, the idea that a shift in the distribution of income such as the one documented in Figure 5.7 is relevant for aggregate demand is gaining support (see also Skidelsky 2010).

4 Conclusions and policy suggestions

In this chapter we have claimed that the 'New consensus' approach to macroeconomics, which results from introducing market imperfections into new classical models of perfect markets and rational behaviour, has been ineffective in predicting the current recession, and is inherently useless to understand the evolution of a real economy where the role of financial markets is relevant for investment and consumption decisions.

We have discussed the common features of alternative views, where the analysis of financial balances is linked both to the evolution of aggregate demand in real markets and to the accumulation of stocks of assets and liabilities.

We have shown how the Levy Institute macroeconomic model, built on a post-Keynesian theoretical ground, has been effective in tracking down the origins of the current recession to unbalances in the growth path of the US economy, which was driven mainly by excessive private sector expenditure financed by borrowing.

Such growth regime, in our view, is the result of neoliberal policies and attitudes which started to gain ground in the 1980s, implying – among other things – a sensible change in the distribution of income, and stagnation in the real wage of middle-class households.

Notwithstanding the failure of mainstream models to predict the recession, most commentators still rely on the 'New consensus' and DSGE models to inform their opinion on how the US is getting out of the recession. A predominant view is that output is recovering, although employment will lag behind, but the worst of the recession is over, and no further action needs to be taken – with some caveats about the external (or 'global') imbalances.

Our view[27] is rather different, since in our projections we focus on the dynamics of the components of demand – rather than on potential output. In our latest exercise, we show that:

- the increase in government expenditure has helped the economy during 2009, and it is likely to have a positive impact in 2010;

- even though government intervention has implied one of the largest increase in deficits in postwar history, its size has not been large enough to compensate for the drop in domestic demand;
- without a sizeable depreciation of the US dollar, the contribution of US net exports to aggregate demand will – again – be insufficient for a recovery in employment;
- given the current credit conditions and debt levels, households are expected to keep a *negative* level of borrowing in the short run. Consumption will therefore stagnate, and if real wages are kept stable – on the face of recent surges in productivity – this will exacerbate the problem of deficient domestic demand;
- investment is not likely to increase if expectations of profits in domestic markets don't improve. Incentives towards the adoption of different ('greener') technologies may help.

It follows that government intervention will still be needed on a large scale to bring unemployment down to reasonable levels. Fiscal policy alone, however, will worsen the external balance again in the medium term (the 'New Cambridge' result), and therefore other policies – such as a stronger devaluation of the dollar vs the currencies of surplus countries – or other policies of a more protectionist nature, will be needed.

To achieve balanced growth in private sector demand in the medium term, a major shift in policies governing the distribution of income will be required, as redistribution from the top income classes to the middle and lower classes is needed to finance any increase in domestic consumption. In addition, a stronger set of incentives for domestic investment would be helpful, especially in those activities – such as the switch to 'greener' technologies and products – where market forces and profit maximisation contrast with social welfare.

Although a growing number of economists suggest that the crisis should be addressed by tackling income distribution, current policies do not seem to move in this direction, and there are as yet no signs of political support towards a change in income distribution, or other policies aimed at increasing the real wage of the median household.

Recent figures from the US showed an increase in consumption, but real disposable income was growing only because of government transfers, with real wages falling over income in line with the drop in employment. The end of government support, in this case, would imply either another drop in consumption, or an attempt from households to resume their borrowing habits, with a new increase in debt and financial fragility.

A large part of government intervention has taken the form of injections of liquidity into the financial sector. This has certainly prevented the crisis spreading further, but recent movement in the market price of equities and commodities may point to another bubble. If international liquidity is not channelled to productive investment, but rather on speculation, the signs of a recovery in early 2010, which many read as the end of the crisis, will prove to be temporary and illusory.

Notes

1. I wish to gratefully acknowledge comments from Wynne Godley and the participants to the conference on 'Global Crisis and Long Term Growth: A New Capitalism Ahead?', Villa Mondragone, 25 June 2009, and the conference on 'The Global Crisis', Siena, 26–7 January 2010. Any remaining errors are my sole responsibility. Financial support from MIUR is gratefully acknowledged.
2. Welt am Sonntag (2007).
3. According to Lavoie (2004). Some early features of the 'New Consensus' were described in Allsopp – Vines (2000) and Taylor (2000). Woodford (2003) is considered to be the best detailed analysis of this approach.
4. 'Fresh water' economists are New-classicals, mainly identified with the 'Chicago School', while 'Salt water' economists are New-Keynesians, and work in the coastal areas of the US. See Krugman (2009).
5. See Bezemer (2009). We will discuss some common features of those economists who 'saw it coming' in section 2.2.
6. Galbraith (2009).
7. See Woodford (2008, 17–18).
8. It is worth noting that Taylor had a radically different view as late as August 2007: 'it is amazing in which excellent condition the world economy is at the moment. There has seldom been a better time'; Welt am Sonntag (2007).
9. Bernanke (2005).
10. An excellent reconstruction of how stock-flow-consistent models relate to the evolution of Keynesian theories is in Dos Santos (2006).
11. Authors in the SFC tradition have used this approach to show that some mainstream and heterodox models were inconsistent. See Godley et al. (1987) or Zezza (2004) among others. Some mainstream economists, notably Sargent (1987), have developed stock-flow-consistent models, which sometimes assume that stocks adjust instantaneously to their desired level to ensure equilibrium.
12. See Dos Santos and Zezza (2008) for a simple model.
13. See Van Treeck (2008) among many others.
14. The classical reference for SFC-PK models is now Godley and Lavoie (2007).
15. See Wolf (2010) for an analysis of the U.K., and Brecht et al. (2010) for euro countries.
17. Theories based on the 'Ricardian equivalence' deny the impact of government expenditure on income, on the basis that additional government spending implies a future increase in taxation, which is discounted by rational

household who increase saving, so that aggregate demand remains constant. The empirical relevance of such theories is, however, questionable.

18. The 'New Cambridge' hypothesis was based on (3.3), and claimed that any increase in government deficit would be mirrored in an external deficit. This result was based on the empirical regularity that the NAFA was stable – in the UK – relative to income, thus suggesting that aggregate expenditure of the private sector was adjusting to both income and the stock of net financial assets. According to our results for the US economy, the hypothesis seems to hold for the medium term. See Zezza (2009).

19. The analysis in Blecker (2009) is, in our view, flawed. The author estimates a VAR of the three balances, possibly with an additional variable, but such a model could not be estimated – in principle – since the three variables are linked by an identity. However, if the variables are approximated, so that the identity does not strictly hold, VAR estimation is feasible, but its usefulness is questionable.

20. The saving rate of the personal sector started to decline approximately in 1985. In the same period the distribution of income started to shift systematically in favour of the richest quintile of the population. For a theoretical model of the relation among the saving rate, borrowing and the distribution of income see (Zezza 2008).

21. Investment can be financed by borrowing, but this does not necessarily imply an increase in debt of the same amount, since investment generates profits which can be used to pay back the loan.

22. It is even more fragile for countries such as Germany, whose trading partners are mainly the other countries in the euro zone, which cannot change their parity against the German currency. A prolonged current account surplus for Germany, matched by current account deficits in other euro zone countries, will undermine the stability of the currency area.

23. See Shaikh et al. (2003) for an early analysis of household debt and the interest payments burden.

24. See Zezza (2007, 2008) for a theoretical analysis including the role of capital gains on real and financial assets.

25. It has been pointed out that if the compensation of a manager is given by her impact on firms profits, such impact may increase with globalization of the market for firms' products, while such process should not have a similar effect on wages of blue collar (and most white collar) workers. According to this view, the change in the structure of relative wages should be the product of competition for managers among multinational firms.

26. See Cynamon - Fazzari (2008), Stiglitz (2008), Barba – Pivetti (20008), and Akerlof (2007) for a somewhat different perspective.

27. Papadimitriou et al. (2009), Zezza (2010).

References

Akerlof, G.A. (2007) 'The Missing Motivation in Macroeconomics', *American Economic Review*, 97(1), 5–36.
Allsopp, C. and Vines, D. (2000) 'The Assessment: Macroeconomic Policy', *Oxford Review of Economic Policy*, 16, 1–32.

Altig, David (2009) 'Economists Got it Wrong, But Why?', 10 September. Available at http://macroblog.typepad.com/macroblog/forecasts/.

Barba, Aldo and Pivetti, Massimo (2008) 'Rising Household Debt: Its Causes and Macroeconomic Implications – a Long-period Analysis', *Cambridge Journal of Economics* 33, 113–37.

Barbosa-Filho, N., Rada, C., Taylor, L. and Zamparelli, L. (2007) *Cycles and Trends in U.S. Net Borrowing Flows: Pro-Cyclical Household Net Borrowing, Counter-Cyclical Government, Consumption and the Current Account, and Elusive Twin Deficits*, SCEPA working paper 2007-5.

Bernanke, B. (2005) 'The Global Saving Glut and the U.S. Current Account Deficit', Sandridge Lecture, Virginia Association of Economics, Richmond, Virginia, 10 March. Available at http://www.federalreserve.gov/boarddocs/speeches/2005/200503102/default.htm.

Bezemer, Dirk J. (2009) '"No One Saw This Coming": Understanding Financial Crisis Through Accounting Models'. Available at http://som.eldoc.ub.rug.nl/FILES/reports/2009/09002/09002_Bezemer.pdf.

Blanchard, Olivier J. (2008) 'The State of Macro', NBER Working Paper No. 14259, August.

Blecker, Robert A. (2009) *The Trade Deficit Trap: How it Got So Big, Why it Persists, and What to Do About It*, EPI Working paper 284, July.

Brecht, Michael, Tober, Silke, van Treeck, Till and Truger, Achim (2010) *Squaring the Circle in Euroland? Some Remarks on the Stability and Convergence Programmes 2010–2013*, IMK Working paper 3/2010.

Cynamon, B.Z. and Fazzari, S.M. (2008) 'Household Debt in the Consumer Age: Source of Growth – Risk of Collapse', *Capitalism and Society*, III, 2, 3.

Dos Santos, Claudio (2006) 'Keynesian Theorising During Hard Times: Stock-flow Consistent Models as an Unexplored "Frontier" of Keynesian Macroeconomics', *Cambridge Journal of Economics*, 30(4), 541–65.

Dos Santos, Claudio and Zezza, Gennaro (2008) 'A Simplified, "Benchmark", Stock-flow Consistent Post-Keynesian Growth Model', *Metroeconomica*, 53(3), 441–78.

Galbraith, James K. (2009) 'Who Are These Economists, Anyway?', *Thought and Action*, Fall, 85–97.

George, Susan (2009) 'A Short History of Neo-liberalism', Conference on Economic Sovereignty in a Globalising World, Bangkok, 24–6 March 1999. Available at http://www.globalexchange.org/campaigns/econ101/neoliberalism.html.

Godley, W. (1999) 'Seven Unsustainable Processes', Levy Institute of Economics, *Strategic Analysis*, January.

Godley, W., Coutts, K. and Anyadike-Danes, M. (1987) 'IS-LM and Real Stock Flow Monetary Models – A Prelude to Applied Macroeconomics Modeling', Cambridge, UK: Cambridge University Department of Applied Economics.

Godley, Wynne and Izurieta, Alex (2002) 'Strategic Prospects and Policies for the U.S. Economy', Levy Institute Strategic Analysis, April.

Godley, W. and Lavoie, M. (2007) *Monetary Economics: An Integrated Approach to Credit, Money, Income, Production and Wealth*. Basingstoke: Palgrave Macmillan.

Hatzius, J. (2005) 'The Private Sector Deficit: Déjà Vu All Over Again, Goldman Sachs', *US Economic Analyst*, no. 05/32, 12 August.

Krugman, Paul (2009) 'How Did Economists Get It So Wrong?', *New York Times Magazine*, 2 September, available at http://www.nytimes.com/2009/09/06/magazine/06Economic-t.html.

Lavoie, Marc (2004) 'The New Consensus on Monetary Policy Seen from a Post-Keynesian Perspective', in Marc Lavoie and Mario Seccareccia, *Central Banking in the Modern World: Alternative Perspectives*. Cheltenham: Edward Elgar, pp. 15–34.

Papadimitriou, Dimitri B., Hannsgen, Greg and Zezza, Gennaro (2009) 'Sustaining Recovery: Medium-term Prospects and Policies for the US Economy', Levy Institute, *Strategic Analysis*, December.

Sargent, Thomas J. (1987) *Macroeconomic Theory*. Boston, MA: Academic Press.

Shaikh Anwar M., Papadimitriou, Dimitri B., Dos Santos, Claudio H. and Zezza, Gennaro (2003) 'Deficits, Debts and Growth: A Reprieve But Not a Pardon', Levy Institute Strategic Analysis, October.

Skidelsky, Robert (2010) 'The Continuing Relevance of Keynes', Lectio magistralis at the University of Rome, 12 February 2010. Available at http://www.uniroma3.it/downloads/inaugurazione/7_Lectio%20magistralis_SKIDELSKY_inglese.doc.

Stiglitz, J.E. (2008) 'Towards a General Theory of Consumerism: Reflections on Keynes' Economic Possibilities for our Grandchildren', in G.S. Becker, L. Becchetti and W.J. Baumol (eds), *Revisiting Keynes: Economic Possibilities for Our Grandchildren*. Cambridge, MA: MIT Press.

Tamborini, Roberto, Trautwein, Hans-Michael and Mazzocchi, Roni (2009) 'The Two Triangles: What Did Wicksell and Keynes Know about Macroeconomics that Modern Economists Do Not (Consider)?', presented at 'The World Economy in Crisis – The Return of Keynesianism?', Berlin, 30–1 October. Available at http://www.boeckler.de/pdf/v_2009_10_30_tamborini_trautwein_mazzocchi.pdf.

Taylor, J.B. (2000) 'Teaching Modern Macroeconomics at the Principles Level', *American Economic Review*, 90(2), May, 90–4.

Taylor, J.B. (2009a) *The Financial Crisis and the Policy Responses: An Empirical Analysis of What Went Wrong*, NBER Working Paper 14631, January. Cambridge, MA: NBER.

Taylor, J.B. (2009b) 'How Government Created the Financial Crisis', *Wall Street Journal*, 9 February.

United Nations (2008) 'System of National Accounts 2008'. Available at http://unstats.un.org/unsd/nationalaccount/SNA2008.pdf.

van Treeck, Till (2008) 'A Synthetic, Stock-flow Consistent Macroeconomic Model of "Financialisation"', *Cambridge Journal of Economics*, 33(3), 467–93.

Welt am Sonntag (2007) 'Interview with John Taylor, by Frank Stocker and Anja Struve'. Available at http://www.ifk-cfs.de/fileadmin/downloads/Media_Lounge/Taylor.pdf.

Wolf, Martin (2010) 'UK Economy Must Perform a Rebalancing Act', *Financial Times*, 13 April.

Woodford Michael (2003) *Interest and Prices: Foundations of a Theory of Monetary Policy*. Princeton, NJ and Oxford: Princeton University Press.

Woodford, Michael (2008) 'Convergence in Macroeconomics: Elements of the New Synthesis', presented at the annual meeting of the American Economics Association, New Orleans, 4 January. Available at http://www.columbia.edu/~mw2230/Convergence_AEJ.pdf.

Zezza, Gennaro (2004) *Some Simple, Consistent Models of the Monetary Circuit*, Levy Institute, Working paper no. 405, May.

Zezza, Gennaro (2007) 'The US Housing Market: A Stock-Flow Consistent Approach', *Ekonomia*, 10(2), 89–111.

Zezza, Gennaro (2008) 'US Growth, the Housing Market, and the Distribution of Income', *Journal of Post Keynesian Economics*, 30(3), 379–407.

Zezza, Gennaro (2009) 'Fiscal Policy and the Economics of Financial Balances', *Intervention*, 6(2), 289–310.

Zezza, Gennaro (2010) 'Getting Out of Recession?', Levy Institute, *Strategic Analysis*, January.

Zezza, Gennaro (forthcoming) 'Income Distribution and Borrowing: Tracking the US Economy with a "New Cambridge" Model", in E. Brancaccio and G. Fontana (eds), *The Global Crisis. Contributions to the Critique of Economic Theory and Policy*. London: Routledge.

6
Re-structuring the Financial Sector to Reduce its Burden on the Economy

Malcolm Sawyer

1 Introduction

The financial crisis of 2007–09 has, unsurprisingly, raised a whole raft of questions about the future of the financial sector, usually focusing on the regulation of the financial sector as a route through which future financial crises may be avoided – or which would at least mitigate the effects of such events. Parts of the debate over regulation have touched on issues of the separation of functions between financial institutions, and of ensuring that banks and other financial institutions are not 'too big to fail'. In this chapter we start with the remarks that the financial sector has grown (relative to the rest of the economy) in the past two to three decades, and consider the roles and purposes of the financial sector. This leads into a consideration of whether the increased resources devoted to the financial sector have been matched by comparable increases in the benefits derived from the financial sector. It is then argued that the financial crisis and the recession, which is seen as arising from the behaviour of the financial sector, also imposes some substantial costs, which are sketched. In the final section we discuss three aspects of ways of re-structuring the financial sector in ways which would reduce its burden on the macroeconomy. First, how to deal with the 'too big to fail' issue which creates moral hazard issues not to mention the costs associated with rescue packages. In effect, it is argued that financial institutions should always be allowed to fail in the sense of being allowed to go bankrupt such that their shareholders are the main losers, with measures in place to permit the activities of the now bankrupt financial institution to continue where necessary. Second, the role of alternative ownership forms is discussed based on the view that mutual and public-owned financial institutions can operate in different and socially preferable ways. Third, the role of taxation in reducing the size of the financial sector and its transactions is discussed.

2 The financial sector in the past two decades

The financial crises of 2007–09 came after three decades or so of developing globalisation and neoliberalism, and an era of financialisation. Epstein (2005, p. 3) defines 'financialization means the increasing role of financial motives, financial markets, financial actors and financial institutions in the operation of the domestic and international economies'. In this chapter the particular attention is on the enhanced scale of financial markets and the resources which they use, and whether there have been economic benefits from that increased scale. Table 6.1 provides some indication of the scale of the financial sector as reflected in the contribution of that sector to GDP, where it can be seen that there is a general tendency for the share in GDP to rise.

The growth of the financial sector over the past two to three decades raises the question as to whether or not the greater resources devoted to the financial sector have been matched by a corresponding increase in the benefits to the economy. At the same time as there has been growth in the financial sector, its structure and mode of operation have been evolving along with a general trend towards deregulation and financial liberalisation. The neoliberal 'atmosphere' promoted and indeed celebrated de-regulation and liberalisation, and viewed regulation as something of a nuisance the extent and effectiveness effects of which were to be minimised. Many have argued that regulation was often undertaken by people and institutions who did not believe in the need for extensive regulation. The now head of the UK's Financial Services Authority (who took up his post on the day that Lehman Brothers collapsed) has written:

> But the belief system of market regulators and financial policy makers in the most financially advanced centres tended to exclude the possibility that rational profit seeking by professional market participants might generate rent extraction and financial instability rather than social benefit – even though several economists had clearly shown why that could be the case. (Turner, 2010, pp. 3–4)

The financial sector had long pushed for deregulation (or self-regulation) and this interacted with the developing neoliberal policy

Table 6.1   Share of financial sector in GDP (%)

	1998	2002	2008
Belgium	4.96	5.01	4.81
Czech Republic	2.99	2.84	2.86
Denmark	4.32	4.25	4.60
Germany	4.82	5.25	4.73
Estonia	2.34	2.71	3.02
Ireland	n.a.	7.61	9.63*
Greece	n.a.	3.39	3.66
Spain	4.15	3.59	3.47*
France	n.a.	4.89	5.19**
Italy	3.61	3.75	4.30
Cyprus	5.43	5.29	5.97
Latvia	2.26	3.55	4.12
Lithuania	1.71	1.99	2.69
Luxembourg	36.71	42.26	51.35
Hungary	2.96	3.09	3.41
Malta	3.75	3.99	5.67
Netherlands	5.62	5.96	5.79
Austria	4.91	4.75	4.70**
Poland	2.75	3.29	3.84
Portugal	4.16	4.60	5.25*
Slovenia	2.96	3.30	3.15
Slovakia	2.02	2.59	2.64
Finland	2.54	2.63	2.17
Sweden	3.41	2.85	2.73*
United Kingdom	6.64	7.49	8.01***
Iceland	3.77	4.89	6.34***
Norway	3.09	2.90	3.53
Switzerland	10.83	10.98	12.10**

* = 2006, ** = 2007, *** = 2005
Source: derived from Eurostat data base.

USA
Finance and insurance: share in national output (%)

1980	1990	2000	2007
4.9	5.9	7.5	7.9

Source: Calculated from *Bureau of Economic Analysis* statistics.

agenda of liberalisation and privatisation. Petit (2010) argues the financial sector:

> has been a major and early promoter of the wave of deregulation that took off in the early 1980s ... Many reasons were given at the

time to support in all countries plans to liberalize financial activities. ... A second argument in favour of the deregulation of the financial sector was that the structures of production had changed. ... There was also a third reason backing the campaign for deregulation. Namely after three decades of a post war expansion, largely fuelled by a process of catching up in continental Europe, there was a general feeling that developed economies were entering a new phase where competitiveness was going to be much less based on price competitiveness and more on qualitative factors (such as design, innovative technological characteristics, after sales service). A deregulated finance did seem in this perspective as a natural co-evolution, matching on many grounds the transformation of the structures of production. (p. 328)

The financial sectors (at least in the UK and the USA) became much more profitable during the 2000s. In the UK, over the period from 2001 to 2007, the share of financial corporations in the gross value added of all corporations rose from 7 per cent to 12 per cent, and the share in operating surplus from 5 per cent to 18 per cent (calculated for Office of National Statistics, *National Income Blue Book 2009*). In the United States, during the 2000s, profits of financial corporations accounted for over one-third of corporate profits (calculated from Bureau of Economic Analysis statistics; various issues) up from around 28 per cent in the period 1987 to 2000.

The traditional roles associated with the financial system are the provision of a payments technology and matching savers and investors, debtors and creditors; and of equal importance the provision of finance to the productive sectors of the economy.[1] It can provide for the sale and resale of financial assets, thereby providing liquidity for savers. It has increasingly been viewed as concerned with the management of risk through provision of insurance functions and the transfer of risk between individuals. 'The main feature of finance is that it is concerned with the mobilization of monetary resources. ... The financial system is also concerned with managing risk, a feature that is particularly stressed by mainstream economists' (Evans, 2009, p. 2). The transport system provides services some of which we may value for themselves (e.g. finding enjoyment and pleasure from a train journey) but many of the benefits of the transport system are derived from someone moving from A to B. My journey to work is rarely pleasurable in itself but enables me to move from my home to place of work. In a similar vein, the financial system can be judged in terms of it facilitating other activities. The provision of an efficient payments system may in some respects be the major role of the financial system in that the immediate justification for propping up banks in difficulty is the effects of people not being paid.

The type of banking which focuses on payments systems and acting as an intermediary between savers and investors has come to be labelled utility or narrow banking. The role of linking savers and investors could also be said to be undertaken by other financial institutions, including the stock exchange. However, in the case of the stock exchange, it has generally not been a source of significant new funds, but rather a combination of enabling entrepreneurs to sell stakes in their companies and – more frequently – a site for the trading of existing equity.

> Since the 1970s, the financial system of the developed capitalist countries have all experienced a major increase in size and complexity as a result of extensive process of innovation, deregulation and internationalization. Most mainstream economists take the view that this has been highly beneficial, that monetary resources have thereby been channelled to those that can employ them most efficiently, and that modern global networks have made it possible to diversity risk so as to strengthen the stability of the system as a whole. ... we take a different view. We consider that the financial sector imposes excessive costs on the rest of the economy, that it does not ensure that capital is made available where it is most needed, and that it has been a key factor in leading to greater inequality and social security. Although the financial sector has succeeded in diversifying certain forms of risk, we believe that it has created new sources of potential instability that increase the risk of a major crisis for the system as a whole. (Evans, 2009, p. 3)

3   The role and costs of the financial sector

The financial sector has absorbed many more resources in recent years and has extracted large profits. Has there been a commensurate increase in the economic benefits provided by the financial sector? If, as discussed in the previous section, two of the main purposes of the financial sector are the provision of a payments system and the linking together of savers and investors, then we would speculate that there has not been any major improvement in the services provided to the real sector by the financial sector. It is difficult to detect any upward trend in household savings over the past two decades – see, for example, figures given in OECD (2010, Annex Table 23), and indeed a rise in consumer debt was a well-known forerunner of the financial crisis. This would suggest that the growth of the financial sector has not stimulated more savings nor has it had more savings to allocate.

It is possible that the efficiency with which the funds from savers are allocated to potential investment has improved – through a reduction in the transactions costs involved, and through improvements in assessment of the use of funds and risks involved leading to 'better quality' investment. For the main industrialised countries, there does not appear to be much change in the volume of investment (relative to GDP) nor in the rate of growth (which might have reflected 'better quality' investment). It is not readily apparent, admittedly at a superficial level, that there have been improvements in the quantity and quality of savings and investment commensurate with the resources employed in the financial sector. Indeed, it could be argued that the ways in which funds were allocated, notably in the direction of consumer debt, played a role in the build-up to the financial crisis.

It is, of course, the rapid growth of new and often complex financial instruments which has attracted much attention.

> Since the 1970s there has been an enormous growth of another type of financial instrument, known as derivatives, which are not concerned with raising finance at all, but rather with unbundling the different characteristics of a security, such as the risk of a change in its price, or of a default. This makes it possible to trade these characteristics without having to trade the underlying security on which they are based. Selling derivatives has become a major source of business for investment banks, who have taken to employing physicists and other graduates with advanced degrees involving maths (so-called 'rocket scientists') to dream up ever more complicated instruments. (Evans, 2009, p. 12)

A dramatic expression of the scale of one part of the financial sector concerns the trade in financial derivatives.

> The total value of all 'over the counter' derivatives outstanding in December 2008, in the world, was ... 591 trillion dollars. World GDP is about 60 trillion so you could say financial speculation economy is notionally ten times the value of the real economy. A more relevant figure is the gross market value of all these bets, a staggering

33 trillion – or half of world GDP. Of these by far the largest slice of the cake is interest rate swaps: 18 trillion in market value, 418 trillion in notional trading. (Mason, 2009)

It could be seen that it was the relatively recent developments in the financial system that were linked closely with the causes of the financial crisis and the forms that were taken by that crisis. It is also those recent developments which raise most questions on the social value of the financial sector. One expression of this has been as follows:

> The financial system of the recent past – with its high leverage, massive trading activities, and ever more complex financial innovation – didn't just go a little bit off course, it blew up spectacularly. And some of the intellectual foundations on which it was based – the reliance on the self-correcting nature of financial markets and on the effectiveness of market discipline in controlling risk-taking – have turned out to be profoundly mistaken. (Turner, 2009)

A number of authors have questioned the social value of these financial innovations. For example,

> Lord Turner [now head of UK Financial Services Authority] ... condemned some financial innovation as 'socially useless', questioning whether 'the world would have been better off without any credit default swaps'. 'There clearly are bits of the financial system ... which have grown beyond a socially reasonable size,' he added. He said that you could tell that by considering 'what percentage of highly intelligent people from our best universities went into financial services'. (http://news.bbc.co.uk/1/hi/business/8223663.stm)

> Lord Turner's view was that there were parts of the wholesale financial services industry – in particular, those relating to structured credit, credit derivatives and fixed income trading – which 'simply grew beyond their socially useful size'. They were 'indulging in innovation which was not socially useful ... but either regulatory arbitrage ... tax arbitrage ... or rent extraction.' As long as that occurs on a more-than-useful scale, he continued, some people would end up 'being paid very large amounts of money for things which are not terribly useful'. The solution, he contended, was likely to lie in

adjusting capital requirements rather than banning entire products. (House of Commons Treasury Select Committee, 2009, p. 26)

In a similar vein George Soros wrote that

> the transaction in question clearly had no social benefit. It involved a complex synthetic security derived from existing mortgage-backed securities by cloning them into imaginary units that mimicked the originals. This synthetic collateralised debt obligation did not finance the ownership of any additional homes or allocate capital more efficiently; it merely swelled the volume of mortgage-backed securities that lost value when the housing bubble burst. The primary purpose of the transaction was to generate fees and commissions. (Soros, 2010)

> Mr Jon Moulton, of Alchemy Partners, labelled innovation in the banking system 'a disease' and did not believe that regulators could keep pace with financial innovation, arguing that a large bank 'with 30 or 40 business lines and huge books of derivatives', was simply too complex. In some cases, he observed, products were 'simply incapable of being analysed by the vast majority of people out there'. ... Professor Buiter commented that there had been an enormous amount of financial innovation that had been pointless and even actively harmful. (House of Commons Treasury Select Committee, 2009, pp. 24–5)

The growth in the scale of the financial sector in many countries and the ways in which its modes of operation and developments in the nature of its offerings raise the obvious questions as to whether the resources devoted to the financial sector have brought commensurate gains in economic well-being and whether the manner in which the financial sectors have changed has brought greater instability. Until 2007, the answer to the latter question would have generally been dismissive of such a possibility, but now the question has to be seriously entertained. Here we have sketched the view that there has not been gains in terms of economic welfare from the increased scale of the financial sector, and that many of its activities are 'socially useless'.

4 Costs of financial crisis

The worldwide recession of 2009–10 can clearly be ascribed to the crisis in the financial sectors, particularly in the US and the UK. The costs of the financial crisis can then be seen through the effects on the levels of economic activity and unemployment as well as the fiscal and other costs associated with the bailout of financial institutions. In many countries which are suffering from recession there was no financial crisis emanating from within its own borders and in other cases difficulties within the financial sector came from their acquisition of 'toxic assets' from American, British and European financial institutions. It could then be argued that the costs of the financial crisis around the world are broader than the costs of loss of economic activity and of financial bailouts which arise within the borders of those countries, and that much of the decline in global output can be viewed as the costs of the financial crises. It is also our contention here that the financial crisis arose from behaviours within the financial sector, and hence the costs imposed by the financial crisis should be viewed as costs of the financial sector imposed on the rest of the economy.

The financial crises of 2007/08 should be viewed as just the latest (and probably the nearest to a full global crisis yet seen)[2] in a long series of financial crises, and serve as a reminder of the systemic nature of financial crises. In that vein, Minsky argued nearly three decades ago that 'Since this recent financial instability is a recurrence of phenomena that regularly characterized our economy before World War II, it is reasonable to view financial crises as systemic, rather than accidental, events. From this perspective, the anomaly is the twenty years after World War II during which financial crises were absent ...' (Minsky, 1982, p. 63): Just before this passage Minsky had listed three threats of financial crisis in the US which were tackled through Federal Reserve interventions: 1966, 1970, 1974–75. More recently, Alan Greenspan remarked that 'The crisis will happen again but it will be different'.[3] The frequency of financial crises can be readily seen from Laeven and Valencia (2008) in their comprehensive listing of banking and other financial crisis for the period 1970–2007 which records 124 banking crises, 211 exchange crises and 64 sovereign debt crises. Those authors also argue that

> The financial crises of the past have led affected economies into deep recessions and sharp current account reversals. Some crises turned out to be contagious, rapidly spreading to countries with no apparent vulnerabilities. Among the many causes of financial crises have been a combination of unsustainable macroeconomic policies (including large current account deficits and unsustainable public debt), excessive credit booms, large capital inflows, and balance sheet fragilities, combined with policy paralysis due to a variety of political and economic constraints. In many financial crises currency

and maturity mismatches were a salient feature, while in others off-balance sheet operations of the banking sector were prominent. (Laeven and Valencia, 2008, p. 3)

The costs of banking crises are often substantial: the above-mentioned authors reviewed 42 banking crises from around the world and estimated that:

- Gross fiscal costs as share of GDP: 15.7 per cent (ranging 0 to 56.8 per cent); net fiscal costs: 13.0 per cent (range 0 to 55.1 per cent).
- Output loss as share of GDP: 20.1 per cent ranging from 0 to 97.7 per cent: this appears to be cumulated over four years (the extreme observation is Thailand 1997), and hence the equivalent on average of output being about 5 per cent lower for each of four years.

Andrew Haldane, Executive Director, Financial Stability, Bank of England, has remarked that the costs of the financial crisis can be evaluated in terms of the fiscal costs or the foregone output of a crisis, and that 'on either measure, the costs of past financial crises appear to be large and long-lived, often in excess of 10% of pre-crisis GDP' (Haldane, 2010, p. 3). But with regard to the present crisis, the fiscal costs may turn out to be relatively small:

The narrowest fiscal interpretation of the cost of crisis would be given by the wealth transfer from the government to the banks as a result of the bailout. Plainly, there is a large degree of uncertainty about the eventual loss governments may face. But in the US, this is currently estimated to be around $100 billion, or less than 1% of US GDP. For US taxpayers, these losses are (almost exactly) a $100 billion question. In the UK, the direct cost may be less than £20 billion, or little more than 1% of GDP. (Haldane, 2010, p. 3)

It is well known that there have been major falls in output and rises in unemployment in 2008 onwards which can be readily attributed to the financial crises. Quoting Haldane again, 'World output in 2009 is expected to have been around 6.5% lower than its counterfactual path in the absence of crisis. In the UK, the equivalent output loss is around 10%' (Haldane, 2010, p. 3). It could be argued that this fall in output is just the downturn stage of a business cycle, and it is compensated by higher output during the upturn stage of the business cycle. Indeed it could be argued that the relatively rapid growth in global output in the years 2003–07 was associated with the credit boom, rising leverage etc. of that era. But experience from previous recessions indicates that effects of recession on lower output may be long lasting. For example, Dow (1998) in his study of the major UK recessions of the twentieth century concluded that

> that in a major recession underemployment results in the deterioration and premature scrapping of physical equipment, and that disbandment or underemployment of a firm's workforce similarly results in the partial destruction of working practices and working relations. ... The capital stock, physical and intangible, takes time to build up, and its destruction cannot be made good rapidly; in effect, therefore, the destruction is quasi-permanent. In this way demand shocks impact on supply. (p. 369)

In the present recession, it has been widely recognised that while there may be a revival of growth around the previously experienced rates, the growth will come from a lower base of output, and that future output may well be on a significantly lower trajectory. From that perspective the costs of financial crisis and recession became quite large. For example, Haldane provides illustrative figures for the present value of global output losses and for the UK based on 'assuming different fractions of the 2009 loss are permanent – 100%, 50% and 25%. It also assumes, somewhat arbitrarily, that future GDP is discounted at a rate of 5% per year and that trend GDP growth is 3%. Present value losses are shown as a fraction of output in 2009.' On that basis his Table 1 'shows, these losses are multiples of the static costs, lying anywhere between one and five times annual GDP. Put in money terms, that is an output loss equivalent to between $60 trillion and $200 trillion for the world economy and between £1.8 trillion and £7.4 trillion for the UK' (Haldane, 2010, pp. 3–4). OECD provides some alternative estimates and selected figures are reported in Table 6.2. This provides a comparison between the growth of potential output in the periods 2006–08, 2009–10 and 2011–17. If again the differences are ascribed to the ongoing effects of the financial crisis, then for the OECD area as a whole, some 0.4 percentage points are knocked off potential growth (2.1–1.7). The final column of Table 6.2 indicates that these forecasts would imply that potential output for the OECD area as a whole will be 4 per cent lower with the forecast growth rates for 2009 through 2017 as compared with what it would be if the growth rate of 2006–08

Table 6.2 Potential output

Annual growth rate of potential output	2006–08	2009–11	2011–17	Output shortfall 2017
USA	2.4	1.5	2.0	4.4
UK	2.2	1.3	1.7	5.1
Canada	2.4	1.6	1.7	6.2
France	1.7	1.2	1.4	3.0
Germany	1.2	0.8	1.1	1.5
Japan	1.0	0.6	0.8	2.2
Euro area	1.7	0.9	1.3	4.2
OECD	2.1	1.4	1.7	4.0

Source: OECD, *Economic Outlook* June 2009, chapter 4 and own calculations.

were continued. Again this would mean that even if the pre-crisis rate of potential output resumed after 2017, (potential) output is 4 per cent lower in perpetuity.

Financial crises clearly have the capacity to impose very substantial costs on the real economy through associated recessions. Yet financial crises are endemic to a financial capitalist economy. In the next section we look at three aspects of policy changes which may at least reduce the frequency of crises.

5 Re-structuring the financial sector

The general thrust of what has been written above is that the expansion of the financial sector over the past three decades or so has not self-evidently brought comparable economic benefits and in a number of countries (including the USA and the UK) has probably become much too large. Further, we have suggested that the financial innovations have often been of little social worth, and indeed products which were said to reduce risk (at least at the individual level) may well have increased systemic risk. The frequency with which financial crises occur is supportive of the general view that 'the processes which make for financial instability are an inescapable part of any decentralized capitalist economy – i.e., capitalism is inherently flawed – but financial instability need not lead to a great depression; "It" need not happen' (Minsky, 1982, p. viii). In a similar vein 'instability is determined by mechanisms within the system, not outside it; our economy is not unstable because it is shocked by oil, wars or monetary surprises, but because of its nature' (Minsky 1986, p. 172). A major response to the financial crisis of

2007/09 has been the call for reforms to the regulation of the financial system, including improved macroprudential regulation, which does not operate on a pro-cyclical basis and incorporates the global reach of financial markets. Regulation faces great problems, including informational problems, responding to innovation in response to regulation and regulatory capture. In recent times, regulators seem to have suffered from a form of 'Stockholm syndrome',[4] whereby the regulator not only acts in the interests of the regulated but also admires the actions of the regulated. One aspect of this is reflected in the statement of the head of the UK Financial Services Authority: 'And in regulators such as the FSA, the assumption that financial innovation and increased market liquidity were valuable because they complete markets and improve price discovery were not just accepted, they were part of the institutional DNA, part of the belief system' (Turner, 2010, p. 3). The approach taken here does not relate to issues of regulation (which is not to dismiss that it has a considerable role) but to issues of structure and size of the financial sector.

The conclusions which we draw from the discussion above is that there is a strong sense in which the financial sector has become too large in many countries and on a global scale with economic benefits generated by the financial sector not commensurate with the resources used by the financial sector. The financial sector imposes costs on the rest of the economy in using resources to produce 'socially useless' products but more significantly through the costs imposed by financial crises including the substantial costs of the 'bailing out' of financial institutions and, more substantially, the subsequent losses of output and employment arising from financial crises. In the policy discussions below we focus on three aspects. First, addressing the 'too big to fail' issue with financial institutions. Second, making use of alternative ownership forms (public and mutual). Third, the extension of taxation to the financial sector.

In many countries the growth of the financial sector over the past two or three decades has been against a background of deregulation and liberalisation. The deregulation and liberalisation have also been accompanied by a decline of the publicly owned banks (particularly significant in many European countries)[5] with the privatisation of banks went alongside other privatisation programmes. In some countries, notably the UK, there was a sharp decline in mutual ownership in the financial sector, coming from a similar belief in the benefits of individual property ownership and the incentives for those who were the collective owners of the mutual (that is, the customers) to acquire individual ownership, which could then be sold. The mutual organisation (although this would also be the case for many local banks) raised much of its funds from the locality in which it was located, and its operations were circumscribed to the provision of banking services, deposit taking and loan provision. However, in other countries, 'the share of cooperative banks has been increasing in recent years; in the sample of banks in advanced economies and emerging markets analyzed in this chapter, the market share of cooperative banks in terms of total banking sector assets increased from about 9 percent in the mid-1990s to about 14 percent in 2004' (Hesse and Čihák, 2007).

> Cooperative banks are particularly numerous and large in Europe. The five largest cooperative banks in the European Union (EU) rank among the EU's top 25 banking groups in terms of consolidated equity. Reflecting the cooperative banks' focus on retail banking, their market share in retail business is even more substantial: for example, five EU member countries have more than a 40 percent market share of cooperative banks in terms of branch networks ... In non-European advanced economies and emerging markets, the share of cooperative banks is generally lower, but there are several countries where they play a non-negligible role. (Hesse and Čihák, 2007)

In thinking about how the financial sector should operate, there is no suggestion that some 'master plan' is put forward. The re-structuring of the financial sector would, however, involve legislation and regulation. But the ideas are more in terms of the direction in which the financial sector could and should be pushed. Here we focus on three sets of ideas. In doing so, there is the assumption that the financial sector has, in many countries, become too large. Hence, objections to proposals below along the lines that this would cause the financial sector to contract (and hence provide less employment, etc.) would, from this perspective, be misplaced. But it does throw up major policy challenges since other industries have to develop to take the place of the financial sector, and industrial as well as macroeconomic policies are required to generate supply and demand conditions needed for full employment. There is also the implicit assumption that the key roles of the financial sector (and notably banking) are the provision of an efficient payments transmission system and the efficient linking of savers and investors.

Dealing with 'too big to fail'

The 'too big to fail' argument states in effect that the failure of an enterprise would have such large negative effects on others that it has to be prevented. These can range over the effects on employment effects in an area, the effects on a country's trading position and the essential nature of the goods or services, which are provided. In the case of financial institutions, it can be employment and other effects, But, more generally, it is the contagion effects from the failure of one financial institution on others through the credit–debt, asset–liability relationships between financial institutions. Further there are the losses imposed on households and from the nature of the services provided in terms of the functioning of the payments system.

A partial response to the issue of losses imposed on households by bank failure comes through deposit insurance for banks. This has, however, generally been limited to relatively small amounts and can raise issues of moral hazard. In a globalised financial system it also raises a question over which national body operates the deposit insurance and for which range of banks (e.g. does a national body in country A provide deposit insurance for a bank owned in country B but operating in country A?). It is clearly also the case that the 'lender of last resort' facility of the Central Bank can address failures arising from liquidity problems (provided that the liquidity problems are in the currency of the country concerned).

The 'too big' element with regard to the financial sector should also be addressed through the operation of competition policy, and specifically through merger policy. In many parts of the financial sector there are issues of market dominance, leading to exploitation of consumers and monopoly profits. There is a good case for a more vigorous competition policy applied to the financial sector, and this could also address issues of vertical integration within financial institutions. There are potential trade-offs between the loss of economies of scale and the exercise of monopoly power. There are also potential trade-offs between the loss of economies of scope and effects which interconnections with an institution have whereby problems in the highly risky parts of the business spread to the rest of the institution and threaten to bring the whole lot down and the conflicts of interest which arise when a range of activities are undertaken within a single organisation.

In the end these are issues which can only be settled through thorough investigations on a case-by-case basis, and no doubt the conclusions would differ from country to country – not least because of some major differences in the degree of competition and concentration across countries. But it may need to be recognized that economies of scale in banking (and in the financial sector more generally) are insubstantial and there should be the presumption that the costs from the exercise of monopoly power (including the associated political power) outweigh the losses from not being able to exploit economies of scale. In this regard, note remarks such as 'economies of scale appear to operate among banks with assets less, perhaps much less, than $100 billion' (Haldane, 2010, p. 16).

The essence of the argument here is that the 'too big to fail' issue should be approached along two lines. First, addressing the issue of size of financial institutions including market share and the scope of activities, Second, the presumption that failing financial institutions should indeed fail with measures to limit the damage which failure of a financial institution should have. The failure of a financial institution imposes costs – on depositors, workers, shareholders. There will inevitably be costs but those costs should as far as possible fall on the owners of the financial institution involved.

There are clearly costs involved in financial institutions going bankrupt, and on the other side there are costs associated with rescue packages, notably fiscal costs and thereby costs to the taxpayers. The costs of the Savings and Loans crisis in the US come readily to mind (at around $160 billion with nearly $125 billion for the financial bailout paid by the US government).[6] But in so far as rescues come through the nationalisation of the financial institutions and hence the acquisition by government of potentially valuable assets, the costs of 'bailouts' are mitigated. Indeed, as hinted above, the substantial costs of financial crisis come from the loss of output, which is often substantial.

The operations of the Federal Deposit Insurance (FDI) in the USA provide a clear example of how to proceed. On the one hand, insurance fees are in effect paid up-front by the financial institutions, which are covered (largely deposit-taking banks). On the other institutional arrangements are in place which permit the takeover of failing banks and their immediate continued operation. This may be followed by the sale of assets, merger with another financial institution and so on. One limitation on this approach may come from the scale of the banks involved, which have tended to be rather small, and the question as to whether it could be extended to the very largest financial institutions.

The analogy may be drawn between what is proposed here and the mechanisms which are (sometimes) in place with regard to public utilities providing vital services such as water, gas, electricity and some transport. A firm that is currently supplying one of those services could be deemed too vital to fail in the sense that the service provided is regarded as vital and where it is not possible at short notice for alternative sources of the service to be provided.

The first key element in what is proposed here is that where what is considered a vital service is being provided for which there is no ready alternative provider, mechanisms should be put in place which permit the financial institution in question to continue in operation until, in effect, alternative arrangements can be made. These alternatives would include the growth of alternative providers, the sale of parts of the business to others and the orderly running down of the unprofitable parts. But the financial institution is allowed to fail – in effect, it goes bankrupt without any compensation being paid to shareholders.

It is widely recognized that deposit insurance and, more generally, a perception that a firm is 'too big to fail' and will consequently be rescued in the case of difficulties generates problems of moral hazard. Greater risk taking is encouraged if the costs of failure are reduced or removed. When an undertaking is successful, the high returns are retained, when an undertaking is unsuccessful, the losses are socialised. A firm that fails and goes bankrupt imposes losses on many – its workers, its creditors and its shareholders.

The arrangements required are that if the functions performed by a financial institution are in some sense vital, those functions continue (and run down in an orderly fashion) following bankruptcy, which imposes maximum losses on the shareholders of the company concerned. There are still costs involved in that bankruptcy imposes costs on a range of people other than the shareholders – creditors not paid, workers losing wages and employment, and so on.

Ownership

There has been a long history of mutual, social and public ownership of banks (broadly defined). At least in the European context, the role of public ownership have been drastically reduced in the past two to three decades, though with some reappearance of public ownership, albeit on an emergency and intended temporary basis, in the past two years. The argument here relates to the long-term role of mutual and public banks rather than as a measure to deal with the threat of collapse by private banks. But, of course, the public ownership, in full or in part, provide an opportunity to re-build mutual and public ownership. The banks now in public ownership could be retained on a long-term basis albeit with a redefinition of their role; an alternative would be to use public ownership as a stage en route to re-mutualisation.

The arguments for the encouragement and development of mutual and public ownership are based on the view that the objectives, roles and nature of mutual and publicly owned financial institutions would differ from those of the privately owned financial institutions. This is not to understate the position that financial institutions are run by managers, whatever the ownership structure, and are subject to the pressures of competition which can bring about similar behaviour by the managers, notwithstanding the differences of ownership structure. For mutual organisations (specifically in the UK) it is argued that 'the ownership structure, regulation and traditional business model of mutual building societies (particularly the dominance of retail funding) makes them less prone to risky speculative activity than is the case with shareholder-owned banks' (Oxford Centre for Mutual & Employee-owned Business, 2009). It has previously been found that 'cooperative banks are more stable than commercial banks. This finding is due to the lower volatility of the cooperative banks' returns, which more than offsets their lower profitability and capitalisation. This is most likely due to cooperative banks' ability to use customer surplus as a cushion in weaker periods. We also find that in systems with a high presence of cooperative banks, weak commercial banks are less stable than they would be otherwise. The overall impact of a higher cooperative presence on bank stability is positive on average but insignificant in some specifications' (Hesse and Čihák, 2007, p. 1).

Banks operating with mutual or public ownership can be a major route through which the key roles of the banking system – namely the provision of payments technology and linking lenders with borrowers and savers with firms undertaking investment – can be reasserted. It is rather pointless to set up (or, in the case of a number of countries where the government has acquired, wholly or in part, 'failing' banks as part of rescue packages, to maintain) publicly owned banks if those banks operate using methods that are essentially the same as privately owned banks. It would be further argued here that the differences in the ways in which public owned banks would operate could not be achieved through regulation. The ways in which public banks could operate would have to depend on the economic objectives of the government and the existing banking system and its shortcomings. The general suggestions, however, would be for publicly owned banks to focus on commercial banking rather than investment banking. Such banks must ensure universal access to the banking system such that everyone has banking facilities readily available to them. It is, however, the provision of investment funds which would be at the heart of their operations.

More than that, however, public banks could also take upon themselves aspects of development banking since they would have both social authority and requisite information about borrowers and the economy. Public banks could thus be part of a general policy to deal with financialization by supporting a revival of production and moving economies away from finance. They would be natural institutions to guide aggregate investment and promote new fields of activity, including 'green' industries in which mature capitalist economies appear to have a comparative advantage. (Lapavitsas, 2010, p. 193)

Mutual and publicly owned banks and other financial institutions would provide a more diverse financial system, and the diversity in terms of objectives, modes of operation and so on could make a contribution to improving the stability of the financial system. There is the potential for these types of financial institutions to focus on what should be the roles of the financial system – the provision of a payments technology, and the channelling of savings into investment.

Taxation

There are three strands to the arguments on the taxation of the financial system. The first is simply that the products of the financial sector are, in general, taxed less than most other goods and services. For example, financial services are frequently exempt from value added taxes (IMF, 2010). The second is similar in that the taxation of financial services/sector (or some parts thereof) is effectively undertaken for reasons of raising revenue, but here with the idea that the tax revenue be hypothecated to provide a 'war chest' to be available as funds for the 'bailing out' of troubled financial institutions. This is subject to two provisos. First, the literal construction of a war chest would be deflationary, and the accounting should be undertaken on a notional basis such that over time the stream of tax revenues from the financial sector more than balances the outgoings on bailouts. Second, as argued above, any rescue of financial institutions should ensure that shareholders bear heavy losses and that a rescue package is focused on reducing the costs of bankruptcy as they fall on workers, customers and other groups.

The third set of arguments relate in a range of ways to using taxation in order to reduce the scale of the financial sector in some way. In this regard, the idea of a financial transactions tax (often now referred to as a 'Tobin tax') is one of long standing. '[t]he introduction of a substantial government transfer tax on all transactions might prove the most serviceable reform available, with a view to mitigating the predominance of speculation over enterprise in the United States' (Keynes, 1936, p. 160). Keynes (1936, pp. 158–9) argues that as a market (foreign exchange markets in this instance) more closely approximates perfect competition (in the sense that transaction costs tend towards zero), the risk increases that speculation ('the activity of forecasting the psychology of the market' as Keynes defines it) will dominate enterprise ('the activity of forecasting the prospective yield of assets over their whole life').

Its recent history starts with Tobin (1974, 1978) and is directed specifically towards the foreign exchange markets. Its aim was, in Tobin's phrase, to 'put sand in the wheels', that is to slow down the volume of transactions in the foreign exchange markets. It was the volatility of the exchange rate under a floating exchange rate system, which was the centre of attention here, and the role of 'noise trading' in the generation of that volatility. It has been a matter of continuing controversy as to whether the volume of transactions does increase or decrease volatility, and also how far the volatility of the exchange rate has detrimental effects on trade and international investment flows. The 'Tobin tax' on exchange dealings has, of course, attracted much attention as a potentially large source of revenue, though with the recognition that such a tax would have to levied on an internationally co-ordinated basis. It is well known that the volume of foreign exchange transactions is of the order of 60 times the volume of international trade. The question here is whether there are significant benefits to this volume of transactions far in excess of that required to finance international trade and long-term capital flows. The possible harmful effects in terms of effects on volatility and thereby on trade have been well rehearsed, even if there are some doubts as to their significance. The question posed here is more whether in light of the resources which are devoted to arranging such transactions there is a corresponding benefit (see, for example, Arestis and Sawyer, 1997, for more discussion on the 'Tobin tax').

Another line of argument to be considered relates to a transactions tax as a form of Pigovian tax, which goes some way towards correcting some externality. There may be two elements here. First, insofar as more transactions in financial assets increase rather than diminish risk (financial fragility) and/or increase the volatility of prices (recognising that the mainstream view would be that the broader the market the lower the volatility). Second, there is the argument (Turner) to the effect that many of the 'products' are 'socially useless'. Since the trading (and indeed the creation) of those products absorbs some resources, then their production should be discouraged. (The idea that some financial products are socially useless needs to be further explored in that people are buying and selling those products, and it is presumed that creating/trading in those products is profitable.)

A transaction tax on trading in financial products can also be seen as a means of raising general tax revenue, some of which could be devoted to 'rescue packages' of the financial sector which often come at considerable cost. It has, of course, to be considered whether a transactions tax could be implemented on a national (or European) scale, or whether as a practical matter it would require to be implemented on a global scale (at least involving, say, the G20 countries).

The title of IMF (2010), 'A Fair and Substantial Contribution by the Financial Sector', in many ways sums up many of the arguments. In that document, two 'forms of contributions' are envisaged. The first is in the form of a 'financial stability contribution', which, it is argued, would be 'linked to a credible and resolution mechanism'. The second is a 'financial activities tax' (which has the appropriate acronym of FAT), which would be 'levied on the sum of the profits and remuneration of the financial institutions' (p. 3).

6   Concluding comments

The main theme of this chapter has related to the costs which the financial sector can impose on the real economy, through the resources which it absorbs and through the ever-present possibility of crisis and recession. As indicated above, the costs of financial crisis are very substantial, and yet there are doubts as to whether the resources used by the financial sector provide social useful output commensurate with the resources deployed. Better regulation can have some role to play in addressing issues of financial instability. But there is the danger of regulatory capture in the sense that the regulators become infected by neoliberalism and the restraints of regulation on profits and innovation. We have briefly considered three other elements of new policies towards the financial sector, which could be summarised as: (i) avoidance of the 'too big to fail' syndrome with failing financial institutions going bankrupt in a setting where the activities of a failing institution can continue; (ii) the stimulation of mutual and publicly owned financial institutions; and (iii) taxation to limit the size and scope of the financial sector.

Notes

1. The relationship between savings and investment is a matter of debate. The tradition view, exemplified in the financial repression literature (McKinnon, Shaw) is a loanable funds approach whereby the links go: savings – bank

deposits – loans – investment. The post Keynesian view runs from investment intentions – loans – investment – bank deposits – savings (Arestis and Sawyer, 2004, for an example). But in either event, the simplified balance sheet of the banks has deposits and loans as the two matching sides of the balance sheet.

2. Crises such as that of the late 1920s/1930s associated with the Great Depression did not have the geographical spread of the present one since, for example, countries such as the Soviet Union were exempt.

3. Interview on BBC Two's 'Love of Money' broadcast at 2100 BST on 10, 17 and 24 September 2009; http://news.bbc.co.uk/1/hi/business/8244600.stm.

4. 'Stockholm syndrome is a term used to describe a paradoxical psychological phenomenon wherein hostages express adulation and have positive feelings towards their captors that appear irrational in light of the danger or risk endured by the victims' (Wikipedia).

5. See Frangakis, Huffschmid and Mencinger (2009) for full discussion on privatisation in the financial sector in Europe. They report (their Table 12.2) 81 bank privatisation in the EU over the period 1982–2000 valued at over $68 billion.

6. Financial Audit: Resolution Trust Corporation 1995 and 1994 Financial Statements, US General Accounting Office. July 1996.

References

Arestis, P. and Sawyer, M. (1997) 'How Many Cheers for the Tobin Financial Transactions Tax?', *Cambridge Journal of Economics*, 21(6), 753–68.

Arestis, P. and Sawyer, M. (2004) *Re-examining Monetary and Fiscal Policies in the Twenty First Century*. Aldershot: Edward Elgar Publishing Limited.

Dow, J.C.R. (1998) *Major Recessions: Britain and the World, 1920–1995*. London and New York: Oxford University Press.

Epstein, G. (2005) *Financialization and the World Economy*. Aldershot: Edward Elgar.

Evans, T. (2009) 'Money and Finance Today', in J. Grahl (eds), *Global Finance and Social Europe*. Cheltenham: Edward Elgar.

Frangakis, M., Huffschmid, J. and Mencinger, J. (2009) 'Bank Liberalization and Privatisation', in Marica Frangakis, Christoph Hermann, Jörg Huffschmid and Károly Lóránt (eds), *Privatisation against the European Social Model: A Critique of European Policies and Proposals for Alternatives*. Basingstoke: Palgrave Macmillan.

Haldane, A. (2010) 'The $100 Billion Question', Comments given at the Institute of Regulation & Risk, Hong Kong, 30 March, http://www.bankofengland. co.uk/publications/speeches/2010/speech433.pdf.

Hesse, H. and Čihák, M. (2007) 'Cooperative Banks and Financial Stability', *IMF Working Paper*, WP/07/2. Washington DC: International Monetary Fund.

House of Commons Treasury Committee (2009). *Banking Crisis: Regulation and Supervision*, Fourteenth Report of Session 2008–09, London.

IMF (2010) 'A Fair and Substantial Contribution by the Financial Sector', paper prepared for Meeting of G20 Ministers, April.

Laeven, L. and Valencia, F. (2008) 'Systemic Banking Crises: A New Database', *IMF Working Papers*, WP/08/224. Washington DC: International Monetary Fund.

Lapavitsas, C. (2010) 'Systemic Failure of Private Banking: A Case for Public Banks'; in P. Arestis and M. Sawyer (eds), *21st Century Keynesian Economics*. Basingstoke: Palgrave Macmillan.

Mason, P. (2009) 'Radical Capitalist Proposes Direct Action at Canary Wharf', http://www.bbc.co.uk/blogs/newsnight/paulmason/2009/08/radical_capitalist_proposes_di.html.

Minsky, H.P. (1982) *Can 'It' Happen Again: Essays on Instability and Finance*. Armonk, NY: M.E. Sharpe.

Minsky, H.P. (1986) *Stabilizing an Unstable Economy*. New Haven: Yale University Press.

OECD (2010) *Economic Outlook*. Paris: OECD.

Oxford Centre for Mutual & Employee-owned Business (2009) 'Converting Failed Financial Institutions into Mutual Organisations' (downloaded from http://www.kellogg.ox.ac.uk/researchcentres/meob.php).

Petit, P. (2010) 'Financial Globalisation and Innovation: Lessons of a Lost Decade for the OECD Economies', in G. Fontana, J. McCombie and M. Sawyer (eds), *Macroeconomics, Finance and Money: Essays in Honour of Philip Arestis*. Basingstoke: Palgrave Macmillan.

Soros, G. (2010) 'America Must Face Up to the Dangers of Derivatives', *Financial Times*, 23 April.

Tobin, J. (1974) 'The New Economics One Decade Older', *The Eliot Janeway Lectures on Historical Economics in Honour of Joseph Schumpeter, 1972*. Princeton, NJ: Princeton University Press.

Tobin, J. (1978) 'A Proposal for International Monetary Reform', *Eastern Economic Journal*, 4 (3–4), 153–9. Reprinted in J. Tobin, *Essays in Economics: Theory and Policy*. Cambridge, MA: The MIT Press).

Turner, A. (2009) 'FSA's Annual Public Meeting Speech', http://www.fsa.gov.uk/pages/Library/Communication/Speeches/2009/2307_at.shtml.

Turner, A. (2010) 'Economics, Conventional Wisdom and Public Policy'. Talk presented at Institute for New Economic Thinking, Inaugural Conference Cambridge, April.

7
Regulate Financial Systems, or Financial Institutions?

Costas Lapavitsas

1 Introduction

Financial regulation could be usefully differentiated into two approaches, first, regulating finance as a system and, second, regulating individual financial institutions. Both contain an aspect of market negation, thus directly influencing the returns to enterprises employed in the sphere of finance. However, the deployment of market negation varies considerably between the two approaches.

Systemic regulation of finance prevailed for nearly three decades following the end of the Second World War. During that period financial regulation had a directed (rather than simply generic) market-negating aspect. Simplifying brutally, the underlying assumption was that the untrammelled operation of financial systems could potentially destabilise capitalist accumulation. Regulatory authorities deployed market negation with the – often unspoken – aim of supporting capitalist accumulation in general. The typical pattern of systemic regulation, consequently, involved an array of mutually interacting measures, such as price and quantity controls, functional specialisation of institutions, and capital controls.

In the course of financial liberalisation and as mature economies became increasingly financialised from the 1970s onwards, systemic regulation of finance lost out to the regulation of financial institutions. Simplifying again, it was assumed that freely operating financial markets were inherently beneficial to capitalist accumulation. Consequently, the regulatory structure that allowed state authorities to direct market negation was dismantled. In its place emerged a market-conforming system regulating the performance of individual financial institutions primarily through imposing constraints on balance sheets.

One remarkable feature of this transformation, however, was that generic market negation has flourished during the same period. Market-conforming regulation of finance might have rejected market negation in its directed form, but has fostered it in its generic form. This meant, above all, lender of last resort interventions, deposit protection for financial intermediaries, and implicit guarantees of the solvency of large financial institutions advanced by the state. The result has been to support the profitability of private financial institutions rather than sustaining capitalist accumulation as a whole.

The crisis of 2007–9 has been a catalytic event in this regard. It has cast light on the transformation of private banking in recent years, particularly the ability of banks to undertake information collection and risk management. It has further revealed the failure of regulation that focuses on financial institutions, while also accentuating generic market negation in the field of finance. Consequently, the crisis has posed afresh the issue of regulating finance as a system. It is argued in this chapter that, under contemporary conditions, it would be difficult to resurrect the older system of directed market negation. For systemic regulation of finance today it would be important also to consider public ownership and control over banks.

The chapter is structured as follows. Section 2 considers the characteristic features of systemic regulation prevailing in the years following the Second World War. The market-negating aspect of this type of regulation is analysed in relation to the generic market-negating aspect of all financial regulation. Section 3 discusses the decline of systemic regulation, the rise of market-conforming regulation of institutions, and the persistence of market negation. Section 4 considers the reasons for failure of market-conforming regulation and the implications for financial regulation in the future. Section 5 concludes by briefly examining public banks as an integral part of systemic regulation of finance.

2   Regulating financial systems, or directed market negation in finance

2.1   Regulating finance to support growth during the 'Long Boom'

Regulation of finance was a characteristic feature of the period of the 'Long Boom' that lasted roughly from the end of the Second World War to the mid-1970s. During that unprecedented period of rapid growth, a range of controls ensured that finance remained a subsidiary part of the economy that provided support to capitalist accumulation. This approach to financial regulation can be called 'regulating financial systems'.

The theoretical and ideological justification for systemic regulation was provided by the dominant Keynesianism of the era. Drawing on the legacy of Keynes, financial speculation was deemed potentially destructive of productive economic activity. Furthermore, 'the euthanasia of the rentier', who presumably undermined productive capitalists, was considered a valid aim of monetary and financial policy (Keynes, 1973: ch. 24). Regulating finance as a system was the counterpart to confident Keynesian management of aggregate demand.

There were three fundamental elements to regulating financial systems, common across advanced countries, but expressed with particular clarity in Japan (Suzuki 1987a). First, price controls were applied to financial operations meaning, above all, interest rate ceilings on financial institution assets and liabilities. On the asset side, interest rates were often determined through a formula based on the lending rate of the central bank, and were kept deliberately low in nominal terms. On the liability side, interest rates on deposits were kept administratively low, to the extent that demand deposits received no interest at all.

At the same time, quantitative controls were applied to lending by financial institutions, directing credit to selected industries and areas of economic activity. Quantitative controls also took the form of administrative setting of several ratios on the balance sheet of financial institutions, above all, the ratio of reserves to deposits. By implication, credit flows and money creation were also constrained.

Second, functional specialisation was imposed on financial institutions. The specific features of functional specialisation varied depending on each country's historical and institutional trajectory. However, commercial and investment banking were generally kept apart, whether through legislation (for instance, the Glass–Steagall Act in the USA and its equivalent, Article 65, in Japan), or through monopoly practices and 'clubbing' exclusivity (as in the UK and elsewhere). Furthermore, long-term investment banking was kept separate from other banking, often with direct state support of its liabilities (long-term bonds), or even direct state ownership of long-term investment banks. Functional specialisation also typically prevailed in financing international trade as well as in agricultural credit, housing credit, and consumer credit.

Third, and perhaps most important, controls on the capital account helped the regulation of international capital flows. This was an integral element of the Bretton Woods system of fixed exchange rates backed by guaranteed convertibility of the US dollar into gold. Regulation of international capital flows (for instance, through outright prohibition of acquiring foreign assets, applying differential exchange rates to financial as opposed to commercial transactions, taxing foreign financial returns, and so on) protected the stability of exchange rates. Control over capital flows created a domestic sphere within which the other two elements of regulation could operate effectively.

The common patterns of regulating finance as system did not preclude differences among financial systems. The long-standing distinction between market-based (Anglo-Saxon) versus bank-based (German-Japanese) financial systems characterised the Long Boom. Bank-based systems were characterised by long-term bank–industry relations based on mutual reputation and supported by cross-shareholding, while stock markets played a subsidiary role. Market-based systems, in contrast, had more prominent stock markets, while bank–industry relations tended to be either at arm's length or shorter-term in nature. But the broad patterns of control applied to both.

Regulating finance as a system was particularly prominent in developing countries. National financial systems were established across a swathe of countries in Asia and Africa emerging from colonialism in the 1950s. Under colonial conditions, the typical financial arrangements included some imperial commercial banks engaging mostly in financing the export trade, plus a central financial authority that oversaw the integration of the colony in the financial and monetary networks of the metropolis. The domestic economy typically had few points of access to the formal credit system. Decolonisation meant establishing national banks, often publicly owned, as well as a central bank. Functional specialisation prevailed among the new institutions, including commercial banks, agricultural banks, long-term investment banks, and export credit banks. Interest rates and quantities of credit were closely regulated.[1]

The theoretical and ideological justification for these policies in developing countries was closely related to the dominant Keynesianism of the time, but also had its own developmentalist dimension. Considerable influence was exercised by Latin American structuralist theories of import-substituting industrialisation, which naturally favoured room for capital controls, while directing credit to promote growth of light industry. Within the World Bank and other multilateral organisations, development was perceived as a matter of planning domestic investment, which typically exceeded domestic savings thus creating the need for financial flows from abroad. Limited theoretical room was allowed for markets, the expectation being that government ministries would directly regulate financial prices and quantities in order to attain planned objectives.

2.2 The market-negating aspect of regulating financial systems

The regulation of finance as a system, thus, entailed direct state intervention in financial prices and flows, both domestically and internationally, as well as demarcating the activities of financial institutions. It also involved the direct ownership of financial institutions by the state. Prices and quantities in the markets for credit were directed towards levels deemed compatible with broader social and economic objectives. Ultimate support for this approach derived from the notion that financial markets left to their own devices tend to produce problematic results for growth, income and accumulation as a whole. Put differently, regulating finance as system amounted to market-negating regulation.[2]

Market-negating regulation, by definition, alters the normal profit-making activities of financial institutions. It affects profitability and the equalisation of returns between the sphere of finance and the rest of the economy, particularly when ceilings are imposed on interest rates. Consequently, the returns of financial institutions have to be protected, including privately owned institutions. Fresh risks are also created for financial institutions as credit is directed to selected sectors, particularly when credit is forced to assume a long-term character. Apart from the evident credit risks, there is a direct impact on maturity transformation through lengthening the assets of commercial banks and other financial institutions. Hence, for financial institutions to deliver long-term lending, liabilities also have to be suitably lengthened and made secure. In a nutshell, regulating finance as a system aims at marshalling financial resources to attain growth and development aims, while transforming financial returns into rents that have state backing.

This dimension of regulating financial systems is stronger under bank-based finance. Securing and regulating the returns of financial institutions evidently requires close interaction between the state bureaucracy, the managers of finance, and the managers of industry. Bank-based systems are more conducive to this type of interaction, given the long-term relations of trust and reputation between industry and finance.[3] The rent-like character of financial returns was evident in several developing countries throughout the postwar years and until the 1980s. It was also prominent in Japan, where banks drew low but fairly secure rent-like returns, backed by the state.[4] In effect, management committees were created at various levels involving the leading representatives of various sections of the capitalist class and leading state bureaucrats, as was most apparent in Japan. These committees supervised competition within the financial system, while also overseeing the interaction between finance and the rest of the economy.

It is apparent that the rent-like aspect of financial returns when finance is regulated as a system could become a source of corruption. Protected and secure returns could generate unusual rewards for the managers of finance and also for the state bureaucrats involved in regulating the financial system. By the same token, direction of credit and regulation of financial prices could invite political favouritism and public corruption. Such phenomena were commonly observed throughout the developing world, but also in developed countries with entrenched bank-based systems. It should be noted, however, that they are far from an exclusive privilege of bank-based finance, or of regulating finance as a system. Market-based finance and regulating financial institutions are also prone to phenomena of corruption, which however acquire a different form for reasons discussed below.

Finally, regulated bank-based systems in and of themselves offer no guarantees of successfully attaining growth and development aims. At the very least they also require a well-educated and efficient bureaucracy, a prevalent spirit of public service – including in running financial institutions – regular renewal of the personnel that operate the levers of control, transparency and public accountability, and so on. These are difficult and complex mechanisms to put in place that also depend on the historical, institutional, customary, and even cultural practices in each country. Above all, they depend on the balance of social forces and the ability of broad layers of working people to exercise democratic control over the complex skein of relations between industry, finance, and the state.

2.3   The generic character of market-negating regulation

Market negation, however, is not an exclusive property of regulating finance as system, and nor of bank-based finance. To a significant extent, state intervention in finance has historically resulted in market negation, irrespective of the framework of regulation, or of the character of the financial system. This type of intervention might be thought of as generic market negation. To be specific, the classic mode of intervention in finance is the 'lender of last resort', which emerged in the British financial system in the second half of the nineteenth century.[5] Marked by the experience of regular decennial crises that were capped by the great disaster of Overend, Gurney, and Co. in 1866, the British state took on board the view that the central bank ought to provide liquidity freely in a crisis.

The ultimate rationale for the lender of last resort is that financial crises are marked by shortage of money to settle existing obligations ('tightness'), and thus risk generalised bankruptcy. If a crisis was allowed to develop into a panic, liquidity risk would affect financial institutions indiscriminately. Hence, the central bank ought to stand ready to provide liquidity until the abating of the crisis. Bagehot (1873) captured this conventional wisdom as early as the early 1870s. Its continuing validity in mature capitalism was amply demonstrated in 2008 following the collapse of Lehman Brothers.

Lender of last resort action by the state is a negation of market processes because it ensures the viability of financial institutions. Participants in capitalist markets presumably have to bear the consequences of their own decisions. Market operations, furthermore, are supposed to result in optimal welfare results on condition of no interference by the state. If financial markets occasionally require the wholesale state provision of liquidity, they self-evidently produce suboptimal results, while participants are protected from their own actions. The problem of moral hazard, therefore, is an inherent aspect of generic market-negating regulation of finance.

In addition to lender of last resort, market negation in the realm of finance has become increasingly prevalent in the form of deposit insurance guarantees by the state. Deposit insurance on a significant scale emerged in the late nineteenth century, and has come gradually to characterise developed financial systems. It can take a variety of legal forms – private and public – and it can be both explicit and implicit. The latter is, in effect, the dominant form in contemporary financial systems, as was shown following the run on Northern Rock building society in the UK in 2007–8.

The need for deposit insurance arises from the structure of commercial banking, which involves the transformation of extremely short-term liabilities into longer-term assets. This transformation creates the insoluble problem of the bank run whereby, if deposit holders converged on a bank demanding cash, the bank would go bankrupt irrespective of its profitability, the quality of its assets, and so on.[6] Deposit insurance guarantees prevent or ameliorate runs by reassuring deposit holders that they would be able to obtain the liquid equivalent of their claim on a bank. This is at bottom a matter of trust since it would be impossible for banks simultaneously to meet all deposit withdrawals, whether guarantees existed or not. For this reason the state is the natural point of reference and guarantor of the existence of trust.

Deposit insurance guarantees by the state are a market-negating measure since they effectively lower the cost of liabilities for banks. They also create the risk of moral hazard, both because bank managers need not ultimately concern themselves with protecting a large part of their sources of funds, but also because the holders of deposits need not ultimately monitor the performance of banks. Consequently, deposit insurance guarantees support bank returns, giving them a rent-like aspect. By the same token, deposit insurance exacerbates moral hazard problems. It is unsurprising that generic market-negating regulation in finance – both as lender of last resort and as deposit insurance guarantees – is associated with money, or liquidity, in the financial system. The dominant form of money in contemporary capitalism is credit money created as a by-product of the lending activities of banks. Commercial banks, regardless of their credit and financial activities, retain a kernel of money-dealing functions, including safekeeping, transmitting, and providing the means of payment and store of value.[7] More broadly, the financial system of advanced capitalist economies rests on the bedrock of the monetary system. If the functioning of money failed, financial markets as a whole would seize up, severely disrupting accumulation. Consequently, the state is directly involved in supporting credit money – turning central bank money into legal tender and guaranteeing its social acceptability – while also attempting to ensure the operation of the monetary system as a whole.

Generic market-negating regulation, be it lender of last resort or imposing deposit insurance guarantees, arises directly due to market processes themselves. Turmoil arising from the operations of financial markets, or the structure of financial institutions, could potentially threaten the operations of the monetary system, further reverberating on the financial system, and causing general economic dislocation. To protect the monetary side of the financial system, therefore, state regulation takes place, which also alters the monetary functions of markets. In this light, market negation can be thought of as the outcome of the spontaneous operations of financial markets and institutions.

Since the early 1980s, however, market-negating regulation has taken a far broader form than the two generic instances mentioned above. Financial institutions have been considered 'too big to fail', and have often been effectively (if tacitly) protected against failure, irrespective of problems of liquidity or deposit withdrawal. Public funds have been repeatedly made available to financial institutions, most prominently during 2007–9, to prevent insolvency. In effect, the state in several advanced capitalist countries systematically protects owners, bond and other liability holders of banks and other financial institutions from the consequences of the commercial actions of the institutions.

The reasons and implications of this policy are discussed in more detail in subsequent sections, but note that such intervention poses far more severe moral hazard problems than protecting depositors, or engaging in lender of last resort activities. In effect, implicit state guarantees of solvency have kept the cost of capital at artificially low levels for banks and other financial institutions. Bank returns have been inflated throughout the period, while banks' managers have been allowed to adopt commercial strategies the worst outcomes of which were eliminated by the state.

Generic market negation of finance contrasts sharply with market negation during the period of regulating finance as a system following the Second World War. The latter occurred as part of an overall policy of forcing finance to sustain growth, and was overseen by a system of formal and informal mechanisms of control involving the state, finance and industry. Rent-like returns to finance were kept low, and the mechanisms of control were imbued with an element of public policy. In contrast, generic market negation in recent decades has occurred while the regulation of finance as a system has been dismantled. Furthermore, it has occurred amidst generalised ideological promotion of free markets, nowhere more than in the financial sector. Far from keeping rent-like returns to finance at a low level, market negation has served to boost them. In effect, financial markets in advanced capitalism have become mechanisms for the organised transfer of profits to small sections of the capitalist class, guaranteed by the state.

3   Regulating financial institutions, or market-conforming regulation

3.1   Decline of regulating finance as a system and rise of financial liberalisation

The approach of regulating finance as a system began to unravel in the late 1960s, and fell apart in the 1970s, together with the dominant Keynesianism of the period. The process began in developed countries, but spread vigorously to developing countries in subsequent decades. There were two fundamental reasons why the 'system' approach to financial regulation became untenable.

The first was the gradual rise of uncontrolled elements of finance during the 1950s and 1960s. A notable phenomenon was the rise of the Euromarkets, allowing US banks to maintain and trade assets outside the regulatory reach of US authorities. But similar phenomena also occurred in Japan with the rise of the 'gensaki' market, that is, an unregulated market for corporations to trade among them temporarily idle funds (Suzuki 1987b). The significance of unregulated markets lay in that they allow financial institutions to bypass regulatory controls on prices and quantities, thus undermining regulation of the system as a whole. Consequently, the management of competition among financial institutions was disrupted. Some institutions were able to make market-driven returns, thus beating others that continued to make controlled returns.

The emergence of such tension might well be an inherent feature of all 'system' regulation of finance. Within Marxist political economy, for instance, finance is treated as a spontaneous outgrowth of capitalist accumulation that mobilises idle money and organises trade credit, thus intensifying accumulation (Itoh and Lapavitsas 1999: ch. 4). Regulation of prices, quantities and functions might place the existing structures of finance under control, but it would not affect the tendency of accumulation spontaneously to generate fresh relations of finance in trade credit as well as in transacting idle money. The result would be tension between controlled incumbent structures and uncontrolled new structures, which would result in systematic differences in returns for financial institutions.

The second reason, albeit clearly related to the first, was the collapse of the Bretton Woods system in 1971–3. Bretton Woods fixed the international value of the dollar by anchoring it to gold at a set price ($35 per ounce). The US state undertook to convert – more or less on demand – dollars held by foreign official bodies at that price. Consequently, exchange rates were in practice fixed, and could change only after protracted pressures and upheaval. A minimum requirement for such a system to hold was to limit cross-border capital flows through a battery of controls. A further requirement was to establish international mechanisms that could provide external assistance in times of pressure on exchange rates, above all, the IMF.

The collapse of Bretton Woods was due in part to the substantial accumulation of US dollars held abroad, which also propelled the growth of the Euromarkets. For our purposes the process of failure is not important. What is important is that, once fixed exchange rates were abolished, the path was opened for the freeing of the capital account. Flexible exchange rates were subsequently marked by unprecedented volatility; at the same time, inflation rates rose, leading to a greater volatility of interest rates. Financial institutions that operated internationally began to press for fewer controls on the movement of capital that would allow them to deal with the risks generated by the new volatilities (Eatwell and Taylor 2000). By the same token, financial innovation was accelerated – a development that would prove of paramount importance in the following period.

Regulating finance as a system became untenable after the lifting of capital controls and in view of the rise of the uncontrolled part of the financial system. That was also the foundation for the gradual drive towards financial liberalisation. There is an ideological dimension to financial liberalisation, briefly mentioned below, but the rise of deregulated finance during the last three decades rested on economic and social forces that began to emerge in the late 1960s. The first major step towards financial liberalisation was the abolition of regulation Q in the USA, which led to a relaxation of interest payments on bank liabilities. More decisively, in 1970, Competition and Credit Control legislation in the UK took a decisive step toward dismantling 'system' regulation of finance in the interests of the international activities of the City of London. The process picked up speed in the 1970s, and became the dominant order in the 1980s.

It is important to note that in developing countries financial liberalisation followed a different, but related path. The established view that controlled finance was in the interests of development declined fairly rapidly in the 1970s. The decisive role was played by MacKinnon (1973) and Shaw (1973), who contradicted the very notion that low interest rates encouraged investment, while also opposing the idea that development funds had to come from abroad. Presumably, higher interest rates would encourage saving and investment, thus obviating the need for external funds. High interest rates would, apparently, further improve the quality of investment by eliminating poor projects.

Such were the intellectual foundations of the pressure to abandon the system of the regulation of finance in developing countries. These ideas were tested very soon and found wanting in Latin America and then more widely across the world. But financial liberalisation acquired new features, eventually becoming an integral part of the Washington Consensus, including a strong emphasis on attracting external (but this time private) funds for development, a notion that was absent from the original formulation of financial liberalisation (Fine, Lapavitsas and Pincus 2001). The underlying principle, however, remained the same, namely that market-negating intervention in finance was counterproductive. Development presumably required market-driven financial activity, within the general approach of 'getting prices right'.

Nonetheless, in large measure financial liberalisation in developing countries has been imposed from the outside. Unlike the spontaneous character of the process of liberalisation in developed countries, liberalised finance arrived in developing countries under heavy pressure from multilateral organisations, above all, the World Bank and the IMF. That is not to say that there has been no domestic constituency in favour of abandoning controls over the financial system. However, the driving force came primarily from the outside and typically prevailed through loan conditionality as certain critical junctures of the last three decades.

3.2   Regulation of institutions and the persistence of market negation

Financial liberalisation (or deregulation) should not be confused with an absence of regulation. Finance has continued to be regulated during the past three decades, both domestically and internationally. But the character of regulation has changed dramatically during this period. A major factor has been the transformation of the theoretical approach to regulation induced by the ascendancy of neoliberalism. The earlier disposition to control financial markets in order to promote growth and development was replaced with its opposite, namely emphasis on the importance of free financial markets. The result was that regulation that used to be market-negating and system-wide became increasingly market-conforming and institution-focused. On the other hand, generic market-negating regulation, far from disappearing, actually became stronger during the same period. In this respect, therefore, the neoliberal approach to regulating financial markets and institutions has generated insurmountable paradoxes.

The dominant analytical approach to finance during the last three decades has been information-theoretic. The theoretical bedrock has been provided by general equilibrium analysis, particularly its conclusions regarding the efficiency properties of free markets. In this context, information asymmetries among market participants are assumed to lead to market failure, and hence possibly to justify state intervention. The pre-eminent asymmetry in financial markets is taken to be between lender and borrower, whereby the latter knows more than the former about the project that a loan is intended to finance. Consequently, suboptimal results might follow from the interaction of lender with borrower, including adverse selection and moral hazard. Information asymmetries of this type provide the theoretical pillar for financial regulation within contemporary economics, including approaches that are generally critical of neoliberalism (see, for instance, Stiglitz 1989, 1998).[8]

Contrary to the interventionist Keynesianism of the 'Long Boom', therefore, there is no presumption that free markets in finance might be inimical to growth and accumulation. The problem, rather, appears to be that markets might not be able to deliver optimal results due to informational weaknesses, which might have institutional roots. It follows that, instead of systemic intervention to keep finance in check, there should be, at most, partial intervention to assuage problems of market failure. Such intervention should be primarily prudential, that is, applying to individual financial institutions to ensure that they could deliver their putative tasks, particularly as these are specified within the analytics of information-theoretic economics. Above all, prudential regulation should supplement the information-collecting and assessing functions of banks, including the ability to monitor borrowers. Prudential regulation is, thus, fundamentally market-conforming regulation.

Market-conforming prudential regulation focuses primarily on the balance sheet of financial institutions – mostly banks – seeking to affect their operations through quantitative or qualitative changes. Regulation, in other words, focuses on the performance of individual institutions rather than the system as a whole. It should be stressed that regulating balance sheets is not an exclusive feature of this approach to regulation. This is, rather, an old form of regulation, which first emerged in the debates surrounding and preceding the Bank Act of 1844. Furthermore, regulating finance as a system in the decades following the Second World War also included quantitative regulation of the asset side of bank balance sheets. Banks were typically subjected to reserve requirements with a view to ensuring liquidity, as well as controlling the money supply. However, the approach of regulating financial institutions that has prevailed during the past three decades has made the focus on balance sheets peculiarly its own, while switching regulatory attention from the asset to the liability side of bank balance sheets.

The main aspect of market-conforming regulation has been to monitor the capital of banks. This approach has been institutionalised in a series of well-known measures codified under Basle I and II, which are currently under review to form perhaps Basle III. The regulatory shift away from assets and toward liabilities reflects a key feature of financial liberalisation, namely the rise of open financial markets within which banks tend to operate.[9] The expanded ability of banks to obtain liquidity by issuing liabilities in open markets appears to have attenuated the age-old requirement to hold sufficient liquid assets. By the same token, access to markets appears to have given banks additional degrees of freedom to manage their assets in order to attain higher profitability. The main task of prudential regulation, therefore, was taken to be ensuring adequate protection for banks by guaranteeing levels of capital on the liability side.

Several parallel developments have turned the focus on bank capital into the standard aspect of contemporary market-conforming regulation. The first is the gradual predominance of the concept of risk in analysing banking coupled with increasing technical sophistication in measuring risk. Needless to say, risk is inherent to banking and bankers have always assessed it in different ways. But developments in the last three decades have been of a different order of complexity. The conventional wisdom of the banker has been given a computationally-intensive scientific veneer, often with the use of mathematical formulae borrowed from physics (Lapavitsas and Dos Santos 2008). Methods of risk assessment have come to depend on market prices, incorporating continuous market changes. Regulatory changes in accounting systems – mark-to-market and fair value – have reinforced the practice of continuous quantitative measurement of risk on the balance sheet. The outcome has been to ascertain the necessary levels of regulatory bank capital with considerable – and entirely misleading – precision, as was codified in Basle II. This system of regulation failed altogether during the crisis of 2007–9, but the underlying approach is far from extinct.

Note finally that generic market-negating regulation has anything but disappeared as prudential regulation rose to ascendancy. Indeed, market-negating regulation has become considerably stronger, providing one of the major paradoxes of financial development in recent years. Deposit insurance has become a permanent feature of liberalised financial markets, and the lender of last resort has become paramount in dealing with crises, as became apparent during the gigantic upheaval of 2007–9. At the heart of contemporary liberalised finance, therefore, lies public subsidisation of financial returns as well as moral hazard. It is probable that the lack of direct state regulation of bank returns and lending has made the impact of these generic weaknesses more severe than they would have been if finance had been regulated as a system.

The worst aspect of market negation under conditions of financial liberalisation, however, is the gradual prevalence of the 'too big to fail' principle in the US and throughout much of Europe. Several large financial institutions have been rescued since the 1970s, whether through private funds that were organised and guaranteed by the state, or directly through the provision of public funds. In effect, the trend towards prudential regulation has ended up guaranteeing the entire liability side of bank balance sheets.

'Too-big-to-fail' makes all other problems of moral hazard pale into insignificance. In effect, equity and bond holders of large private financial institutions can expect to be protected from losses through state regulation. It is apparent that this development directly contradicts the ideology of financial liberalisation that has underpinned the approach to regulation in recent decades. From a mainstream perspective, the justification for it could be the avoidance of 'system risk', that it, the risk that the size of the institutions involved could cause a generalised collapse. Yet, if private financial institutions are capable of generating such gigantic negative externalities, the regulatory response ought to include placing these institutions under public control. Market-negating regulation could also reach its logical limit of denying the market altogether.

4   The failure of market-conforming regulation of financial institutions

The crisis of 2007–9 represents a failure of market-conforming regulation of institutions for two main reasons. First is the systematic bypassing of Basle II regulations by banks. Large, internationally operating banks, which typically deployed value-at-risk and mark-to-market techniques, were able to overcome capital adequacy regulations through financial innovation. As was already mentioned, banks participated in asset securitisation by setting up new institutions that issued asset-backed liabilities which were effectively backed by the banks themselves. Bank assets were moved off-balance-sheet and capital adequacy requirements continued to be ostensibly satisfied. Banks were thus able to participate in the exceptionally profitable (for a period) processes of mortgage and other securitisation.

This process has been frequently referred to as 'regulatory arbitrage', and the implicit assumption is that it arose from design faults and a lack of foresight on the part of regulatory authorities, or the abandonment of sensible 'business models' by banks.[10] There is no doubt that Basle II gave large banks the freedom to use in-house techniques of risk measurement, at the same time transforming capital adequacy into a target that banks aimed to bypass rather than meet in order to protect themselves. Regulation thus actively encouraged large banks to securitise assets in order to 'churn' regulatory capital. Banks were able to continuing lending and making profits while appearing to meet the capital adequacy requirements. But it is pure hindsight to ascribe this development either to the inadequacies of regulators, or to a temporary lapse in bank operating practices.

The bypassing of Basle II in the course of the bubble of 2001–7 is a typical instance of the financial system spontaneously undermining regulation by creating new, unregulated activities that have higher returns. Once the unregulated area (in this case primarily the 'shadow banking system' in the US) took root, the regulated activities became progressively untenable in the old form. This phenomenon has nothing to do with regulatory deficiencies and is an integral part of the development of capitalist finance. The role of the financial system, as was already mentioned, is continually to mobilise idle money and trade credit in order to sustain accumulation and extract financial profit. The institutional mechanisms through which these processes take place are continually altered and renewed by competing capitals. If regulation is imposed on parts of the financial system, new mechanisms spontaneously emerge which undermine the regulation imposed. It is misleading to imagine that prudential or other rules could be designed that could permanently avoid this fate. The most that the regulator could hope for is continually to contest the tendency of the financial system to by-pass regulations.

The second, and more fundamental, reason for the failure of market-conforming regulation of institutions in 2007–9 is also related to the collapse of the underlying theoretical assumption regarding the nature of banks and financial markets. Contemporary analysis of finance, as was mentioned above, is information-theoretic. Banks are perceived to be specialists in information gathering and assessing that monitor borrowers and manage risks. Financial markets, more generally, are also assumed to price and distribute risk. In this light, the aim of prudential regulation is to improve information flows while protecting the solvency of financial institutions by safeguarding capital adequacy.

The financial bubble and the subsequent crisis of the 2000s have severely dented the credibility of this approach to finance and financial institutions. Securitisation has undermined the notion that banks are specialists in information gathering and assessing.[11] In the course of the bubble banks acquired assets without even a perfunctory examination of quality, purely because they expected to move these assets off-balance-sheet through securitisation. Even worse, banks proceeded to set up new financial institutions that issued asset-backed debt against the very loans that had not been properly examined in the first place.

The ostensible justification was that securitisation had made it possible to subcontract monitoring onto ratings organisations, credit enhancers, and so on. In practice, and as became clear in the course of the crisis, subcontracting led to the effective abandonment of monitoring across the chain of transactions that marked securitisation. But even if the final outcome had been less severe and the major crisis of 2007–9 had been averted, a fundamental problem would have remained. Namely, what is the economic role of banks in advanced capitalist economies if the monitoring of borrowers is systematically subcontracted onto others? Given the fundamental informational failure of banking, the regulatory focus on capital adequacy is an irrelevance, or a mechanism for regulating activities the economic content of which had become blurred.[12]

Along similar lines, the crisis of 2007–9 has further shown that the management of risk by financial institutions as well as by financial markets has failed altogether. This was immediately recognised by some among the mainstream, who adduced the crisis to a 'mispricing' of risk (Goodhart 2008). Unfortunately, the problem is a lot more profound. There is no obvious institutional or regulatory reason why risk should have been thus 'mispriced'. It appears that financial institutions and markets failed to gather requisite information, particularly 'soft', or 'relational' information that would have been a staple of the assessment of credit risk in the past. Banks relied extensively on the spuriously scientific credentials of computationally-intensive risk measurement methods. These phenomena occurred in the context of free competition among banks, thus reflecting systemic failure of financial institutions rather than some temporary or accidental mishap. Once again, the regulatory focus on capital adequacy is an irrelevance.

Given the failure of prudential regulation of institutions, what are the likely patterns of financial regulation in the coming period? Note first that there is a paucity of ideas among the mainstream in this regard. The still prevalent approach, insofar as that can be gauged from the proposals for a Basle III code, appears to be the strengthening of market-conforming institutional regulation (BIS 2009). The proposals add an emphasis on the degree of capital adequacy as well as on placing limits on the overall size of bank balance sheets, but there is no fundamental change of approach. In view of the preceding discussion, this is an inadequate response to the regulatory failure represented by the crisis of 2007–9.

The deeper problems posed by the failure of regulation have led some among the mainstream to engage in a quest for new approaches to 'systemic' regulation (Haldane 2009). At present, however, this means little more than speculative analyses of the financial system as 'network' or as a biological system, which offer no obvious paths to financial regulation. For still others, the search for 'systemic' regulation amounts to strengthening 'macroprudential' regulation (Borio 2009). For the moment, it is not clear what this would mean, other than seeking a range of early warning signals of crisis, or a range of discretionary levers of intervention in case of crisis. In effect, it would be necessary to have an omniscient regulator that would be able to exercise discretion if and when necessary.

The bafflement of the mainstream and its inability to break out of the narrow confines of the Basle approach create room to reconsider genuine systemic regulation along the lines discussed in part 2 of this chapter. Already there has been extensive discussion regarding the separation of investment from commercial banking.[13] There is little doubt that mixing commercial with investment banking has proven deeply problematic in 2001–7 – particularly in Anglo-Saxon systems – since it sustained the excesses of securitisation. Separating the two types of banking would be a step toward recreating the functional demarcation that characterised systemic regulation of finance in the postwar years.

The point is, however, that systemic regulation during its historic high period operated as a complex whole. Functional specialisation effectively limited the operations of banks because it operated within a system of controlling price and quantity of credit as well as capital flows. If systemic regulation is to be renewed along similar lines, this would require the creation of a complex set of mechanisms and not simply one part of the earlier whole, e.g. functional specialisation. It is apparent, furthermore, that capital controls, if they were to be truly operational, would have to be re-imposed as part of a global effort, not in a fragmented manner.

Recreating systemic regulation under current conditions would thus face structural problems as well as difficulties of coordination and ideological opposition. Capital flows are a gigantic component of the contemporary world economy. Furthermore, private banks have changed profoundly during the past three decades, while failing irrevocably in the course of the crisis of 2007–9. In these circumstances, recreating market-negating systemic regulation is likely to impose broader requirements on public intervention that in the years of the 'Long Boom'. Specifically, it is likely to require creation of public banking on a large scale. System regulation of finance in the years to come could be sustained by maintaining the core of the banking system under public control, while also deploying the older techniques of price, quantity, function and capital flow controls. Needless to say, the processes and mechanisms through which such a change could take place require detailed discussion. But the failure of market-conforming regulation of institutions calls for precisely this kind of theoretical and policy debate.

5   Instead of conclusion: public banks as part of systemic regulation of finance

Public ownership of banks has been far from rare even under conditions of financial liberalisation. Public banking, for instance, has remained very significant in Germany throughout the last three decades, and that includes a large long-term investment bank (KfW). Public takeovers of large private banks have occurred repeatedly in mature countries during the last few decades, particularly as a result of banking crises, for instance in Japan and Sweden. The banks that came under public ownership were typically rescued in order to be returned to private ownership. At the peak of the banking crisis of 2007–9, the issue of extending public ownership over stricken banks was discussed even in the US.[14] Its proponents advocated takeover as a temporary counter-crisis measure with the ultimate aim of returning banks to private ownership. These proposals met with little success, partly due to adroit bank lobbying, which contributed to the current state of regulatory immobility.

The crisis, however, has forced the UK government to take majority stakes in the Royal Bank of Scotland and Northern Rock, plus a minority stake in Lloyds-HBOS. These constitute a significant proportion of British banking and could potentially act as a basis for broader public ownership and control over the banking system. But the approach of the UK government hitherto has been to rescue these banks in order to return them to full private ownership at the earliest opportunity. The government has consistently refused to take over actual bank management that would aim to support the performance of the economy as a whole. This is unfortunate since public ownership and control of banks would allow for the re-establishment of systemic regulation of banking under current conditions.

The most obvious way in which public banks could play this role would be by managing credit to support economic activity beyond plain regulation of the price and quantity of credit. As was shown in section 4, private banks have failed in the delivery of elementary commercial banking functions. Public banks could become major providers of commercial banking functions to small and medium-sized enterprises as well as to individuals. Small and medium-sized enterprises (SMEs) typically borrow for fixed and circulating capital, while borrowing by individuals allows for smoothing of consumption profiles. The steady provision of commercial credit to SME and individuals could sustain aggregate demand, support employment and contribute to counter-cyclical policy. This would be market negation with the conscious aim of supporting output and employment.

Under conditions of financialisation the provision of this type of credit could be thought of as a public utility, reminiscent of transport, electricity and water.[15] The circulation of personal income in mature countries, for instance, has come to rely on the steady supply and repayment of individual credit. To be sure, the analogy with public utility does not hold fully since credit in not a normal commodity but a set of economic relations based on trust and anticipation. With that proviso in mind, the point remains that public banks could in principle regulate the ubiquitous flows of individual (and SME) credit to achieve socially-set objectives.

To be more specific, public banks could provide credit for housing, education, and health as well as for the smoothing of general consumption. Such credit would be supplied on a commercial basis with regular repayment at publicly determined rates of interest. It would be natural for lending terms to vary according to the objectives of social policy. Public banks could certainly adopt the techniques of information collection for income, employment, and personal conditions, while still deploying credit scoring and risk management. There is no reason to think that they would perform worse than failed private banks in these respects.[16]

Public banks could pursue further market negation by adopting aspects of long-term development banking. They could obtain funding to support such credit in a variety of ways, including preferential access to deposits and the issue of publicly guaranteed bonds. Deposit insurance guarantees by the state are already in place for private banks with the perverse effect of supporting private returns and exacerbating moral hazard. If these were removed from private and applied to public banks, they would ensure a steady supply of funding for the latter. Given secure financing, public banks would be able to contribute to broader management of long-term credit aimed at rebalancing mature economies by reducing the predominance of finance. The direction of rebalancing would probably include 'green' activities, for which there is strong popular demand, including non-fossil-fuel forms of energy, less reliance on private cars, raising the energy efficiency of private homes, reducing industrial pollution, and so on. These aims require major public investment, which public banks would be in a position to finance.

Development credit provided by public banks would inevitably pose the problem of interaction with open markets in finance, and thus with private banks. As was discussed in section 2, market negation affects the returns of financial institutions, raising the issue of comparability between public and private financial institutions. It further raises the problem of avoiding 'regulatory arbitrage', that is, the bypassing of controls in order to generate higher returns. There is no permanent solution for these problems within a capitalist economy. However, the mere existence of public banks would facilitate systemic control over the rest of the financial system, including price and quantity of credit as well as controlling the functional specialisation of remaining private banks.

Finally, there would be risks of corruption for public banks, possibly as the result of political influence. But fully represented and democratically expressed public interests could be effective mechanisms in controlling such risks. In the context of banking, in particular, public service can be a stronger and more reliable motive than personal gain, which has failed decisively in recent years. Finance has been one of the least democratic areas of contemporary economies during the last three decades, with disastrous results. Establishing public banks should be more than mere nationalisation, and certainly not the simple replacement of failed private managers by state bureaucrats. It would be desirable to set the remit of public banks socially and collectively, imposing transparency on decision making and full accountability to elected bodies. Public banks might then become an effective element of systemic regulation of finance.

Notes

1. For a historical discussion in the context of Africa see, for instance, Brownbridge and Harvey (1998).
2. Throughout this chapter restrictions applying on banks with regard to obtaining a license (entry), branching, setting up a bank holding company, and so on, are ignored. These are powerful instruments of intervention on the part of state authorities but do not amount to restrictions on the normal business of banking capital, which is the main concern of this chapter.
3. Typically captured by the term 'Main Bank' for the Japanese system (Aoki and Patrick 1994; Hoshi and Kashyap 2001).
4. For an excellent analysis of the rent-like character of the returns of Japanese banks during the High Growth Period see Inaba (2008).
5. General policy intervention in the sphere of money and finance emerged considerably earlier. As early as the 1830s the Bank of England operated the 'Palmer Rule' on its gold reserves relative to its liabilities. The rule took a rigid form in the Bank Act of 1844.
6. The inevitability of bankruptcy in case of a bank run was demonstrated by Diamond and Dybvig (1983).
7. Marxist political economy has long stressed this aspect of banking (Lapavitsas 2003: ch. 4).
8. A further justification for regulation might be that financial failure has significant externalities on the rest of economic activity. But the theoretical

foundations of this view are not nearly as well-worked out as those of information asymmetries.

9. Elsewhere this has been called an element of the financialisation of contemporary capitalism (Lapavitsas 2009).
10. A view expressed with clarity by Acharya and Richardson (2010).
11. For an analysis of this point from a political economy perspective see Elkholy (2010).
12. And that is without even mentioning inefficiency and predatory charging in the retail monetary services offered by private banks, including money transfers, deposit keeping, payments, and so on. The inefficiency of banks has been noted by mainstream economics (Berger and Mester 2003).
13. For instance, Kay (2009).
14. For instance, Posen (2009).
15. A suggestion already made by Erturk et al. (2009).
16. Needless to say, public banks could easily provide a full range of monetary services to households, including payments, safe-keeping and value transfers, while plugging into the existing clearing mechanisms, and without the predatory charges of private banks.

References

Acharya, V. and Richardson, M. (2010) *Repairing a Failed System: An Introduction*, New York University Stern White Papers, http://whitepapers.stern.nyu.edu/summaries/intro.html.

Aoki, M. and Patrick, H. (1994) *The Japanese Main Bank System: Its Relevance for Developing and Transforming Economies*. Oxford: Oxford University Press.

Berger, A. and Mester, L. (2003). 'Explaining the Dramatic Changes in Performance of US Banks: Technological Change, Deregulation, and Dynamic Changes in Competition', *Journal of Financial Intermediation*, 12(1), 57–95.

Bagehot, W. ([1873] 1978) *Lombard Street*, in vol 9 of *The Collected Works of Walter Bagehot*, edited by N. St John-Stevas. London: The Economist.

BIS (2009) *Strengthening the Resilience of the Banking Sector*, Basel Committee of Banking Supervision, Consultative Document, Geneva: BIS.

Borio, C. (2009) 'The Macroprudential Approach to Regulation and Supervision', VoxEU, http://www.voxeu.org/index.php?q=node/3445.

Brownbridge, M. and Harvey, C. (1998) *Banking in Africa*. Oxford: Currey; Trenton: Africa World Press; Nairobi: East African Educational Publishers; and Kampala: Fountain Publishers.

Diamond, D. and Dybvig, P. (1983) 'Bank Runs, Deposit Insurance and Liquidity', *Journal of Political Economy*, 91, 401–19.

Eatwell, J. and Taylor, L. (2000). *Global Finance at Risk*. Cambridge: Polity Press.

Elkholy, S. (2010) 'Political Economy of Securitization and Development: The Case of Egypt'. Unpublished PhD Thesis, University of London.

Erturk, I., Froud, J., Johal, S., Leaver, A. and Williams, K. (2009) *Memorandum to the House of Commons – Treasury*, http://209.85.229.132/search?q=cache:eN9HSiTRwusJ:www.publications.parliament.uk/...

Fine, B., Lapavitsas, C. and Pincus, J. (eds) (2001) *Development Policy in the Twenty-first Century: Beyond the Post-Washington Consensus*. London: Routledge.

Goodhart, C.A.E. (2008) 'The Background to the 2007 Financial Crisis', *International Economics and Economic Policy*, 4, 331–46.

Haldane, A. (2009) 'Small Lessons from a Big Crisis', BIS, http://www.bis.org/review/r090710e.pdf.

Hoshi, T. and Kashyap, A. (2001) *Corporate Financing and Governance in Japan: The Road to the Future*. Cambridge, MA: MIT Press.

Inaba, K. (2008) 'The Transformation of Japanese Commercial Banking: Information Gathering and Assessing', unpublished PhD Thesis, University of London.

Itoh, M. and Lapavitsas, C. (1999) *Political Economy of Money and Finance*. London: Macmillan.

Kay, J. (2009) 'Narrow Banking: The Reform of Banking Regulation'. Centre for the Study of Financial Innovation, 88. UK: Heron, Dawson & Sawyer.

Keynes, J.M. ([1936] 1973) *The General Theory of Employment, Interest and Money*. London: Macmillan/Palgrave.

Lapavitsas, C. (2003) *Social Foundations of Markets, Money and Credit*. London: Routledge, pp. 1–170.

Lapavitsas, C. (2009) 'Financialised Capitalism: Crisis and Financial Expropriation', *Historical Materialism*, 17(2), 114–48.

Lapavitsas, C. and Dos Santos, P.L. (2008) 'Globalization and Contemporary Banking: On the Impact of New Technology', *Contributions to Political Economy*, 27, 31–56.

McKinnon, R. (1973) *Money & Capital in Economic Development*. Washington, DC: Brookings Institution.

Posen, A. (2009) 'A Proven Framework to End the US Banking Crisis Including Some Temporary Nationalizations', Testimony Before the Joint Committee of the US Congress Hearing on 'Restoring the Economy: Strategies for Short-term and Long-term Change', 26 February, http://www.iie.com/publications/papers/posen0209.pdf.

Shaw, E.S. (1973) *Financial Deepening in Economic Development*. Oxford: Oxford University Press.

Stiglitz, J. (1989). 'Markets, Market Failures and Development', *American Economic Review*, 79(2), 197–202.

Stiglitz, J. (1998) 'More Instruments and Broader Goals: Moving Toward the Post Washington Consensus', the 1998 WIDER Annual Lecture, Helsinki, 7 January.

Suzuki ,Y. (1987a) *The Japanese Financial System*, Oxford: Clarendon Press.

Suzuki, Y. (1987b) *Financial Reform in Japan – Developments and Prospects*, Bank of Japan Monetary and Economic Studies, 5(3), December.

8
Institutional Investment and Financial Regulation: An International Comparison

Ramona Meyricke

1 Introduction

The last thirty years have been a period of remarkable change in global financial markets, over which liberalisation, technology and consumer needs have critically shaped financial systems. Liberalisation of financial systems was largely a consequence of the hypothesis that government restrictions interfere with credit allocation and lead to a lower quantity and quality of investment (McKinnon, 1973). Liberalisation involved the removal of government regulations and controls on the exchange rate, international capital flows and the banking sector. Concurrent with liberalisation, demographic and workforce trends altered customers' financial needs and led to changes in financial distribution channels, products and suppliers; technology made financial transactions easier to access, faster and further reaching (Australian Government, 1997). Together, these changes have increased: short-termism, the correlation of investors' beliefs and the susceptibility of the financial system to crises (Brock, 1999; Carmichael, 1999). Since the late 1970s there has been an increase in the frequency of banking crises across the world. Evidence suggests that this is because, in most cases, liberalisation was not accompanied by an adequate regulatory framework, so it led to increased risk-taking (Kaminsky and Reinhart, 1999).

Over the same period, institutional investors (IIs), such as insurance companies, pension funds and investment funds, have established themselves as major players in international capital markets. IIs now own a large proportion of financial assets in most developed economies and exert significant influence over financial markets and corporate finance (Impavido et al., 2001a; Gompers and Metrick, 2001). The rise of institutional investment has been associated with a shift away from bank-based finance to market-based finance and with increased competition between commercial banks and non-bank financial institutions (Davis, 1996). In light of these factors, the problem addressed in this chapter is whether regulation of IIs could have prevented, or reduced the impact of, the Global Financial Crisis (GFC). Institutional investment can increase financial instability if it is not accompanied by an adequate supervisory framework. Herding behaviour, characteristic of IIs, can increase asset price volatility (Sias, 2004). IIs may also contribute to liquidity crises and banking crises (Davis, 2003). Investment behaviour, however, is influenced by the structure of the financial system and the regulatory framework. Financial regulation creates incentives and constraints on the behaviour of all investors and profoundly affects the structure and scale of financial activities (Australian Government, 1997).

This chapter explores the hypothesis that the GFC was caused in part by shortcomings in the financial regulation of IIs. It is argued that financial instability was increased by the failure of regulation to prevent institutional investment behaviours that amplify asset price volatility. After outlining the characteristics of IIs and the magnitude of their activities globally, the ways in which institutional investment can affect asset price volatility and financial stability are reviewed. Next, the role of institutional investment and financial regulation in the GFC is analysed. The impact of the GFC and financial regulations are compared across four countries with similar levels of institutional investment (as a percentage of GDP), but different regulatory frameworks: Australia, Canada, the UK and the US. Particular attention is paid to the regulatory frameworks in Australia and Canada, whose banks emerged from the GFC relatively unscathed.

Regulation of IIs is identified as a key factor that has increased financial resilience in Australia and Canada. The conclusion is that financial regulation cannot successfully prevent financial crises unless it monitors all systemically important financial institutions, not just banks. In addition, in a rapidly changing financial system, financial regulators require adequate resources to identify emerging risks and the authority to intervene early in order to prevent levels of asset price volatility that threaten financial stability.

2 An overview of institutional investment

2.1 Macro characteristics

Institutional investors (IIs) have established themselves as major players in the capital markets of most developed countries and some developing countries, such as Chile and Peru (Davis, 1996). IIs are specialised financial institutions who act on behalf of beneficiaries to manage pooled savings towards a specific objective (in terms of risk, return and maturity). IIs can be distinguished by their liabilities, which influence their investment behaviour (IMF 2005). For example, defined benefit pension funds have long-term liabilities as their beneficiaries cannot withdraw their funds until retirement, death or disability. This means that they can invest based on long-term fundamentals and pay less attention to short-term movements in financial markets. In comparison, money market funds are short-term vehicles, as beneficiaries can withdraw their funds at short notice, so short-term movements in financial markets influence their investment decisions.

Between 1995 and 2007, IIs' assets increased as a percentage of GDP in all OECD countries (Table 8.1). In 2005, IIs were in control of financial assets in excess of US$45 trillion – or 150 per cent of OECD countries' GDP (IMF 2005). This increase is in part because the population of most OECD countries is ageing. This has increased the need for long-term savings products, such as savings accounts in pension funds or annuities provided by life insurers (Davis, 1996). As IIs have a medium- to long-term investment horizon, typical institutional investment funds include a large portion of equity shares (partly to allow beneficiaries to benefit from share market returns). As shown in Table 8.2, in the major developed economies (Germany, France, Japan, the UK and the US) almost half of all pension funds' and investment companies' assets are invested in equity shares (IMF, 2005).

Accordingly, in many countries, higher levels of institutional investment explain the rapid growth of share markets over the past 20 years (Impavido et al., 2001a). In the UK, IIs own around 45 per cent of equity listed on UK share markets (HM Treasury, 2001). In the US, in 1996, IIs already controlled over half of the equity listed on US share markets (Gompers and Metrick, 2001). IIs demand for equity has contributed to the rapid development of global share markets, and has increased the opportunities for listed firms to obtain finance by issuing shares or corporate debt (Impavido et al., 2001b).

Institutional investment has also driven changes in the banking system and credit markets. Since 1970, the size of the financial system (measured by the value of total financial claims relative to GDP) and the percentage of financial claims that are intermediated have grown sharply (Davis, 2003). Over the same period, the share of financial assets controlled by the banking sector decreased as IIs increased their share of financial assets (Davis, 2003). Historically, banks were the sole providers of financial functions such as the pooling and allocation of

Table 8.1 Financial assets of institutional investors in OECD countries as a percentage of GDP (Gonnard et al., 2008)

	1995	1996	1997	1998	1999	2000	2001	2002	2003	2004	2005	2006	2007
Australia	82.6	90.5	102.4	110.2	122.2	126.1	126.0	118.3	120.6	129.6	141.5	152.3	–
Austria	43.5	50.2	57.6	65.0	78.6	84.1	87.0	90.7	97.9	105.8	125.3	130.3	128.2
Belgium	31.0	35.8	44.3	70.5	79.8	83.0	84.6	80.1	87.0	95.6	105.0	110.7	111.1
Canada	94.0	107.9	118.6	126.2	131.6	128.1	125.2	117.7	122.2	127.5	134.1	144.4	146.4
Czech Republic	16.7	17.5	15.5	13.5	15.9	16.3	13.8	16.8	17.1	19.5	19.0	18.4	22.4
Denmark	83.2	89.7	100.0	106.8	120.5	123.3	121.1	118.9	130.4	150.3	172.6	176.6	181.3
Finland	50.4	59.1	63.7	70.0	90.9	86.1	82.5	83.1	92.9	103.4	120.9	133.1	132.4
France	75.9	84.6	95.0	104.5	123.5	130.7	129.6	123.9	131.6	147.6	160.2	174.0	171.4
Germany	56.4	63.4	74.6	84.0	97.0	99.3	99.3	97.2	105.2	107.3	116.0	119.1	117.3
Greece	11.5	15.4	23.5	26.9	36.2	30.1	25.5	22.2	23.0	22.6	19.3	16.7	15.3
Hungary[2]	3.4	4.3	7.5	8.9	11.0	12.6	14.2	16.2	16.4	19.0	24.5	28.4	32.9
Iceland	–	–	–	–	–	–	105.5	112.1	129.5	145.0	167.9	180.3	198.1
Ireland	–	–	–	–	–	–	334.1	331.5	362.8	389.3	483.4	549.0	555.3
Italy	25.9	33.4	44.9	65.5	96.8	94.3	90.6	84.8	90.0	90.9	97.1	98.1	86.7
Japan	98.7	94.5	101.5	102.1	110.8	106.1	104.2	107.4	117.5	123.5	145.2	148.4	–
Korea	–	–	–	–	–	–	–	67.6	64.9	68.6	73.9	80.1	91.6
Luxembourg[3]	37.1	54.8	77.7	93.8	104.2	108.6	114.2	106.9	117.7	129.9	149.6	–	–
Mexico[2]	1.3	1.3	1.3	1.4	5.3	4.6	6.6	7.0	7.4	7.3	8.2	9.7	–
Netherlands	146.0	158.5	170.4	181.4	197.9	189.5	176.3	159.1	171.3	182.4	201.8	206.4	196.9
New Zealand	–	–	–	–	–	–	–	–	–	–	–	–	–
Norway	42.8	43.6	46.4	45.4	51.8	44.8	43.3	42.3	48.0	50.3	54.8	58.3	61.9
Poland[4]	1.4	1.8	2.4	3.1	4.4	6.8	9.4	13.0	15.8	18.5	23.6	30.1	–

(continued)

Table 8.1 Continued

	1995	1996	1997	1998	1999	2000	2001	2002	2003	2004	2005	2006	2007
Portugal[2]	18.1	21.3	47.4	52.7	53.8	52.1	50.6	49.9	53.6	54.4	63.1	66.6	65.4
Slovak Republic[4][5]	–	–	–	–	–	0.6	6.5	7.3	9.7	11.8	15.6	16.2	–
Spain	33.5	43.7	54.8	62.9	63.3	59.2	58.0	56.2	60.5	63.5	66.1	64.6	60.5
Sweden[3]	48.6	58.3	66.9	73.7	87.1	87.0	127.7	108.0	120.5	128.8	150.7	159.3	–
Switzerland	–	–	–	–	206.9	214.1	212.5	192.7	208.8	219.3	253.6	–	–
Turkey	0.8	1.2	1.2	1.4	2.4	2.3	3.3	3.9	5.5	5.6	6.1	4.4	–
United Kingdom	162.1	170.6	192.5	200.3	224.9	210.3	191.8	165.4	175.4	181.4	207.4	–	–
United States	140.8	151.6	166.9	180.7	195.4	185.1	177.4	163.1	181.7	187.8	191.2	202.5	211.2
QECD (17) total[6]	110.2	116.8	129.4	139.0	152.8	146.8	141.5	132.9	145.8	152.2	162.6	–	–

1. Investment companies, insurance companies, pension funds and other forms of institutional savings, non-consolidated data.
2. Excluding investment companies: Hungary (1995–96), Portugal (1995–97) and Mexico (1995–98).
3. Including only insurance companies: Luxembourg (1995–2005), Sweden (1995–2000).
4. Excluding pension funds: Poland (1995–98), Slovak Republic (2000–05).
5. Excluding insurance and pension funds: Slovak Republic (2000).
6. OECD (17) total excludes countries for which data are not available or comparable over the period 1995–2005.

Table 8.2 Asset allocation of institutional investors in Germany, France, Japan, the UK and the US (in per cent) (IMF, 2005)

	Pension Funds		Insurance companies		Investment companies	
	1997 (%)	2003 (%)	1997 (%)	2003 (%)	1997 (%)	2003 (%)
Domestic equity	44	37	21	20	39	37
Foreign equity	11	11	3	5	9	10
Real estate	2	3	0	0	0	0
Other	4	15	21	17	11	10
Domestic bonds	33	27	50	49	38	38
Foreign bonds	3	6	5	9	3	5
Cash	3	1	0	0	0	0

savings, monitoring borrowers, managing financial risk and facilitating the trading of goods and services (Levine, 1999). Financial liberalisation and the growth of securitised debt markets, however, meant that non-bank institutions could provide many of the same services as banks at lower cost. Subsequently, banks changed their business models in order to remain competitive. Most US banks now maintain short-term balance sheets, with tradable assets and liabilities so that they can quickly adjust the size and composition of their balance sheet (Cecchetti, 2008). There has also been a decrease in banks' net interest margins, as some banks reduced their profit margins to remain competitive with IIs while others shifted their focus from interest-earning to fee-earning activity (Impavido et al., 2001b).

2.2 Micro characteristics

IIs manage the pooled savings of many individuals in a distinctive manner. Pooling savings enables greater portfolio diversification, economies of scale and access to capital markets and large indivisible assets, such as commercial property. The size of institutional investment funds also means that IIs have considerable power and influence in market transactions. They may be able to exert control over companies in which they hold a majority share, or to negotiate better terms on debt contracts. IIs also face some restrictions because they manage pooled savings of beneficiaries who do not have direct control over how their money is invested. IIs have a legal responsibility to act in the best interests of the beneficiaries; that is, to maximise risk-adjusted returns within the beneficiaries' time horizon (ICGN, 2007).

IIs have a distinct investment process involving several agents, each with different roles and responsibilities (ICGN, 2007). Typically the investment process will include:

1. A board who oversee the investment process and monitor agents.
2. Asset managers, employed by the board, who are responsible for the investment of funds in line with a mandate setting out investment objectives and limitations.
3. Service providers who assist with designing or executing the investment mandate.
4. Custodians who administer and maintain records for the funds' assets. (HM Treasury, 2001)

Investment is guided by a mandate which sets out the investment objectives and restrictions. Each objective will usually include a target return to be achieved over a particular time horizon, expressed relative to an index e.g. to achieve a five-year average return of 2 per cent over the FTSE100. Asset managers rely on the same public information as individual investors, but they can process greater amounts of information more rapidly than individual investors. This is an advantage that IIs have over individual investors (Hughes et al., 2005).

Structural and incentive problems along the institutional investment chain may encourage behaviour that conflicts with the objective of maximising risk-adjusted returns and/or distorts financial markets (HM Treasury, 2001). For example, institutional investment in the UK has focused on listed shares and gilts at the expense of other assets such as venture capital, companies outside the major indices and high-yield bonds (HM Treasury, 2001). Institutional investment is also associated with behaviour that can increase asset price volatility, such as herding[1] and short-termism (Sias, 2004). Issues with institutional investment that can distort financial markets include:

1. Trustee boards generally lack adequate support and investment expertise. This leads to poor evaluation of advisers, unclear contractual structures with incentives for herding and short-termism, an overreliance on advisers, and insufficient resources devoted to asset allocation.
2. There are few checks and balances along the investment chain. This is because knowledge of investment issues is generally low and competition between service providers is distorted. (HM Treasury, 2001)

Short-termism and herding increase asset price volatility and can cause a small shock to have a large effect on capital flows (IMF, 2003; Chari and Kehoe, 2000). Institutional investment is rife with structures which generate strong incentives for short-termism and herding (HM Treasury, 2001). In principle, IIs have long-term horizons; however, evidence suggests that there is mismatch between the perceived investment horizon of trustees (who believe that they operated under long-term horizons) and the actual investment horizon of asset managers, whose performance is evaluated over a short-term horizon (HM Treasury, 2004). Evidence shows that institutions turn over their portfolios and trade more often than individuals (Schwartz and Shapiro, 1992). In relation to herding, there are several theories as to why investors herd. Investors are likely to herd if:

1. They infer information from each other's trades (Sias, 2004);
2. They are attracted to securities with specific characteristics (Gompers and Metrick, 2001);
3. There are reputational costs for acting differently from the herd, or other incentives to ignore private information and follow the behaviour of others[2] (Scharfstein and Stein, 1990).

Empirical evidence suggests that institutional herding results primarily from institutions inferring information from each other's trades (Sias, 2004). In addition, inflows to IIs increase the demand for the large and liquid stocks, and this can increase asset price correlation (Gompers and Metrick, 2001). Also the performance structure of most fund managers encourages them to seek returns relative to other managers, or to an index, rather than achieving highest absolute return; this creates strong incentives to invest in the same type of assets (Hughes et al., 2005).

Banks also herd, but for different reasons. The failure of one bank can exert a negative externality on other institutions (Brunnermeier et al., 2009). These externalities may be caused by at least five different factors: informational contagion, loss of access to funding for the failed bank's customers, interbank connections, debt-deflation and liquidity spirals and credit channel effects (Brunnermeier et al., 2009). Over all, these externalities mean that the failure of one bank can depress the general level of economic activity, which reduces deposits and profits for all surviving banks. Given the externalities arising from bank failure, banks prefer to fail (or survive) together, so they invest in the same type of assets and therefore have correlated asset returns (Acharya, 2009). A further incentive for banks to fail together is that government assistance (e.g. guarantees or recapitalisation facilities) is usually greater in the case of widespread bank failures. If an institution fails alone, it is less likely to receive government support than if many banks fail together.

Herding by any group of institutions can result in poor investment decisions across an entire industry. It also increases the correlation of asset returns and asset price volatility.[3] IIs are very large and have control over sufficient financial assets to move asset prices and significantly influence financial market dynamics (IMF, 2005). In principle, the long-term nature of IIs' liabilities means that they can invest based on long-term fundamentals rather than short-term market movements. This has the potential to lower financial market volatility and increase financial stability (Impavido et al., 2001a). In practice, however, issues with the institutional investment process can lead to short-termism and herding which increase financial instability.

3   Impacts on financial stability

Financial instability can be defined as widespread disruption to the functioning of the financial system capable of impeding the performance of an economy. Financial crises are a manifestation of financial instability. Theory and evidence support the view that financial crises are caused by market mechanisms which amplify asset price volatility, rather than by external shocks or macroeconomic policies (Acemoglu et al. 2003; Brunnermeier et al., 2009). Asset price volatility is inevitable in a system where prices are based on expectations of uncertain future profits. The arrival of new information, or a change in existing information, will change investors' expectations and hence the price. The IMF (2005) identifies four factors that can turn asset price volatility into financial instability: incentive structures that encourage herding and short-termism, lack of robust risk management, market infrastructure weakness and lack of transparency. These factors are important because they contribute to mechanisms that amplify asset price volatility. The interaction between asset price volatility and the liquidity of interrelated institutions is the crucial mechanism underlying most financial crises (Brunnermeier et al., 2009). Liquidity cycles amplify and spread asset price volatility across markets. A liquidity cycle usually progresses as follows:

1. Asset price falls reduce cash inflow or increase cash outflow;
2. This creates a liquidity problem where there is insufficient cash to meet current liabilities;

3. Firms are forced to sell assets to generate cash inflow, which pushes down asset prices;

4. Further asset price falls create further liquidity problems; and so on.

Liquidity spirals can spread through direct linkages, such as interbank loans (Allen and Gale, 2004). A negative shock to the balance sheet of one bank may cause them to liquidate assets (loans). As well as lowering prices, this may create liquidity problems for the counterparty to the asset. It also presents a systemic risk because banks will fail if their liquidity demands exceed the supply of liquid assets. Diamond and Rajan (2005) show that volatility can spread even if there are no explicit links between banks, via the negative spillover effect of bank failures on aggregate demand and liquidity. In summary, a financial crisis can be broken down into four stages (Currie, 2005): 1. initial asset price falls; 2. asset price falls spread from one market to another; 3. the effect of price falls on financial intermediaries leads to failures which endanger the system via their effects on liquidity of interrelated institutions and 4. this creates risk of core banking and payments system failure.

Financial instability will be increased by any factor that increases or amplifies asset price volatility. Asset price volatility and correlation between international markets has increased since the 1970s (Dees et al., 2007). This is partly due to interconnections arising from globalisation and related changes in market structures (Bordo et al., 1999). Asset price volatility also increases with the widespread use of leverage, which amplifies asset price returns (Kaminsky et al., 2003), or when institutional herding is common (IMF 2005). So systems of large, interconnected institutions that herd are likely to be more volatile than those with smaller institutions whose actions are uncorrelated. IIs can also give rise to financial instability or liquidity cycles if they shift their asset allocation at the same time, or encourage greater risk-taking in the financial sector by competing with banks (Davis 2003).

Figure 8.1 summarises how certain structural changes and characteristics of institutional investment impact on financial stability. This analysis identifies underlying risk factors that increase financial instability, rather than specific instruments or rules involved in a particular crisis.

Any factors that increase liquidity risk or encourage institutions to sell assets into falling markets will amplify market volatility (Brunnermeier et al., 2009). Factors such as leverage, shortage of liquidity, informational contagion and lack of transparency can turn asset price volatility into financial instability (IMF, 2005). Pro-cyclical regulations or risk management can also amplify asset price shocks (IMF, 2005). For example,

Structural changes	Institutional characteristics (risk factors) affecting financial stability	Effects on financial stability
Technological and financial innovation	• Correlation of beliefs • Herding • Interconnection	Increase in asset price volatility
Demographics and consumer demands	• Lack of transparency • Leverage	Increase in amplifying market dynamics such as:
Regulation, accounting rules and risk management practices	• Model uncertainty • Short-termism • Synergies among the above	• Liquidity spirals • Informational contagion • Counterparty contagion • Credit channel effects

Figure 8.1   Structural changes underlying financial instability

capital adequacy requirements that increase when asset prices are declining will force banks to raise capital at a time when income may be declining and it may be hard to raise external finance due to suppressed demand. This increases pressure on banks to sell assets in order to raise capital. Financial markets dominated by IIs will be more volatile and prone to financial crises if institutional investment increases leverage, inter-connection, shortage of liquidity, a lack of transparency and herding, all of which amplify asset price volatility.

In summary, IIs now control sufficient financial assets to move asset prices and significantly influence financial market dynamics (IMF, 2005). IIs compete with banks, providing many of the same functions. To remain competitive with IIs, many banks now maintain short-term balance sheets with tradable assets and liabilities (Cecchetti, 2008). Short-termism and herding behaviour, characteristic of IIs, increases the susceptibility of the financial system to crises. In addition, IIs may trigger liquidity cycles if they all shift their asset allocation at the same time or if they encourage greater risk-taking by banks via competition (Davis, 2003).

4   Institutional investment, regulation and the Global Financial Crisis

A range of potential causes of the GFC have been proposed, including: financial regulation, asset price bubbles in property and equity markets, international macroeconomic imbalances, macroeconomic policies and institutional features (Rose and Spiegel, 2009). This section focuses on the interaction between IIs and financial regulation. It explores the hypothesis that the GFC was partly caused by the failure of regulation to mitigate investment behaviours that increase financial instability. The GFC was triggered by huge losses on credit securities that caused the failure of Lehman Brothers. The credit securities involved several factors known to amplify asset price volatility: a shortage of liquidity, a high degree of leverage and interconnectedness, and a lack of transparency and documentation which exacerbated informational contagion (Blanchard, 2008). Financial regulation should limit the risk factors and amplification mechanisms that increase systemic risk (Blanchard, 2008). There is, however, some evidence that regulatory changes increased risk-taking in the lead up to the GFC.

Competition between bank and non-bank institutions intensified due to regulatory changes which spurred the growth of a large unregulated 'shadow banking system' (Jones, 2000). In the US, the repeal of the Glass–Steagall Act in 1999 removed regulations that prevented commercial banks from undertaking trading activity; so commercial banks, investment banks and IIs could all offer the same services. Banking, brokerage, insurance and securities companies merged into integrated financial conglomerates. Financial integration increased competition between banks for wholesale deposits and loans and reduced the scope for traditional bank intermediation (Davis, 2003). In addition, the adoption of the Basel Accord increased banks' operating costs relative to non-bank institutions. The Basel Accord assigned risk weights to different types of bank assets, and banks were required to hold higher capital for assets such as commercial loans. The innovation of loan securitisation[4] meant that non-bank institutions could lend money to borrowers, and that any financial institution could sell its loans on, or place them off-balance sheet (Trichet, 2009). The Basel Accord created incentives for loan securitisation, because banks could reduce their capital requirements by securitising loans through off-balance sheet vehicles that were not subject to regulatory costs (Jones, 2000). Securitised products allowed banks to generate higher profits than traditional loans, and did not have the same capital requirements. Securitisation, however, weakened incentives for prudent credit risk assessment and ongoing monitoring (Trichet, 2009). Finally, the GFC also revealed problems with the documentation of securitised products and a lack of knowledge of their risks. These factors point to weaknesses in financial regulation (Demirgüc-Kunt, 2009).

Regulatory changes increased the competition between banks and other financial institutions, which also encouraged banks to relax lending standards and to increase their level of risk-taking (IMF, 2005). Banks responded to increased competition from non-bank institutions by increasing their activity in the functions traditionally performed by IIs. This was done by increasing off-balance sheet, fee-earning activity such as the securitisation of loans and the trading of derivatives, and reducing traditional on-balance sheet, interest-earning activity (Cecchetti, 2008). A period of low interest rates also squeezed banks' interest income and made fee-earning activity more attractive. Banks tried to capitalise their advantage in loan origination by issuing more short-term loans and increasing loan securitisation in order to earn income from fees and avoid capital charges. In the short-term, loan securitisation appears to reduce the maturity mismatch on bank balance sheets. The structure of these securities, however, generally increased banks' interest rate risk and refinancing risk (Gorton, 2008).

In addition to a build-up of risk within the banking sector, the availability of bank credit at low interest rates fuelled a credit boom. Household borrowing and financial institutions' leverage increased. In the UK, increased household indebtedness was associated with higher house prices and house purchases (Benito et al., 2007). The loans made to households were packaged, moved off bank balance sheets and sold as securities. Large volumes of securitisation were possible because (i) households were willing and able to borrow; and (ii) there were many IIs willing to buy credit securities, often with borrowed money (Macfarlane, 2008). There was also an increase in the degree of leverage within the financial sector (Macfarlane, 2008). Leverage amplifies returns. Faced with increased competition and squeezed loan margins, financial institutions sought to increase their returns by increasing leverage (IMF, 2005). The build-up of leverage occurred mainly within the shadow banking system, in institutions such as investment banks and hedge funds (Jones, 2000). It was difficult to measure because these institutions were not obliged to report on their off-balance sheet activities, but it is reflected in the growth in securitised debt markets (see Figure 8.2). Regulatory changes in 2004, which allowed US investment banks to be supervised on a consolidated basis, led to a jump in leverage that was associated with increased purchases of credit securities (Blundell-Wignall et al., 2009).

Leverage amplifies gains and losses. Incentive structures throughout the financial system, however, are such that investors have unlimited potential benefit from gains but are protected from losses. For example, traders' salaries are often structured as a base salary plus a bonus equal to a percentage of any financial gains made; total pay increases if gains are made, but does not fall below the base salary if a loss is made. Also, in the

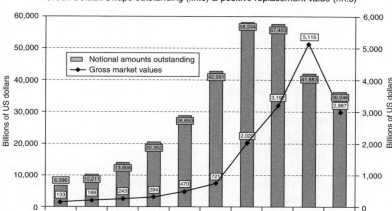

Figure 8.2 Credit defaults outstanding (Blundell-Wignall et al., 2009)

Note: Notional amounts are all the debt exposure covered. Gross market values on the right-hand side refer to how much money would actually change hands after netting if derivatives were sold on the reporting date at prevailing market prices.

Source: BIS OECD.

banking system at large, it was assumed that governments would act as the lender of last resort to prevent banks from becoming insolvent. This encourages banks to make riskier loans because if loans are profitable the banks benefit, but if there is a widespread default the government pays (Rose and Spiegel, 2009). Incentive structures that capped losses encouraged excessive risk-taking and partly caused the GFC (Bernanke, 2009).

As well as failing to mitigate risky lending and excessive leverage, some regulations also amplified the crisis. Feedback effects that reinforced liquidity spirals arose from mark-to-market accounting, and risk management or trading systems which forced institutions to reduce leverage following an asset price fall (Brunnermeier et al., 2009). Finally, pro-cyclical capital requirements meant that banks were forced to find more capital in illiquid credit markets because the risk of their loans increased (Kashyap and Stein, 2003). These feedbacks intensified the squeeze on bank balance sheets. Asset values dropped, credit market liquidity dried up and capital requirements increased simultaneously.

5 International comparison of financial regulation

This section compares the role of financial regulation in the GFC across Australia, Canada, the UK and the US. These countries have similar levels of institutional investment but different regulatory frameworks. Particular attention is paid to Australia and Canada, whose banks emerged from the GFC almost unscathed. The focus is on financial risk and regulation, rather than economic factors.

Following the subprime crisis in 2008, only 11 of the top 100 banks in the world (ranked by assets) were rated AA. However, all of the major Australian banks were in this group (MacFarlane, 2008). In addition, no Australian or Canadian banks needed government recapitalisation throughout the GFC. By contrast, as at October 2009, the UK government had spent US$81 billion on recapitalisation and the US government spent US$806 billion on recapitalising banks (Blundell-Wignall et al., 2009).[5] Most of the banks that experienced intervention by the public authorities during the GFC focused heavily on mortgage finance or structured finance (Honohan, 2008). Figure 8.3 shows a breakdown of bank balance sheets from seven banks, each located in a different country. Bank of America, Citigroup, Barclays, UBS and Deutsche Bank all belong to countries that figured prominently in the GFC. Only Westpac, an Australian bank, and Santander, a Spanish bank, are located in countries that did not need large amounts of government assistance. The difference between these banks and the others is that they had a higher proportion of loan assets, a lower proportion of derivatives and securities and relied more on deposits than other liabilities to fund lending. That is, they followed a 'traditional' banking model where deposits fund loans, rather than using wholesale funding to finance various debt securities. Banks like Westpac and Santander avoided the large losses suffered by most banks (Blundell-Wignall et al., 2009).

The Australian Prudential Regulation Authority (APRA) identifies three underlying reasons for the resilience of the Australian system: structural factors, strong financial institutions and good regulation (Lewis, 2009). In terms of market structure, mortgage lending in Australia is different to the US in several respects. In the US, mortgage originators had very little accountability or incentive to properly assess credit risk because they could easily absolve themselves of any risk by passing it onto another institution. This 'originate to distribute' model never took off in Australia. This is partly because APRA requires that, if a third party originates a loan, the lending institution must ensure that the originator applies the institutions' own credit assessment standards (Lewis, 2009). In addition, APRA introduced significantly higher capital charges for high risk or 'subprime' loans in 2004 (Lewis, 2009). Finally, in some US states mortgages are non-recourse loans; so if the funds recouped from sale of the mortgaged property are less than the outstanding debt, the

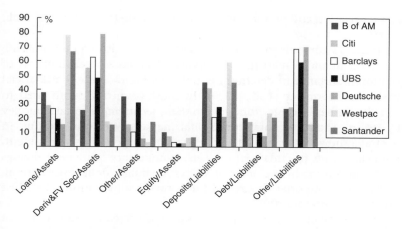

Figure 8.3 Breakdown of bank balance sheets (Blundell-Wignall et al., 2009)

lender may not have recourse to the borrower after foreclosure. Non-recourse loans are more likely to default than loans where the lender has recourse to the borrower (Gent and Kudlyak, 2009). In Australia mortgages are full recourse, which provides enhanced security for lenders. In summary, Australian mortgage securitisation markets are low risk relative to their US counterparts. Australian corporate debt markets are small because few Australian companies are large enough to be rated by credit rating agencies. Furthermore, Australian investors were less likely to invest in US subprime securities due to 'home bias' preference to invest in Australian assets (Mishra, 2008). Finally, the Australian economy and stock market experienced strong growth over the last decade mainly due to exports of resources benefitting from strong commodity prices (The Economist, 2008).

From an institutional perspective, the Australian banking system is an oligopoly dominated by four large banks. These banks are protected from mergers or acquisitions by the 'Four Pillars' policy. This limits competitive pressure on these banks, reducing the need to engage in high-risk activity to remain profitable. In terms of regulation, Australian regulators place less reliance on quantitative models for risk management and did not adopt Basel II until 1 January 2008 (Lewis, 2009). Excessive reliance on risk management models can increase asset price volatility because market-sensitive models all use the same market data inputs; so all banks relying on these models will try to reduce their exposure at the same time. In turn this increases asset price volatility and correlation and prompts model-driven selling (Brunnermeier et al., 2009).

Australia's compulsory retirement savings laws also had a stabilising effect on financial markets. The ability of banks to recapitalise is of central importance in determining the extent and depth of a financial crisis (Brunnermeier et al., 2009). In most countries, funds used to recapitalise banks came from government, as attempts to raise money by issuing shares or bonds on capital markets were unsuccessful. In Australia, however, banks and non-financial corporations were able to raise capital on the financial markets. Compulsory retirement savings contributions are in the order of $70bn Australian dollars per annum, and were an important source of funds for recapitalisation (The Allen Consulting Group, 2009).

The Australian financial system was also protected by regulation that limited the build-up of risk in non-bank financial institutions. APRA has no institutional boundaries in its scope. It regulates all financial institutions on a functional basis, focussing on core risk types: credit, market, governance and insurance (Carmichael, 2002). This focus helped to prevent risk accumulating in non-bank institutions, such as insurance companies, in the way that it had done in the US. In addition to specific regulations, e.g. of capital adequacy and risk assessment, APRA also has a strong focus on corporate governance. APRA checks that board members are suitably skilled to manage the risks of their business and encourages boards to understand the risks of their business. If the board cannot understand and manage the risk of a product it should be a 'no go' area (Laker, 2009).

In the UK, on the other hand, regulatory and corporate governance failures created financial instability (Buiter, 2007; Walker, 2009). Buiter (2007) argues that the 'tripartite' structure of Britain's financial regulation is flawed because it puts the information about banks with the Financial Services Authority (FSA) separate from the agency with the liquid financial resources to provide short-term assistance to banks (the Bank of England). A government review into the GFC recommended that the FSA increase its focus on the quality of governance and risk management (Walker, 2009). Finally, on a practical note, in 2006 the FSA was supervising 29,759 firms (McCallum, 2006), whereas APRA is only supervising about 4,500 firms (APRA, 2010).[6] Compared to the FSA, APRA can spend more time monitoring each fund for a given level of resources.

The aspects of prudential regulation central to the health of the Australian financial system are very similar to those factors that maintained the resilience of Canadian banks throughout the GFC.

The legal mandate of the Canadian regulator, the Office of the Superintendent of Financial Institutions Supervision (OSFI), is a key strength of the Canadian system of regulation (Currie, 2005). OSFI's mandate focuses on solvency and early intervention. OSFI has a lot of freedom to act, and the independence and authority to act quickly and effectively in a financial crisis. OSFI has an early-warning system and could respond to a build-up of high-risk loans within a bank by forcing the bank to reduce its leverage ratio (Financial Times, 2009). OSFI also monitors bank leverage very closely. This was identified as an important back stop in the financial crisis, and an essential supervisory tool in addition to risk-based capital adequacy requirements.

Canadian banks are subject to tough capital requirements and restrictions on leverage. In the third quarter of 2008, average Canadian banks had capital adequacy ratios of 9–10 per cent, above the 8 per cent minimum required (Financial Times, 2009). OSFI suggests this is because they spent a lot of time working through Basel II and internal risk assessment models with banks, so that they understood how much capital was required to be held against their loan book (Financial Times, 2009). The quality of personnel is also a key focus, with OSFI recruiting from the public and the private sector, and adding more resources to prevent reliance on top-level staff and the boards of the institutions they are regulating (Financial Times, 2009). OSFI moves quickly to improve and fix shortcomings in the financial regulatory framework. For example, OSFI integrated regulation of banks and insurers in 1995, six years before the Joint Forum of the Basel Committee on Banking Supervision made recommendations to this effect (Currie, 2005).

In summary, the Australian and Canadian regulators share a focus on risks to solvency across all financial institutions, not just banks. They both focus on early intervention and a style of working closely with the board to improve corporate governance. Finally, APRA and OSFI both had adequate human resources, legal authority and the independence to act quickly to prevent a build-up of risk in the financial system. In addition to structural factors, financial regulation partly explains why Australian and Canadian banks did not engage in as much 'high-risk' activity as their UK or US counterparts.

6   Structure of financial regulation: institutional versus integrated

This section compares the structure of financial regulation in Australia, Canada, the UK and the US, and its success in reducing financial instability. In a broad sense, financial regulation includes direct regulation of institutions and instruments and indirect measures such as taxation law, or codes of conduct developed by professional associations. The cost of a financial crisis is potentially very large and includes disruptions to economic activity, credit losses and fiscal costs. The main goal of financial regulation, therefore, is to ensure the stability of the financial system as a whole (Brunnermeier et al., 2009). The underlying function of financial regulation is to address four main sources of market failure: anti-competitive behaviour, market misconduct, asymmetric information and systemic instability (Carmichael, 2002). The first two failures pertain to 'business conduct' while the second two pertain to the 'safety and soundness' of the financial system. The focus of this section is on regulation primarily concerned with the safety and soundness of financial institutions, that is, prudential regulation.

Traditionally, prudential regulation followed an 'institutional model', where a single regulator was assigned to each institutional group (defined by legal status) with responsibility for correcting some or all sources of market failure (G30, 2009). The US is the most extreme example of this type of structure. In the US there are multiple prudential regulators, whose jurisdiction is defined by institutional groups and also by state; each regulator has responsibility for a different set of regulatory functions (Carmichael, 2002). The US framework of state regulation limited the degree and the effectiveness of oversight of financial institutions (G30, 2009). In addition, different regulatory models for banks and insurers impede effective supervision (Bernanke, 2009). Regulators had little power to curtail non-bank activity in the US system, and could do little to prevent risky lending in the lead up to the GFC (IMF, 2005).

In developed financial systems, similar products and services are provided by different types of institutions. This means that common principles of financial regulation should apply to bank and non-bank financial institutions, because both types of institutions can cause market failure (BIS, 2001). Accordingly, many countries have shifted to an 'integrated' or 'functional' approach to financial regulation, where a single regulator is assigned to correcting one or more of the four sources of market failure, for all institutions subject to that particular failure. The majority of integrated regulators assign one regulator to each source of market failure, some combine two or more of these functions into one agency. In contrast to the US where there are multiple financial regulators, in Australia, Canada and the UK there is a single prudential regulator for all financial institutions (the APRA, OSFI and FSA respectively) (IMF, 2006).

Table 8.3 Responsibilities of the integrated prudential regulator in Australia, Canada and the UK (Carmichael, 2002)

Responsibility for regulating	Australia	Canada	UK
Asymmetric Information Failure:			
Prudential Policy	Y	Y	Y
Prudential Implementation	Y	Y	Y
Market Misconduct Failure:			
Market Conduct (General)	N	P	Y
Market Conduct (Fundraising)	N	N	Y
Disclosure	N	P	Y
Systemic Instability Failure:			
Payments system	N	N	N
Competition Failure:			
Competition Policy	N	N	N

"Y"   full responsibility.
"N"   no responsibility.
"P"   partial responsibility, i.e. shared with another agency or government.

As shown in Table 8.3, the main difference between Australia and Canada is that the duties for prudential regulation and business conduct have been separated in the Australian system (with APRA responsible for prudential regulation and another regulator responsible for business conduct and disclosure); whereas OSFI has partial responsibility for general business conduct. In the UK, one regulator, the FSA, is solely responsible for prudential regulation and business conduct. The FSA has more responsibilities than the Australian or Canadian prudential regulators, who are responsible for fewer firms and have less responsibility to regulate business conduct and disclosure.

The large losses suffered by UK banks illustrate that integrated financial regulation is insufficient on its own to achieve financial stability. The FSA have acknowledged failures pertaining to over-reliance on rules that focussed on institutions at the expense of systemic risk, and to flaws in the rules used to monitor capital and liquidity (Ross, 2009). Following the GFC, the FSA plans to adopt a more 'intrusive' approach to regulation, asking more challenging questions as well as being more willing to intervene where necessary. This approach includes increasing resources devoted to the supervision of high-impact firms, and an increasing focus on business strategies and system-wide risks, the technical competence of staff and on the details of bank accounting (Ross, 2009). These measures should make the approach of the FSA a more proactive and informed one.

As IIs control a significant portion of the assets within the financial system, the way in which they are regulated affects financial stability. In addition, regulating IIs has an indirect influence on the behaviour of all investors who rely on IIs for finance, such as private equity funds and hedge funds. Rather than focussing on individual institutions, history would suggest that a focus on sources of market failure, or risk types, is more effective at ensuring the safety and soundness of the financial system. An integrated approach to financial regulation, however, is not enough to achieve the objective of financial stability. Regulators need clear objectives and a focus on financial risk, sufficient resources to identify emerging risks and the authority to intervene early in order to prevent a build up of risk.

7　Risk-based regulation

The financial system is constantly evolving. If firms are prevented from using one particular instrument, it is likely that they will pursue their objectives using other instruments (Acemoglu et al., 2003). In such a system, regulatory structures that can respond to emerging risks are necessary to maintain financial stability. Forward-looking, principles-based (or risk-based) legislation is more flexible than a quantitative or rules-based approach, and can change faster to meet regulatory needs. This section reviews the evolution of financial regulation in Australia to highlight how a risk-based approach can enhance financial stability.

Australian financial regulation has undergone significant reforms as a result of past crises. The commercial property crisis of the early 1990s was a trigger for change in Australian financial regulation. Australian banks were hit hard by this crisis: Two large, state government-owned banks failed, as did the second-largest building society, the largest credit union, three merchant banks, a mortgage trust and a friendly society (Macfarlane, 2008). In response, the Australian government commissioned an inquiry to recommend ways to improve financial regulation (Australian Government, 1997). The inquiry identified technological innovation, consumer needs and regulation as the critical shapers of global financial systems over the twenty-first century. The recommendations of the review were to:

1　Increase flexibility in regulatory structures so they are more responsive to the forces changing the financial system;
2. clarify regulatory goals;

3. increase the accountability of the agencies charged with meeting those goals; and
4. ensure that regulation of similar financial products and conglomerates is consistent.

Following this inquiry, in 1998 the Australian government reoriented financial regulation away from an institutionally based approach towards a functionally based approach. The new measures were designed to ensure that regulation was consistent with the basic goals of maintaining financial system safety and stability, and better focussed on its underlying objectives, while still encouraging competition. These changes did not prevent the failure of a major Australian insurer, HIH, in 2001, which generated losses in the order of five billion Australian dollars as a result of overvaluations of assets and the underestimation of liabilities (Reuters, 2001). A Royal Commission was called in 2001 to investigate the causes of the collapse and to determine how to reduce the risk of other financial failures. Subsequent investigations revealed that the failure was caused in part by an aggressive acquisition strategy, which included entering unfamiliar foreign markets and by a complex structure, involving more than 200 subsidiaries, which convoluted the financial accounts (Cagan, 2001).

The HIH Royal Commission made a number of recommendations relating to the reform of prudential regulation. The recommendations focused on improving corporate governance, financial reporting and the consistency of regulation between financial institutions and states (Australian Government, 2004). Reforms were made to ensure consistency of regulation between insurance companies and banks, and between 'insurance-like' product providers and insurance companies, as well as removing state legislation so all insurers were regulated consistently on a national level. APRA now monitors by risk type, focussing on all sources of credit risk, market risk and liquidity risk present in the financial system (Currie, 2005).

APRA also responded to the collapse by committing to strengthen the skills of its staff and to develop a more proactive and sceptical approach to supervision – for example, by reviewing supervisory processes and continually questioning staff assumptions, views and conclusions. APRA strengthened the capacity of its staff to supervise and regulate financial institutions by setting up specialist teams, and recruiting people from industry into front-line supervisory roles (Laker, 2009). APRA also implemented a 'Probability and Impact Rating' (PAIR) system which informs their approach, and assists in making risk judgements and focusing supervision where it is most needed. A fund receiving an extreme PAIR rating will typically have a concentration of investments in one product or market, and high exposure to volatility. APRA also has powers to intervene in the management of financial institutions before risks build up to a critical level (Laker, 2009).

The financial system is evolving constantly, so regulation needs to respond to emerging risks in order to maintain financial stability. In Australia, following the collapse of HIH, rigid rules were rescinded and replaced with a system of regulation focused on: identifying emerging risks, enabling early regulatory intervention and strengthening corporate governance. This partly explains the resilience of banks in Australia throughout the GFC (Lewis, 2009).

8　Summary and conclusions

IIs control sufficient financial assets to directly influence financial market dynamics through their investment activity, and to indirectly influence many financial institutions as purchasers and suppliers of credit (Davis, 1996). Structural and incentive problems involved in institutional investment may distort financial markets and increase asset price volatility. In particular, asset price volatility can be increased by the excessive use of leverage, which amplifies asset price returns (Kaminsky et al., 2003), and by herding behaviour (IMF, 2005). Evidence from the GFC suggests that a financial system dominated by large, highly connected financial institutions, with incentive structures that encourage herding, is likely to be more volatile than one with smaller institutions that act independently of one another.

Financial regulation incentivises and constrains the behaviour of actors in the financial system and affects the type and the scale of financial activities (Australian Government, 1997). It is argued that financial instability was increased by the failure of financial regulation to keep up with the structural changes taking place in financial markets. In particular, financial instability was increased by a failure to regulate the following features of institutional investment which cause and amplify asset price volatility: excessive risk-taking, leverage, herding and short-termism.

The impacts of the GFC differed across Australia, Canada, the UK and the US. These four countries have comparable levels of institutional investment but different regulatory structures. In the US, a firm's legal status (for example, bank or insurance company) determines the financial regulations that apply. In Australia, Canada and the UK, however, regulators apply consistent regulations across bank and non-bank financial institutions.

The Australian and Canadian regulators focus on early intervention and a style of working closely with industry, and they both have adequate human resources, legal authority and the independence to act quickly to prevent a build up of risk in the financial system. These factors most likely prevented a build up of risk in Australian and Canadian banks.

In conclusion, financial regulation cannot prevent financial crises unless it encompasses all systemically important institutions and the risks that are inherent in their activities. As IIs are major players in global financial markets, regulation should address the aspects of their activity that may threaten financial stability. A rapidly changing financial system necessitates regulation that is responsive to changes in financial markets. Regulators need adequate resources to identify emerging risks and the authority to intervene early in order to prevent a build up of risk. Finally, regulation should seek to strengthen corporate governance and instil a focus on risk management within the boards of institutions. As responsibility for the management of any institution ultimately rests with its board.

Notes

1. Herding is defined as a group of investors following each other's trades.
2. Acting like others suggests that you have received the same information and arrived at a similar conclusion; taking a contrarian position is more likely to be perceived as incorrect (Scharfstein and Stein 1990).
3. Asset price volatility is usually defined as the standard deviation of changes in the log of asset prices (IMF 2003).
4. Securitisation involves packaging loans together in a pool, then issuing 'securities' that are backed by the pool of loans. The funds obtained from selling the securities are lent to the ultimate borrowers and used to pay fees; when the ultimate borrowers make loan repayments these are passed onto the owners of the securities, after the deduction of fees.
5. This is in addition to other costs on asset purchases, guarantees, and facilities, as well as indirect economic costs.
6. 180 Authorised Deposit-taking Institutions, 150 general insurers, 4,430 Superannuation Entities, and 32 Life insurers.

References

Acemoglu, D., Johnson, S., Robinson, J. and Tchaicharoedn, Y. (2003) 'Institutional Causes, Macroeconomic Symptoms: volatility, Crises and Growth', *Journal of Monetary Economics*, 50, 49–123.
Acharya, V. (2009) ''A Theory of Systemic Risk and Design of Prudential Bank Regulation', *CEPR Discussion Paper Series*, No. DP7164.
Allen, F. and Gale, D. (2004) 'Financial Intermediaries and Markets', *Econometrica*, 72, 1023–61.

The Allen Consulting Group (2009) *Better Living Standards and a Stronger Economy: The Role of Superannuation in Australia*, Report to the Association of Superannuation Funds of Australia.

Australian Government (1997) *Australian Financial System Inquiry Final Report*. Canberra: Australian Government Publishing Service.

Australian Government (2004) *Recommendations of the HIH Royal Commission*. Canberra: Australian Government Publishing Service.

Benito, A., Waldron, M., Young, G. and Zampolli, F. (2007) 'The Role of Household Debt and Balance Sheets in the Monetary Transmission Mechanism, *Bank of England Quarterly Bulletin*, 2007, no. 1, pp. 70–8.

Bernanke, B. (2009) 'Lessons of the Financial Crisis for Banking Supervision', *Federal Reserve Bank of Chicago Conference on Bank Structure and Competition*, 7 May. Available at: http://www.federalreserve.gov/newsevents/speech/bernanke20090507a.htm.

Blanchard, O. (2008) 'The Crisis: Basic Mechanisms, and Appropriate Policies', *MIT Department of Economics Working Paper*, No. 09-01.

Blundell-Wignall, A., Wehinger, G. and Slovik, P. (2009) 'The Elephant in the Room: The Need to Deal with What Banks Do', OECD Journal: *Financial Market Trends*, no. 2, pp. 1–27.

Bordo, M.D., Eichengreen, B. and Irwin, D. (1999) 'Is Globalization Today Really Different Than Globalization a Hundred Years Ago?', *NBER Working Paper*, No. 7195.

Brock, H. (1999) 'Explaining Global Market Turmoil: A Fresh Perspective on its Origins and Nature', in D. Gruen and L. Gower (eds), *Capital Flows and the International Financial System*. Australia: Reserve Bank of Australia.

Brunnermeier, M., Crockett, A., Goodhart, C., Persaud, A. and Shin, H. (2009) 'The Fundamental Principles of Financial Regulation', *Geneva Report on the World Economy*, no. 10.

Buiter, W. (2007) 'Lessons from the 2007 Financial Crisis', *CEPR Discussion Paper*, no. DP6596.

Cagan, P. (2001) 'HIH Insurance: A Case Study", *E Risk*. Available at: http://www.erisk.com/learning/CaseStudies/HIHCaseStudy.pdf.

Carmichael, J. (1999) 'Overview of the Global Banking and Finance System: Current Features and Future Trends', *52nd International Banking Summer School*, 30 August. Available at: http://www.apra.gov.au/Speeches/99_04.cfm.

Carmichael, J. (2002) 'Experiences with Integrated Regulation', *APRA Insight*, 1st Quarter.

Cecchetti, S. (2009) 'Crisis and Responses: The Federal Reserve in the Early Stages of the Financial Crisis', *Journal of Economic Perspectives*, 23(1), 51–75.

Currie, C. (2005) 'Towards a General Theory of Financial Regulation: Predicting, Measuring and Preventing Financial Crises', *School of Finance and Economics Working Paper Series*, no. 142. Sydney: University of Technology Sydney.

Demirgüç-Kunt, A. and Luis, S. (2009) 'Are all the Sacred Cows Dead? Implications of the Financial Crisis for Macro and Financial Policies', *World Bank Policy Research Working Paper Series*, no. 4807.

Diamond, D. and Rajan, R. (2005) 'Liquidity Shortages and Banking Crises', *Journal of Finance*, 60, 615–47.

Davis, E.P. (1996) 'The Role of Institutional Investors in the Evolution of Financial Structure and Behaviour', *LSE Financial Markets Group Special Paper No. 89.* London: London School of Economics.

Davis, E.P. (2003) 'Institutional Investors, Financial Market Efficiency, and Financial Stability', *European Investment Bank Papers,* no. 4/2003.

Dees, S., Holly, S., Pesaran, M.H. and Smith, L.V. (2007) 'Long Run Macroeconomic Relations in the Global Economy', *Cambridge Working Papers in Economics,* no. 0703, Cambridge: University of Cambridge.

Financial Times (2009) 'View from the Top with Julie Dickson, Canadian Bank Regulator', *Financial Times Online transcript,* 18 December. Available at: www.ft.com/cms/s/0/75b43310-ebee-11de-930c-00144feab49a.html.

G30 Working Group on Financial Reform (2009) *Financial Reform: A Framework for Financial Stability.* Washington, DC: G30.

Ghent, A. and Kudlyak, M. (2009) 'Recourse and Residential Mortgage Default: Theory and Evidence from US States', *Federal Reserve Bank of Richmond Working Paper,* no. 09-10.

Gonnard, E., Kim, J. and Ynesta, I. (2008) *Recent Trends in Institutional Investors' Statistics.* Paris: OECD.

Gompers, P. and Metrick, A. (2001) 'Institutional Investors and Equity Prices', *Quarterly Journal of Economics,* Vol. 116, No. 1, pp. 229–59.

Gorton, G. (2008) 'The Subprime Panic', *Yale ICF Working Paper,* no. 08-25.

HM Treasury (2001) *Institutional Investment in the United Kingdom: A Review.* London: HM Treasury.

HM Treasury (2004) *Myner's Principles for Institutional Investment Decision-Making: Review of Progress.* London: HM Treasury.

Honohan, P. (2008) 'Risk Management and the Costs of the Banking Crisis', *National Institute Economic Review,* 206(1), 15–24.

Hughes, A., Kidman, M. and Wilson, G. (2005) *Masters of the Market,* 2nd edn. Australia: John Wiley & Sons.

Impavido, G., Musalem, A. and Tressel, T. (2001a) 'Contractual Savings Institutions and Banks' Stability and Efficiency', *World Bank Policy Research Working Paper,* no. 2751.

Impavido, G., Musalem, A. R. and Tressel, T. (2001b) 'Contractual Savings, Capital Markets, and Firms' Financing Choices', *World Bank Policy Research Working Paper,* no. 2612.

International Monetary Fund (2005) *Global Financial Stability Report,* September. Available at: http://www.imf.org/External/Pubs/FT/GFSR/2005/02/pdf/chp3.pdf.

International Corporate Governance Network (2007) *Statement of Principles on Institutional Shareholder Responsibilities.* Available at: http://www.icgn.org/best-practice/.

Jones, D. (2000) 'Emerging Problems with the Basel Capital Accord: Regulatory Capital Arbitrage and Related Issues', *Journal of Banking and Finance,* 24(1–2), 35–58.

Kaminsky, G. and Reinhart, C. (1999) 'The Twin Crises: The Causes of Banking and Balance-of-payments Problems', *American Economic Review, American Economic Association,* 89(3), 473–500.

Kaminsky, G., Reinhart, C. and Vegh, C.A. (2003) 'The Unholy Trinity of Financial Contagion', *NBER Working Paper,* no. 10061.

Kashyap, A. and Stein, J. (2003) 'Cyclical Implications of the Basel II Capital Standards', Chicago: Graduate School of Business, University of Chicago.

Kindleberger, C. (1996) *Manias, Panics, and Crashes: A History of Financial Crises*. New York: John Wiley and Sons.

Laker, J. (2009) 'The Global Financial Crisis and Beyond', Speech to the Australian British Chamber of Commerce, 26 November. Available at: http://www.apra. gov.au/Speeches/APRA_The-global-financial-crisis-and-beyond.cfm.

Lewis, D. (2009) 'How APRA is Responding to the Global Financial Crisis', Banking Seminar held at Edmund Rice Centre for Social Justice and Community Education, 25 March. Available at: www.apra.gov.au/Speeches/upload/ 2009-March-25-Presentation-to-ERC-Paper-2.pdf.

Levine, R. (1999) 'Financial Development and Economic Growth: Views and Agenda', *World Bank Policy Research Working Paper*, no. 1678.

Macfarlane, I. (2008) 'The 2008 Lowy Lecture on Australia in the World'. Australia: Lowy Institute.

McCallum, C. (2006) 'Risk Based Regulation: The FSA's Experience', Speech to ASIC, 13 February.

McKinnon, R. (1973) *Money and Capital in Economic Development*. Washington, DC: Brookings Institution.

Mishra, A. (2008) 'Australia's Equity Home Bias', *Australian Economic Papers*, 47(1), 53–73.

Phllipon, T. (2009) 'An Overview of the Proposals to Fix the Financial System', 15 February. Available at: http://www.voxeu.org/index.php?q=node/3076.

Reinhart, C. and Rogoff, K. (2008) 'Is the 2007 US Sub-prime Financial Crisis So Different? An International Historical Comparison', *American Economic Review*, American Economic Association, 98(2), 339–44.

Reuters (2000) 'Australia's HIH Wound Up, Losses Up to A$5.3 Billion', 27 August.

Ross, V. (2009) 'Lessons from the Financial Crisis', *Chatham House Conference on Global Financial Regulation*, 24 March. Available at: http://www.fsa.gov.uk/ pages/Library/Communication/Speeches/2009/0324_vr.shtml.

Schwartz, R. and Shapiro, J. (1992) 'The Challenge of Institutionalization of the Equity Market', in A. Saunders (ed.), *Recent Developments in Finance*. New York: New York Salomon Center.

Sias, R. (2004) 'Institutional Herding', *The Review of Financial Studies*, 17(1) (Spring), 165–206.

The Economist (2008) 'Down Under: The Air Goes Out of One of the Last Remaining Booms', 24 July. Available at: http://www.economist.com/countries/australia/ fromtheeconomist.cfm.

Walker, D. (2009) *Walker Review of Corporate Governance of UK Banking Industry*. London: HM Treasury.

9
Rethinking the Lending of Last Resort Function: A Historical and Contemporary Perspective

Germana Corrado

1 Introduction[1]

The renewed interest in reforming the international monetary and financial system is not surprising if we look at the unexpected succession financial crises in the last decade of the twentieth century and at the first global crisis of the twenty-first century. Why did these crises occur? Most observers and policymakers agreed that the financial sector fragility has played a central role in explaining the outbreak of the more recent crises. In fact, the financial crises of the 1990s were distinctive in that they were primarily rooted in poorly regulated bank-based financial systems (Freixas et al., 2000; 2004; Calomiris, 2000; Arestis et al., 2001; Eichengreen, 2002); and the widespread of the 2008 economic and financial crisis has again dramatically highlighted the fear that the interbank market might not function properly failing to recycle the emergency liquidity provided by the central banks. This might be seen as a form of bank run that origins when financial intermediaries refuse to renew credit lines to other intermediaries, thus putting at risk the survival of the system (Freixas and Parigi, 2008). Undoubtedly, if on the one hand it seems that there has been considerable progress after the twentieth century financial crises in setting and implementing new international financial standards, on the other hand much less progress has been made with respect to strengthening safeguard measures against the widespread of financial crises.

This chapter offers a new insight on the role of emergency liquidity assistance provided by central banks since one of the main issues emerging from the ongoing debate is not whether a Lending of Last Resort (hereafter LOLR) policy should exist but how to best organise the LOLR function at national and international level (Goodhart, 1999, 2009).

In fact, from the economic and financial crisis that began in the summer of 2007 we have learnt that the LOLR support practices have been deeply reshaped, as central banks have been forced to adapt some of the orthodox prescriptions of the traditional LOLR doctrine. For example, the Federal Reserve System has put in place unprecedented measures to increase the list of collateral eligible for lending and to extend emergency liquidity assistance to investment banks, government-sponsored entities, money market mutual funds as well as to a large insurance company; while the Bank of England participated in the bailout and, ultimately, the nationalisation of a depository institution, Northern Rock. The LOLR support has been then offered to financial institutions unable to secure funds through the regular circuit and this suggests that a new role for the LOLR is emerging which is distant from the theoretical and institutional perspective of central banks' emergency liquidity assistance (IMF, 2008). As highlighted by policymakers and economists, the global scope of the last financial crisis is forcing a reassessment of the LOLR function and the nature of liquidity shortages in a world of multiple currencies and large cross-border financial flows (Obstfeld, 2009).

The first part of this chapter offers an overview of the evolution of the lender of last resort role over time while the second part focuses on how to design LOLR intervention. We introduce a stylised model where LOLR support is contingent on banks' monitoring effort and we show that when the lender of last resort's commitment to intervene is matched with some operational discretion, according to a 'constructive ambiguity' approach, then the provision of emergency liquidity may be crucial to enable liquidity-distressed but 'well-behaved' banks to survive. However, such LOLR practices should take into account the systematic moral hazard behaviour of the banking sector and retain some degree of flexibility (i.e., operational discretion) so that central banks can play a strictly limited role of lenders of last resort rather than of lenders of 'first' resort.

2 Alternative views of the LOLR function: a historical and contemporary analysis

Different views on the LOLR function can be summarised in the following way: (i) the classical position embodied in the Bagehot's statement, (ii) Goodfriend and King's view and the case for open market operations, (iii) the view of Goodhart (and others) and the case of a LOLR facility available to both illiquid and insolvent banks, (iv) and finally the free-banking view that refuses the notion of emergency liquidity support assessing that a competitive financial market guaranties a panic-proof banking system.

2.1 Bagehot's maxim

Let us briefly review the first three views of the academic literature on LOLR intervention listed above, starting from Bagehot's (1873) well-known statement on LOLR support actions. Bagehot accepts and broads Thornton's view (1802) in pointing out those principles according which a central bank should act as a lender of last resort to the domestic banking system. He argued that

Nothing, therefore can be more certain than the Bank of England.. in time of panic must advance freely and vigorously... The end is to stay the panic and for this purpose there are two rules. First these loans should only be made at very high rate of interest... Secondly that at this rate these advances should be made on all good banking securities, and as largely as the public ask for them. (Bagehot, 1873, pp. 96–7)

The above classical doctrine on LOLR practices may be summarised by the following statement: *'Lend freely to temporarily but solvent banks at a high interest rate and on good collateral.'*

This maxim suggests that the following elements should always characterise the domestic LOLR activities, at least from a theoretical point of view: (i) the central bank is the only lender of last resort in a monetary system; (ii) the central bank should lend any amount, but at a penalty rate,[2] in order to discourage borrowing by those institutions that can obtain liquidity from the market; (iii) making clear in advance the readiness of the central bank to lend freely; (iv) lending to anyone with good collateral (solvent banks) valued at pre-panic prices; (v) preventing illiquid banks from failing: only *solvent* banks should be eligible for LOLR support.

These Bagehotian principles have been further adopted and developed by several authors, including Friedman and Schwartz (1963), Schwartz (1986) and Meltzer (1986). Undoubtedly, these rules are a reference point for the literature on emergency liquidity lending, but over the last two centuries they have been deeply reshaped.[3] In fact, over the years there has been some bending of the rules governing the decisions of the lender of last resort in respect of how much to lend, to whom and the conditions to apply. And therefore the LOLR practices can be better described as a toolbox with the choice of the specific tool to be used left largely to the discretion of the crisis manager according to a case-by-case assessment (Giannini, 1999; Schwartz, 2002).

2.2   The non-interventionist approach

Some economists advocate that LOLR facilities should be exercised solely at a macroeconomic level through Open Market Operations (hereafter OMOs) and not through a discount window lending to specific institutions in order to prevent or at least refrain moral hazard behaviours (see among others Friedman, 1959; Humphrey, 1975; Meltzer, 1986; Goodfriend and King, 1988; Bordo, 1990; Kaufman, 2002; Schwartz, 1988). This view argues that the provision of emergency lending by central banks to distressed individual banking intermediaries is misguided while the interbank market is widening and deepening enough to ensure a better allocation of liquidity from banks in surpluses to those which are facing liquidity problems but they are still creditworthy. Monetary authorities should never lend to individual banks because private lenders are more able to identify the illiquid but solvent banks to bail out. This is defined as the 'non-interventionist' approach to the LOLR support practices, implying that in the event of a bank panic the central bank acting as a lender of last resort should regulate the aggregate level of the money stock via pure OMOs. According to this view, the LOLR intervention is confined to ordinary monetary policy practices aiming at injecting temporarily high-powered money into the market in order to satisfy the increasing market demand of liquidity and to avoid an upward jump of the interest rates; while it is left to the market the function to lend to individual illiquid but sound banks while allowing potentially insolvent intermediaries to default.

This 'money view' is justified by assessing that the central bank must not divert from its final objective of maintaining price stability, an objective that might be not pursued strongly enough if monetary authorities are involved in a direct emergency lending intervention to individual distressed financial institutions. The basic arguments addressed by the non-interventionist view might be then summarised as follows: (i) bailing out banks implies negative incentive effects due to the excessive risk-taking on behalf of the bank managers; this implies that severe moral hazard problems arise from LOLR interventions at a microeconomic level; (ii) the presence of well-developed and liquid financial markets justifies the conduct of LOLR operations only at a macroeconomic level. Beyond this view there is the strong assumption that the interbank market works efficiently, even in times of stress, so that all those issues related to market failures are not at all taken into account. However, one of the most peculiar aspects of the recent sub-prime crisis has been that the interbank market has experienced liquidity problems for a prolonged period of time (Fernández de Lis; 2008). Financial regulation has perhaps focused too much on solvency and capital issues, and has neglected liquidity, which was taken for granted in the most developed markets.

2.3 Myths about the LOLR function

The third view even accepting the principle of a central bank emergency lending to individual financial institutions,[4] the so-called 'banking view', nevertheless goes over the Bagehotian principle of emergency liquidity support to illiquid but solvent banks. In fact, this strand of literature points out that the monetary authorities have no clear-cut rule for distinguishing an illiquid but potentially solvent bank from an illiquid but insolvent one (see among others Goodhart, 1988 and 1999; Goodhart and Huang, 1999; He, 2000). This approach highlights that the distinction between insolvency and illiquidity is an unhelpful myth on LOLR loans and it argues that because of the difficulty of evaluating the assets of a distressed institution, a central bank usually has to take a decision on the LOLR support to meet an immediate liquidity problem when it knows that there is a doubt on its insolvency (Goodhart, 1988). Hence, this view clearly explodes the myth that some early commentators of Bagehot's work built by arguing that it is generally possible to distinguish between an insolvent and an illiquid financial institution and that LOLR has to be provided *only* to the latter. But this is a mistaken interpretation of Bagehot's proposals. In fact, Goodhart (1999) argues that Bagehot's proposal related simply to the collateral that the applicant could offer and when the central bank discounts good bills for a financial intermediary, it did not and could not at the same time estimate also its solvency. Moreover, the failure of a bank or more than one bank is likely to generate a widespread panic among people which is likely to resolve with a loss of confidence in the whole financial system. In order to prevent or limit systemic risks a central bank should rescue insolvent institutions through LOLR. This view highlights that even if a bank is potentially solvent at the time of the liquidity assistance, nevertheless it may become insolvent later because of the subsequent deterioration of the fundamentals as a result of the far-reaching nature of the financial crisis. Hence, a bank which is solvent *ex ante* may not be so *ex post*. But even in the case that the institutions which received LOLR support have then to be closed, nonetheless emergency liquidity lending could still serve a useful public purpose, in providing time for authorities to arrange for an orderly closure of failing institutions (see Freixas et al., 1999). In fact, the aim of LOLR facilities is to safeguard the financial system as a whole, not any single institution, against systemic risk. Authorities should provide LOLR support when the failure of an institution, either by itself or through spreading the contagion to other institutions (domino effects), damages the financial system stability. The 2008 financial crisis has shown that it would be erroneous to adopt a narrow definition of LOLR support, stating that it should be limited to the funding of illiquid but solvent depository institutions. In fact, the lender of last resort role has to be a broad one encompassing the closure or bailout decision defining the lender of last resort as an agency that has the faculty to extend credit to a financial institution unable to secure funds through the regular circuit.

Although a distinction between illiquidity and insolvency cannot be generally made by the authorities at the outset of a crisis, a practical rule should be followed by the crises lender. This practical rule should rely almost entirely to the conduct of an *ex ante* banking supervision surveillance that allows the central bank, if it is also endowed with supervisory powers on the national banking system, or the supervisory agency, if monetary and supervisory powers are separately exercised, to have complete and reliable information made available prior to the crisis on well-managed and badly managed banks.

2.4   Rules *versus* discretion

Within the debate on rules *versus* discretion in the conduct of economic policy, literature has shown the superiority of a commitment to a set of clear and verifiable rules (transparency) rather than the adoption of a discretionary economic policy (see, among others, Kydland and Prescott, 1977). This is justified by the introduction of the rational expectation hypothesis, which implies that agents have the same relevant information as the authorities and are therefore able to anticipate and offset the effect of a discretionary policy. Hence, the policymakers should commit themselves to clear rules and establish credibility by being consistent in their behavior.

But, by looking through the central banks' statements or through the existing banking legislation, we discover that there are only a few countries where a set of detailed rules regarding the LOLR operations are specified clearly, like, for example, the United States, Bulgaria and Hong Kong. Whereas the national banking and central bank legislation and regulations in most countries contain only general statements on LOLR support, in the above countries it is stated that the central bank may intervene, carrying out LOLR intervention whenever it is necessary for the maintenance of the financial stability. However, it is not specified in detail how this support should be provided. For example, in the euro zone we cannot detect any provisions on LOLR facilities either in the treatise establishing the monetary and economic union among the European countries or in the statute of the European Central Bank. In fact, in the Maastricht Treaty there is no explicit provision for the LOLR function; and although it does not completely rule out LOLR, nothing has been decided on how the responsibility to make decisions and to take action should be allocated across the European System of Central Banks (ESCB).

This suggests that a non-rule-based (discretionary) approach seems to be the common practice in handling banking sector problems, even if the literature is recently becoming aware of the possibility of reconciling the two approaches that are not mutually exclusive. In fact, although there are good reasons for ambiguity in LOLR facilities which are mostly related to the necessity of granting flexibility of response to the policymakers in case of systemic risks, nevertheless this operational autonomy in LOLR operations should be matched by accountability in order to reduce the likelihood of forbearance, especially in the emerging economies where there are strong political pressures on the application of banking safety nets. The lack of any pre-commitment to a specific course of action in the provision of emergency lending services to distressed financial institutions gives also rise to time-inconsistency problems. In fact, while it is in the interest of the authorities to deny their willingness to provide a liquidity safety net, *ex post* they may find it optimal to intervene (see Freixas et al., 1999). These considerations suggest that a balance of ambiguity and transparency in conducting LOLR operations is needed in order both to restrict the bankers' ability to shift the risk and the ability of the LOLR to socialise losses. This is will be more widely discussed in the next paragraphs.

3 The moral hazard problem: transparency *versus* ambiguity in LOLR facilities

One important issue arising from LOLR support practices is the moral hazard problem with respect to both borrowers' actions (i.e., banking intermediaries) who engage in risk-shifting activities, and uninsured investors' actions (i.e., creditors and partially insured depositors) who have less incentive to monitor banks due to the implicit guarantee which is brought about by LOLR bailout policies.

In fact, it is recognised that emergency lending to distressed financial institutions provides a form of insurance which modifies agents' incentives (bank managers, owners and creditors). This is the moral hazard issue related to hidden actions or *ex post* asymmetric information. This problem was already emphasised by Thornton (1802) and Bagehot (1873) who argued that if proper measures were not taken the establishment of a LOLR facility could strengthen rather than lessen the potential for a financial collapse. Literature has further worked out on the broader aspects of LOLR facilities but it has given only an insightful but incomplete review of the moral hazard issue in relation to LOLR operations. Moreover, the economic analysis of the moral hazard problem arising from the introduction of deposit insurance schemes has been widely developed both from a theoretical and an empirical point of view. Despite some clear differences both the provision of deposit insurance and LOLR facilities can in turn be led back to the classic insurer's problem (Moore, 1999). It can then be argued that any insurance generates a moral hazard, but this does not mean that such a safety net guarantee is not rational and that its cost is not often much lower than the systemic risk which was avoided (Giannini, 1999).

3.1 The 'constructive ambiguity' approach

In order to offset or at least reduce moral hazard one possible way followed by many central banks has been the use of 'constructive ambiguity'. This term is referred to the practice of not disclosing rules regarding not only whether or not the lender of last resort will intervene in rescuing a troubled institution, but also the conditions to access to such a financial safety net. In fact, many central banks maintain some ambiguity on how, when and whether they will provide LOLR support. It is argued that both the safety nets and the market discipline will better work in a context in which authorities maintain a policy of 'constructive ambiguity' with respect to what they will do, and how and when they will do it (Giannini, 1999). Hence, in order to avoid moral hazard problems the access to LOLR facilities should be made uncertain, or something to be determined ad hoc in each crisis. Hence, the 'ambiguity' in carrying out emergency lending is referred not so much to whether or not a rescue will take place, but rather to the terms and conditions the rescue will carry with it. In other words, the term constructive ambiguity may be interpreted as an unpredictable or random strategy.

Some arguments have been recently advanced in favour of ambiguity in keeping LOLR operations. Firstly, an increased flexibility of response by the authorities is associated with increased expected variance in the outcomes; this means that the risk-averse agents will be more prudent than they would be if they were confident of being rescued by the lender of last resort (Cordella and Levy Yeyati, 2006; Broda and Levy Yeyati, 2006; Corrado, 2004). Secondly, in the absence of full information and in circumstances in which it is necessary to take prompt and decisive action, as in the case of LOLR support, authorities might be not able to distinguish if a bank is illiquid, but potentially solvent, or just insolvent (Goodhart and Huang, 1999). Therefore, in order to minimise the risk of bank runs and widespread bank failures (systemic threats) authorities need discretion in deciding the extent of LOLR facilities. This means that flexibility has the property of leaving to the agency acting as a crisis manager some discretion in applying the appropriate rescue package chosen on the basis of a case-by-case assessment (Schwartz, 2002). Hence, a cookbook approach – that is, setting out in advance a set of well-defined operational rules – is largely inefficient in managing the problems of financial markets (Freixas et al., 2000).

3.2 A reconciling view

This view asserts the need for setting out *ex ante* clear rules which establish the necessary but not sufficient conditions for the access to LOLR facilities in order to limit the extent of emergency liquidity assistance. *Ex ante* transparency does not rule out discretionary in the managing of banking problems as there will be ambiguity even in the handling of an individual bank in cases where problems in that bank are leading to systemic threats. Therefore, the specification of the preconditions for LOLR support does not reveal inconsistent with an operational discretion in case of systemic risk, when whatever rules have been set out they may be override by the authorities (Enoch et al., 1997). Furthermore *ex post* transparency[5] through a set of well-designed accounting standards might be helpful for balancing this operational autonomy left to the monetary authorities (or agency) who act as lenders of last resort. This transparency aims at publicly providing full information on what the lender of last resort has done also with regard to the remedial actions or sanctions that the central bank – or the supervisory agency – has taken against the bank(s) rescued. These rules for public disclosure after the banking crisis outbreak are designed for granting accountability and auditing on LOLR support actions. And it is argued that this information has to be fully and clearly given to the public without any delay as soon as this is feasible and without causing additional problems for the banking system (Fischer, 1999; He, 2000).

The 2008 global economic and financial crisis, which began in summer 2007 with the US subprime crisis, seems to be a very good example of when markets need to know *ex ante* the exact conditions of support from the central bank, especially when the turmoil originates from a generalised lack of confidence. Furthermore, economists and policymakers recognise that accurate information on central bank emergency lending might act as a double-edged sword, since it might help restore confidence as happened in the case of Bear Stearns, but in other cases it can severely undermine public confidence and precipitate the bank's failure as happened in the case of Northern Rock. It is quite difficult to assess which factors will lead to one or another of the above scenarios, but perhaps the perception of resolute help frm the authorities is most important as it appears to lead to a swift and effective solution of market distress. In fact, the liquidation of Northern Rock in such a fragile banking environment would most likely have triggered domino and contagion effects in the credit market since its closure might have impaired public confidence in the broader financial system. Thus, it seems that current practices in carrying out LOLR support take into account mostly considerations of systemic risk that might involve potential spillover effects leading to widespread bank runs (Solow, 1982). All of the considerations listed above highlight that LOLR support appears now to be a very complex architecture whose constitutive elements are: (i) a high degree of operative discretion; (ii) effective supervisory surveillance;[6] (iii) accountability;[7] and (iv) some degree of punishment to the rescued institutions.

4   LOLR facilities in an international context

Financial crises of the scale and severity we have seen in recent years have posed a major threat to the construction of a strong global financial system. The international community has responded by calling for the reform of the international financial and monetary architecture. A major element of architectural reform must be more effective policies and incentives at a supranational level in order to prevent, promptly manage and resolve disturbances on the international financial markets. Within this issue we look at the more recent debate on the need for international LOLR arrangements suited to provide financial assistance to international banks or to foreign debtor countries that face a liquidity crisis (see, among others, Claassen, 1985; Sachs, 1995; Fischer, 1999; Giannini, 1999; Mishkin, 1999; Calomiris, 2000). Literature has stressed the potential role of a worldwide agency able to make LOLR loans. It has been argued that in the last few years the International Monetary

Fund (IMF) is acting increasingly as a fully-fledged international lender of last resort (see, among others, Fischer, 1999). But despite the recently operative changes, more attention should be given to some aspects that hinder the IMF's ability to act as an international lender of last resort, like the absence of full powers of (i) supervisory surveillance, (ii) enforcement and (iii) effective conditionality. All of these elements constitute the building blocks on which emergency liquidity support facilities should be set up. In fact, some authors like Schwartz (2002) and Capie (2002) remark that the IMF is not and will not be a true LOLR because it cannot print money, therefore since its resources are limited it cannot lend freely against good collateral to a crisis-hit country. Another source of critics of the potential role of the IMF as a lender of last resort for crisis-hit countries emerges from the observation that the IMF should lend against good collateral, but the latter is an ill-defined concept when the borrower is a government instead of a bank or a firm (Eichengreen, 2002). Therefore, neither the IMF nor any other agency acting as a universal lender of last resort seem likely to be forthcoming – at least in the short run. Several alternative ways to cope with international financial crises have been then proposed; among them there is the regional lender of last resort hypothesis according to which emergency liquidity support facilities should be provided by a geographically localised supranational institution to crisis-hit countries belonging to a well-defined regional block. This geographical division of the worldwide areas into a system of regional financial agreements should coincide with the current three-block trading configuration: Asia, Europe and the Americas. This solution may be defined as a 'Do It Yourself' (DIY) LOLR support that serves as a self-insurance mechanism against liquidity crises. Such insurance can be provided in several ways: (i) building up large foreign currency reserves; this was already done, for example, by China and Korea after the 1990s crises; (ii) a second approach is to create contingent credit facilities with international banks, or set up collateralised loan facilities (Feldstein, 1998); and (iii) the creation of regional self-insurance funds. The implementation of regional agreement for taking measures against the collapse of distressed economies should be a fundamental step towards the establishment of a more stable international financial market. In fact, the crises of the late 1990s in Asia, Latin America and Russia have shown clearly that the current international financial system has failed in providing such an effective crisis protection and management mechanisms.

Of course, a regional lender of last resort is only a partial and not fully satisfactory solution to the problem of achieving international financial stability because of the important limits that this option sets.

But let us comment here on two points that the literature has focused on until in respect of regionalism in monetary operations related to LOLR support. The first issue is given by the potential benefits arising from the geographical closeness of the borrowing countries linked by a deep economic integration which makes them aware of the great potential dangers of not injecting quickly a huge amount of liquid funds to stem a crisis. Secondly, it seems that LOLR support can be provided in a more efficient way when it is managed by a small number of participants bound by cultural and economic ties. Certainly, a deeper regional cooperation in monetary and financial affairs (i.e. monetary regionalism) may enhance financial stability in some regions of the word by giving a more effective protection against the spread of financial crises. Still there are costs associated with forbearance whenever the regional emergency liquidity LOLR is carried out to rescue one or more countries belonging to the block. In fact, since a regional lender of last resort knows that area-wide severe contagion effects spread from one country to another of the region leading to systemic risk, then it is less willing to wait for intervening, and therefore 'regional authorities might overemphasise financing to the detriment of adjustment' (Giannini, 1999).

5   A closed economy model of bank default and lending of last resort support

We consider an infinite time-horizon economy[8] where a continuum of banks operate; they act as corporations in the interest of their shareholders, collecting deposits[9] and lending to capital-producing firms seeking to maximise their profits. In each period banks use these short-term funds (deposits) to finance a large number of domestic high-risk investment industrial projects I_t giving a verifiable return R_t in case of success, and nothing in case of failure. Like in Holmöstrom and Tirole's analysis (1993), we assume that there are two types of projects: a 'good' project with a high probability of success p_H and a 'bad' project with a low probability of success p_L; the bad project gives to the borrower (the firm) a non-verifiable private benefit and this is a source of moral hazard. Banks are also endowed with a monitoring technology while individual agents are not. Thus, the credit market is characterised by asymmetric information and intermediated lending; and banking intermediaries are able to monitor borrowers at a total cost $C(n_t)$, where n_t denotes the fraction of monitored projects (borrowers), with $0 \leq n_t \leq 1$. Only by monitoring the borrowers (firms) banks can force them to choose the investment technology with the higher probability of success.

The representative bank will get a (gross) return R_t with probability p_H on each monitored project at an average monitoring cost equal to $C(n_t)/n_t$. On the remaining unmonitored loans there is a higher risk of default with p_L denoting the probability that the borrower goes bankrupt on the 'bad' investment project, where $p_H > p_L$.

The bank has the incentive to monitor a project whenever the following condition is satisfied:

$$p_H R_t - \frac{C(n_t)}{n_t} \geq p_L R_t \tag{1}$$

In (1) the monitoring cost function, $C(n_t)$, is assumed to be continuous, twice differentiable with positive first and second derivatives with respect to n_t, hence $\frac{\partial C(n_t)}{\partial n_t} \geq 0$ and $\frac{\partial^2 C(n_t)}{\partial n_t^2} > 0$. Thus, $C(n_t)$ is an increasing and convex function of the fraction n of monitored projects at time t.

Finally we assume that the funds (deposits) collected by the bank net of the reserves required by the central bank are used to finance firms' investment projects. So that the following equality holds in each period:

$$I_t = (1 - \gamma)D_t \tag{2}$$

Relationship (2) is the resource balance constraint of the bank. In (2) D_t denotes the amount of deposits collected by the bank; γ is the reserve requirement coefficient on bank deposits;[10] and I_t is the total amount of loans made to domestic firms.

Given the market deposit rates the bank maximises the following discounted stream of profits, V_t, in each period by choosing the number of monitored projects (borrowers), n:

$$V_t = \max \sum_{t=0}^{\infty} [\rho S(n_t)]^t \Pi_t \tag{3}$$

where Π denotes bank's expected profits, $\rho < 1$ is the discount factor and S is the bank's survival probability which depends on the bank's monitoring activity.

By assuming time-invariant policies so that the bank's problem is stationary and, given also its recursive nature, the bank's value can be restated as follows:

$$V = \max \frac{\Pi}{1 - \rho S(n)} \tag{4}$$

in (4) the term Π denotes nominal profits which are defined as follows:

$$\Pi = \int_0^\infty \max\left\{0, \; \left[\varepsilon I\left(nRp_H + (1-n)Rp_L - C(n)\right) - (1-\gamma)DR^D\right]\right\} f(\varepsilon)d\varepsilon \qquad (5)$$

that given (2) can be rewritten as follows:

$$\Pi = \int_0^\infty \max\left\{0, \; D(1-\gamma)\left[\varepsilon\left(nRp_H + (1-n)Rp_L - C(n)\right) - R^D\right]\right\} f(\varepsilon)d\varepsilon \qquad (6)$$

where ε denotes firms' productivity shock with support $(0,\infty)$ and probability density function $f(\varepsilon)$, R^D is the (gross) deposit rate, I is the total cost of the risky industrial projects financed by the bank; each project promises an uncertain return R. Due to the recursive nature of the problem time subscripts have been dropped.

The assumption is that only by exerting its monitoring effort is the bank able to force the borrower to choose the 'good' investment technology, and n denotes the fraction of monitored projects on which the bank will get the repayment R with a higher probability p_H. Productivity shocks and uncertainty on the repayments of bank's loans are then the only sources of risk in this model.

By using condition (2) and assuming that the aggregate supply of deposits collected by banks is fixed and it is normalised to 1, that is $D = 1$, we can derive from (6) the value of the shock to firm's output below which the bank will get zero profits:

$$\varepsilon^* = \frac{R^D}{\left[nRp_H + (1-n)Rp_L - C(n)\right]} \qquad (7)$$

where (7) defines the threshold value of the shock below which bank's liabilities exceed bank's assets and the bank is subject to default.

Under (2) and (7), the current profit (6) can be restated as:

$$\Pi = \int_{\varepsilon^*}^\infty (1-\gamma)\left[\varepsilon\left(nRp_H + (1-n)Rp_L - C(n)\right) - R^D\right] f(\varepsilon)d\varepsilon \qquad (8)$$

According to (8) the monitoring effort exerted by the bank, which is measured by the number of monitored borrowers (projects), is the choice variable of the above bank's decision problem.

5.1 A blanket lending of last resort support

If we assume that a bank insurance[11] exists, such as LOLR facilities, then the bank's survival probability $S(n)$ is now equal to:

$$S(n) = G(n) + (1 - G(n))L \qquad (9)$$
$$= (1 - L)G(n) + L$$

where $G(n)$ is the probability that the bank does not default, and L is the probability that the LOLR will intervene in case bank defaults covering the gap between assets and liabilities at no cost. The bank's survival probability is then given by the sum of the probability of no default plus the probability that, if returns are zero, the LOLR intervenes to rescue the distressed intermediary.[12]

For now we assume that the lender of last resort will intervene with a given probability L that is we consider a 'blanket' LOLR support.[13] Later in this chapter, we will make the probability of LOLR assistance contingent on bank monitoring activity in order to curb the distortions (i.e. moral hazard problems) that arise from standard bank insurance policies.

The optimal level of bank monitoring is given by the level of n that maximises the objective function (4) subject to (2), (1) with $0 \le n \le 1$.

We differentiate (4) with respect to the fraction of monitored projects, n, getting the following FOC:

$$\frac{\partial V}{\partial n} = \frac{1}{1 - \rho S}\left(\frac{\partial \Pi}{\partial n} + \rho \frac{\partial S}{\partial n} V\right) = 0 \qquad (10)$$

In (10) the derivatives $\dfrac{\partial \Pi}{\partial n}$ and $\dfrac{\partial S}{\partial n}$ are respectively equal to:[14]

$$\frac{\partial \Pi}{\partial n} = (1 - \gamma)[R\Delta p - C'(n)]G(n)\bar{\varepsilon} \qquad (11)$$

$$\frac{\partial S}{\partial n} = (1 - L)\frac{\partial G}{\partial n} \qquad (12)$$

where $\Delta p = p_H - p_L$ and terms $\bar{\varepsilon}$ and $G(n)$ are respectively defined as:

$$\bar{\varepsilon} = \frac{\int_{\varepsilon^*}^{\infty} \varepsilon f(\varepsilon)d\varepsilon}{G(n)} \qquad (13)$$

$$G(n) = \int_{\varepsilon^*}^{\infty} f(\varepsilon)d\varepsilon \qquad (14)$$

In (13) $\bar{\varepsilon}$ denotes the firm's (borrower) average output conditional on the event that the intermediary does not default, and $G(n)$ is the probability of not defaulting.

The derivative of current profits with respect to the number of monitored borrowers (11) is positive as long as the difference between the expected return from the 'good' and 'bad' investment projects, $R\Delta p$, is greater than the marginal cost of bank monitoring, $C'(n)$.

In (12) the derivative of the probability of no default with respect to the fraction of bank's monitored projects, $\frac{\partial G}{\partial n}$, reads as:[15]

$$\frac{\partial G}{\partial n} = R^D \left(\frac{R\Delta p - C'(n)}{Z^2} \right) f(\varepsilon^*) d\varepsilon^* \qquad (15)$$

where the compound term $Z = [nRp_H + (1-n)Rp_L - C(n)]$.

Analogously to (11), we see that in (15) the probability of surviving is positively related to n as long as the difference between the expected return from the 'good' and 'bad' investment projects, $R\Delta p$, is greater than the marginal cost of monitoring, $C'(n)$, faced by the bank. There is an intertemporal effect that incentives the bank to exert higher levels of monitoring as the expected bank's future value increases by the term $\rho S' V$ when the monitoring effort and thus the probability of not defaulting, G, rise.

Relationships (12) and (15) show that in the presence of LOLR support the derivative of the survival probability, S, with respect to the fraction of monitored projects is positive under condition (1) but that it is smaller than in the absence of LOLR facilities. This implies that LOLR might induce banks to shrink their monitoring activity leading to severe moral hazard problems. In fact, a blanket guarantee like LOLR support might induce a risk-taking behaviour from intermediaries, that in the model takes the form of a decrease in the level of bank monitoring.

Proposition 1 *Under a blanket LOLR intervention the level of bank's monitoring effort is lower than otherwise.*

To show this result, we choose a quadratic monitoring cost function $C(n)$ which is strictly increasing in the fraction of monitored projects and convex this implies that monitoring costs rise at an increasing rate with respect to the number of monitored borrowers:

$$C(n) = \rho n^2 \qquad (16)$$

Using (16), we can rewrite (11) and (15) as follows:

$$\frac{\partial \Pi}{\partial n} = (1-\gamma)G(n)[R\Delta p - 2\rho n]\bar{\varepsilon} \tag{17}$$

$$\frac{\partial G}{\partial n} = R^D \left(\frac{R\Delta p - 2\rho n}{Z^2} \right) f\left(\varepsilon^*\right) d\varepsilon^* \tag{18}$$

Using (12), (17) and (18), the FOC (10) reads as follows:

$$\frac{\partial V}{\partial n} = \frac{1}{1-\rho S} \left(\frac{\partial \Pi}{\partial n} + \rho(1-L)\frac{\partial G}{\partial n}V \right) = 0$$

$$\tag{19}$$

$$\frac{\partial V}{\partial n} = \left(\frac{R\Delta p - 2\rho n}{1-\rho S} \right) \left[\bar{\varepsilon}(1-\gamma)G(n) + \frac{\rho V(1-L)}{Z^2}R^D f\left(\varepsilon^*\right)d\varepsilon^* \right] = 0$$

The presence of a form of free bank insurance, such as LOLR facilities, plays a key role as it affects the probability of bank's survival by increasing it as shown in (19). In fact, in accordance with the standard literature on deposit and bank insurance (Grossman and Hart, 1982), we show that the possibility of a bailout reduces bankers' incentive to exert effort and improve the performance of the firm; and it indirectly encourages bank's management to reduce the monitoring on the entrepreneurial projects which they have financed. These findings rely on the assumption that the LOLR support is available to banks irrespective of the level of monitoring of high-risk investments, so that the chances of preserving the insurance benefits in the event of a shock to firm's output are enhanced, without any increase in the cost of monitoring to the bank. In the following section we will analyse how a state-contingent emergency liquidity support might affect the above results.

5.2 A state-contingent lending of last resort support

In the previous section we saw that, by increasing the probability of survival, a 'blanket' LOLR intervention may induce banks to shrink the monitoring effort. Therefore, a LOLR facility that works as an implicit guarantee both to bank and to depositors exacerbates moral hazard inducing excess risk-taking by the financial intermediaries. Now we make LOLR support contingent on the level of bank monitoring effort, n. In sum, now we consider a LOLR policy that evaluates the monitoring activity exerted by the financial intermediaries when it is asked to intervene and rescue them (Lee and Sharpe, 2006). Therefore, the bank's survival probability with a contingent LOLR intervention, S_{cl}, can be rewritten as follows:

$$S_{cl}(n) = G(n) + (1 - G(n))L(n) \qquad (20)$$

where $G(n)$ has been defined in (14) and in the term $S_{cl}(n)$ the subscript cl denotes the bank's survival probability when the LOLR intervention is contingent on the number of monitored projects, n. Therefore, the probability of LOLR intervention, L, is now a function of bank monitoring.

If we assume that LOLR support to distressed financial intermediaries follows a Beta distribution with a *pdf*:

$$L(n) = \left\{ \begin{array}{cc} \dfrac{n^{\alpha-1}(1-n)^{\beta-1}}{B(\alpha,\beta)} & \text{for } 0 < n \le 1 \\ 0 & \text{otherwise} \end{array} \right\} \qquad (21)$$

The Beta distribution is a family of continuous probability distributions defined on the interval $[0,1]$ parameterised by two positive shape parameters, typically denoted by α and β. The parameters are set in order to have a strictly increasing probability density function, that is $\alpha = 1$, $\beta < 1$ or alternatively $\alpha > 1$, $\beta \le 1$. The beta function, $B(\alpha,\beta)$, appears at the denominator as a normalisation constant to ensure that the total probability integrates to unity, $\int_0^1 L(n) \, dn = 1$. Relationship (21) shows that the probability of bailing out is not more exogenous but it is contingent on the fraction of monitored loans, n, and it is *strictly* increasing with bank monitoring activity, n. This formulation may be reconciled with a so-called 'constructive ambiguity' approach according to which the lender of last resort should retain some discretion as to when, under which circumstances and to what extent rescuing a distressed bank. As highlighted above, this provision of emergency liquidity may be crucial to enable distressed but 'well-behaved' banks to survive and finance high-quality investment projects.

Proposition 2 *With a contingent LOLR the bank's survival probability, S_{cl}, increases as the level of bank monitoring, n, increases; and the increase in S_{cl} is greater than in presence of a 'blanket' LOLR assistance.*

Proof. We differentiate bank's survival probability, S_{cl}, with respect to the fraction of monitored projects:

$$\frac{\partial S_{cl}}{\partial n} = (1-L)\frac{\partial G}{\partial n} + (1-G)\frac{\partial L}{\partial n} \tag{22}$$

where given the state-contingent probability of LOLR intervention as defined in (21) the derivative $\frac{\partial L}{\partial n}$ is then equal to:

$$\frac{\partial L}{\partial n} = \frac{(\alpha-1)n^{\alpha-2}}{B(\alpha,\beta)} \tag{23}$$

where the parameter values $\alpha > 1$ and $\beta = 1$ have been set to ensure a *pdf* strictly increasing with the number of monitored projects n. By plugging both (23) and the derivative of the probability of no default, $\frac{\partial G}{\partial n}$, with respect to the fraction of monitored projects (18) into relationship (22), we get:

$$\frac{\partial S_{cl}}{\partial n} = (1-L)R^{D}\left[\frac{R\Delta p - 2\rho n}{Z^{2}}\right]f(\varepsilon^{*})d\varepsilon^{*} + (1-G)\frac{\partial L}{\partial n} \tag{24}$$

where the last right-hand-side term $\frac{\partial L}{\partial n} = \frac{(\alpha-1)n^{\alpha-2}}{B(\alpha,\beta)} > 0$.

According to (24) the bank's survival probability is positively correlated with the level of bank monitoring. And by comparing (24) with (12) we see that with a state-contingent LOLR intervention the bank's survival probability is higher than in presence of a 'blanket' LOLR assistance since it increases with the monitoring activity exerted by the bank.

This is captured by the last positive term $(1-G)\frac{(\alpha-1)n^{\alpha-2}}{B(\alpha,\beta)}$ on the right-hand side of (24). In fact, as shown by Cordella and Levy Yeyati (2006) and Broda and Levy Yeyati (2006), a state-contingent LOLR policy by decreasing the probability of a crisis (failure) might enhance the expected continuation value of the borrower and the payoff of engaging in safer investment projects. Therefore, if the main source of moral hazard problems is a reduction in loan monitoring, then the lender of last resort should not intervene in any case making available any amount of liquidity to financial markets. Instead, with state-contingent LOLR support facilities, the probability that central banks will intervene to rescue banks increases as the level of bank monitoring increases. This implies that the lender of last resort is more willing to bail out the distressed banking intermediary exerting higher levels of monitoring effort. And the lender of last resort will punish those intermediaries that put lower levels of effort into monitoring borrowers, by reducing the probability of intervening. Therefore, we stress that LOLR actions should take into account the systematic moral hazard behaviour of the banking sector and retain some degree of flexibility so that the central bank can play a strictly limited role of a lender of last resort rather than of a lender of 'first' resort (Berlemann et al., 2002).

But a LOLR policy contingent on bank's monitoring activity is difficult to implement in practice. First, because the level of monitoring effort cannot be observed directly and then we need to construct some measure of the quantity and/or quality a bank's monitoring effort. For example, based on the fact that the key input into the monitoring process is bank labour, some authors use as a proxy for bank's monitoring effectiveness the amount banks invest in the agents responsible for their loan monitoring, that is, their employees. The underlying assumption is that the quantity and quality of the bank's staff do reflect bank's monitoring effort (Lee and Sharpe, 2006; Coleman et al., 2006). Secondly, the constructive ambiguity is a quite complex notion that is difficult to pin down and formalise; it also puts a large degree of discretion in the hands of the lender of last resort. As Freixas et al. (1999) pointed out, this lack of transparency enables the authorities to avoid having to justify treating differently what the general public may perceive as identical situations. In fact, any attempt to design and put into practice some guidelines for LOLR intervention might fail if there is not a well-defined set of rules for constraining or, indirectly, encouraging financial intermediaries to act more prudently. This would prevent that those banks which have been shrinking the monitoring activity get unlimited support from the LOLR and gamble for resurrection by investing in the continuation of a project with a negative expected net present value.

6   Summary and conclusions

The outbreak of the recent global economic and financial crisis has shown that rethinking the international monetary and financial architecture has become a very urgent need. If on the one hand it seems that there has been considerable progress over the last few years since the twentieth century's financial crises in setting and implementing new international financial standards, on the other hand much less progress has been made with respect to strengthening safeguard measures against the widespread of financial crises, such as LOLR facilities. How to best organise LOLR support actions remains an important task to carry on. We introduce a simple model that shows how LOLR policy contingent on the level of banks' monitoring, might effectively curb risk-taking behaviour. We highlight that when the lender of last resort commitment to intervene in the case of default is matched with some operational discretion according to a 'constructive ambiguity' approach then a large injection of emergency liquidity may be crucial to enable the survival of distressed but well-behaved banking intermediaries. And the perception of such resolute and generous support in terms of the liquidity injected by the authorities might lead to a swift and effective solution of financial market distress. However, central banks should take into account the systematic moral hazard behaviour of the banking sector and therefore retain some degree of flexibility in order to play a strictly limited role of lenders of last resort rather than of 'first' resort.

Notes

1. Affiliation: Assistant Professor, University of Rome Tor Vergata, Department of Economics and Institutions, Via Columbia 2, 00133 Rome, Italy.
2. The emphasis given to the need of high interest rate led some authors, as Humphrey and Keleher (1984), to argue that Bagehot proposed that the interest rate charged should be always a penalty rate, i.e. at a rate above the current market rate. But Goodhart (1999) and other authors point out that the charged interest rate should be above that in effect in the market prior the panic, but not necessarily above the contemporaneous market rate. Therefore, the penalty rate should be defined relative to the interest charged during normal (pre-crisis) times.
3. For a historical and contemporary analysis of the notion and the conduct of LOLR see Goodhart and Illing (2002).
4. In contrast to the 'money view', it is suggested that the term LOLR should be used only for central bank liquidity support to individual banks (see Goodhart, 1999).
5. For example the Bank of Japan, the Bank of England and the Bank of Finland disclose in their annual reports some details of the LOLR operations provided (e.g. amounts, collateral, name of institutions etc.).
6. This refers to *ex ante* detailed information on the banking system.
7. This refers to *ex post* information disclosure.
8. For a version of the model in an open economy setting see Corrado (2004).
9. The assumption that bank deposits are covered by full deposit insurance simplifies the analysis by making the deposit rate an exogenous variable. It also allows us to abstract from depositors' decision problem and to focus on bank's problem.
10. Changes in bank's legal reserve requirement could be a mean to reduce the impact of a shock on the economy.

11. If bank's returns do not cover the value of the outstanding liabilities (deposits) the lender of last resort will provide the funds needed to repay depositors.

12. In absence of LOLR intervention the probability of surviving is instead equal to $G(n)$ with $G(n) < S(n)$ and $G'(n) < S'(n)$. Therefore, the presence of LOLR support increases the bank's survival probability and this might create incentives for risk-taking behaviour.

13. In this analysis we abstract from the distinction between illiquid and insolvent banks and thus from the problem of whether the LOLR should intervene to rescue the formers leaving the insolvent banks defaulting.

14. By applying Leibniz's rule, the derivative of the expected current profit (8) with respect to the fraction of monitored projects is:

$$\frac{\partial \Pi}{\partial n} = -(1-y)\left\{Z\varepsilon^* - yR^D\right\}\frac{\partial \varepsilon^*}{\partial y} + (1-y)\int_{\varepsilon^*}^{\infty}\varepsilon\left[R\Delta p - C'(n)\right]f(\varepsilon)d\varepsilon \qquad \text{(n.1)}$$

where $Z = [nRp_H + (1-n)Rp_L - C(n)]$. Since in (n.1) the first term goes to zero, we get expression (11) in the text.

15. By applying Leibniz's rule, the derivative of the probability of not defaulting (14) with respect to the fraction of monitored projects is:

$$\frac{\partial G}{\partial n} = -f\left(\varepsilon^*\right)d\varepsilon^*\frac{\partial \varepsilon^*}{\partial n} \qquad \text{(n.2)}$$

From (n. 2) after some computations we get the expression (15) in the text.

References

Arestis, P., Baddeley, M. and McCombie, J. (2001) *What Global Economic Crisis?* New York: Palgrave.

Bagehot, W. (1873) *Lombard Street: A Description of the Money Market*. London: H. S. King.

Berlemann, M., Hristov K. and Nenovsky, N. (2002) 'Lending of Last Resort, Moral Hazard and Twin Crises: Lessons from the Bulgarian Financial Crisis 1996/1997', William Davidson Working Paper No. 464.

Bordo, M. D. (1990) 'The Lender of Last Resort: Alternative Views and Historical Experience', *Economic Review, Federal Reserve Bank of Richmond*, 76(1), 18–29.

Broda, C. and Levy Yeyati, E. (2006) 'Endogenous Deposit Dollarization', *Journal of Money, Credit and Banking*, 38(4), 963–88.

Calomiris, C. (2000) 'Blueprints for a New Global Financial Architecture', in L. Auernheimer (ed.), *International Financial Markets: The Challenge of Globalization*. Chicago: University of Chicago Press.

Capie, F. (2002) 'Can There Be an International Lender of Last Resort?', *International Finance*, 1(2), 311–25.

Claassen, E. M. (1985) 'The Lender of Last Resort Function in the Context of National and International Crises', *Weltwirtschaftliches Archiv*, 121(3), 217–37.

Coleman, A. D. F., Esho, N., and Sharpe, I.G. (2006) 'Does Bank Monitoring Influence Loan Contract Terms?', *Journal of Financial Services Research*, 30(2), 177–98.

Cordella, T., and Levy Yeyati, E. (2006) 'A (New) Country Insurance Facility', *International Finance*, 9(1), 1–36.

Corrado, G. (2004) 'Lending of Last Resort, Bank Monitoring and Financial Dollarization', *International Finance Review*, 5. Published in H. Arbeláez and R. W. Click (eds), *Latin American Financial Markets: Developments in Financial Innovations*. Oxford: Elsevier, pp. 163–88.

Eichengreen, B. (2002) *Financial Crises and What to Do About Them*. Oxford: Oxford University Press.

Enoch, C., Stella, P. and Khamis, M. (1997) 'Transparency and Ambiguity in Central Bank Safety Net Operations', IMF Working Paper, WP/97/138. Washington, DC: International Monetary Fund.

Feldstein, M. (1998) 'Refocusing the IMF', *Foreign Affairs*, 77 (March/April), 20–33.

Fernández de Lis, S. (2008) 'The Subprime Crisis and the Lender of Last Resort', Analysis of the Real Instituto Elcano: International Economy & Trade, ARI 106/2008.

Fischer, S. (1999) 'On the Need for an International Lender of Last Resort', *Journal of Economic Perspectives*, 13(4), 85–104.

Freixas, X. and Parigi, B.M. (2008) 'Lender of Last Resort and Bank Closure Policy', CESifo Working Paper no. 2286, April.

Freixas, X., Parigi, B.M. and Rochet, J.C. (2000) 'Systemic Risk, Interbank Relations and Liquidity Provision by the Central Bank', *Journal of Money, Credit and Banking*, 32(3), Part 2 (August), 611–38.

Freixas, X., Parigi, B.M. and Rochet, J.C. (2004) 'The Lender of Last Resort: A 21st Century Approach', *Journal of the European Economic Association*, 2(6), 1085–115.

Freixas, X., Giannini, C., Hoggarth., G. and Soussa, F. (1999) 'Lender of Last Resort: a Review of the Literature', *Financial Stability Review*, November.

Friedman, M. (1959) *A Program for Monetary Stability*. New York: Fordham University Press.

Friedman, M. and Schwartz, A.J. (1963) *A Monetary History of the United States*. Princeton, NJ: Princeton University Press.

Giannini, C. (1999) 'Enemy of None but a Common Friend of All? An International Perspective on the Lender of Last Resort Function', *Princeton Essays in International Finance*, 214.

Goodfriend, M. and King, R.G. (1988) 'Financial Deregulation, Monetary Policy and Central Banking', *Federal Reserve Bank of Richmond Economic Review*, 74(3), 363–80.

Goodhart, C.A.E. (1988) *The Evolution of Central Banks*. Cambridge, MA: MIT Press.

Goodhart, C.A.E. (1999) 'Myths About the Lender of Last Resort', *International Finance*, 2(3), 339–60.

Goodhart, C.A.E. (2009) *The Regulatory Response to the Financial Crisis*. Cheltenham, UK: Edward Elgar Publishing Ltd.

Goodhart, C.A.E. and Huang, H. (1999) 'A Model of the Lender of Last Resort', IMF Working Papers 99/39. Washington, DC: International Monetary Fund.

Goodhart, C.A.E. and Illing, G. (2002) *Financial Crises, Contagion and the Lender of Last Resort. A Reader*. Oxford: Oxford University Press.

Grossman, S. and Hart, O. (1982) 'Corporate Financial Structure and Managerial Incentives', in J. McCall (ed.), *The Economics of Information and Uncertainty*. Chicago: University of Chicago Press, pp. 107–37.

He, D. (2000) 'Emergency Liquidity Support Facilities', IMF Working Paper, WP/00/79. Washington, DC: International Monetary Fund.

Holmöstrom, B. and Tirole, J. (1993) 'Financial Intermediation, Loanable Funds, and the Real Sector', *Quarterly Journal of Economics*, 112, 663–91.

Humphrey, T.M. (1975) 'The Classical Concept of the Lender of Last Resort', *Federal Reserve Bank of Richmond Economic Review*, 61 (February), 2–9.

Humphrey, T.M. and Keleher, R.E. (1984) 'The Lender of Last Resort: A Historical Perspective', *Cato Journal*, 4(1), 275–318.

International Monetary Fund (2008) 'Global Financial Stability Report: Containing Systemic Risks and Restoring Financial Soundness', in *World Economic and Financial Surveys*, April.

Kaufman, G. (2002) 'Lender of Last Resort: A Contemporary Perspective', in C.A.E. Goodhart and G. Illing (eds), *Financial Crises, Contagion and the Lender of Last Resort: A Reader*. Oxford: Oxford University Press, pp. 169–85.

Kydland, F.E. and Prescott, E.C. (1977) 'Rules Rather than Discretion: the Inconsistency of Optimal Plans', *Journal of Political Economy*, 85(3), June, 473–92.

Lee, K. and Sharpe, I.G. (2006) 'Does the Bank's Monitoring Ability Matter?', Australian Prudential Regulation Authority Working Papers, WP2006-04.

Meltzer, A.H. (1986) 'Financial Failures and Financial Policies', in G. Kaufman and R.C. Kormendi (eds), *Deregulating Financial Services: Public Policy in Flux.* Cambridge, MA: Ballinger.

Mishkin, F. (1999) 'Global Financial Instability: Framework, Events, Issues', *Journal of Economic Perspectives*, 13(4), 3–20.

Moore, G. (1999) 'Solutions to the Moral Hazard Problem Arising from the Lender of Last Resort Facility', *Journal of Economic Surveys*, 13(4), 443–76.

Obstfeld, M. (2009) 'Lenders of Last Resort and Global Liquidity. Rethinking the System', *Development Outreach Magazine*, World Bank Institute, December.

Sachs, J. (1995) 'Do We Need an International Lender of Last Resort?', Princeton University, Frank Graham Memorial Lecture, Princeton, NJ.

Schwartz, A. (1986) 'Real and Pseudo-Financial Crises', in F. Capie and G. Woods (eds), *Financial Crises and the World Banking System.* London: Macmillan, pp. 11–40.

Schwartz, A. (1988) 'Financial Stability and the Federal Safety Net', in W.S. Haraf and G.E. Kushmeider (eds), *Restructuring Banking and Financial Services in America.* Washington, DC: American Enterprise Institute for Public Policy Research, pp. 34–62.

Schwartz, A. (2002) 'Earmarks of a Lender of Last Resort', in C.A.E. Goodhart and G. Illing (eds), *Financial Crises, Contagion and the Lender of Last Resort: a Reader.* Oxford: Oxford University Press, pp. 449–68.

Solow, R. (1982) 'On the Lender of Last Resort', in C.P Kindleberger and J.P. Laffargue (eds), *Financial Crisis: Theory, History and Policy.* Cambridge: Cambridge University Press, pp. 237–48.

Thornton, H. (1802) *An Enquiry into the Nature and the Effects of the Paper Credit of Great Britain.* London: Hatchard.

10
The Necessity of Reforming the International Monetary System

Fernando Ferrari-Filho

To my mother, Elza, in memoriam

1 Introduction

The current international financial crisis is a crisis of globalised finance, meaning that a crisis in one specific segment of the financial system – specifically the United States subprime mortgage market – eventually spreads worldwide. The effects of such a crisis are not neutral in economic and social terms, added to which the benefits of financial globalisation have come to be called seriously into question. While this crisis is associated with an absence of regulation, particularly by the State, it has been action by *Big Bank* and *Big Government*[1] that has prevented it from developing into a depression. This chapter evaluates the present international financial crisis and interpretations of it, and indicates that surmounting it will depend on a series of post Keynesian type measures. To that end, it describes very briefly the origins of the crisis, and developments and lessons from it, then presents the conventional and post Keynesian views of foreign exchange and financial crises, especially as regards the present international financial crisis. Lastly, on the one hand, it sets out the main conventional and heterodox arguments for the necessity of restructuring the international monetary system and some proposals for reform of that system and, on the other hand, in the light of post Keynesian theory, following Davidson (2002), it presents a proposal for restructuring the international financial system. That proposal, in the author's view, is capable of preventing future foreign exchange and financial crises, while at the same time assuring the conditions for macroeconomic stability, understood as sustainable economic growth with full employment, price stabilisation and external equilibrium.

2   A brief analysis of the current international financial crisis: origins, consequences and lessons[2]

2.1   Origins

Internationalisation of the financial system has substantially altered the nature and determinants of world economic dynamics: the combination of deregulated financial markets and the attendant emergence of financial innovations (such as securitisation and derivatives), freely mobile capital and flexible and volatile foreign exchange and interest rates, on the one hand, have limited the action of domestic macroeconomic policies and, on the other, have been one cause of recurrent balance of payments and foreign exchange crises in emerging economies (particularly those that took place in the 1990s), crises of both liquidity and solvency, and the recent international financial crisis.

When markets are integrated to the point of creating a 'single' world money and credit market – under conditions where there are no stabilising financial and foreign exchange rules and where traditional macroeconomic policy tools become increasingly insufficient to contain currency exchange and financial collapse at the world level – this process of financial globalisation comes to result ultimately in crises of effective demand and unemployment.

The present international financial crisis – which incidentally originated from losses caused by mounting mortgage loan defaults on the United States subprime market (high-risk real estate finance market) and produced knock-on effects worldwide, because a large part of those mortgages has been securitised and distributed to investors on the global market – is above all a crisis in financial globalisation understood as a tendency to create a global financial market and to intensify capital flows among countries. This process can be traced back to the 1970s crisis in the Bretton Woods international monetary system, to deregulation of financial markets in the course of the 1980s, and to the liberalisation of foreign exchange markets and capital flows from the 1990s onwards.

As a result of the process of financial deregulation, foreign exchange market liberalisation and capital mobility, 'a strong trend towards "financialization" and rent-seeking started to take shape in capitalist economies', where companies, financial institutions and consumers 'began to subordinate their spending, investment and savings decisions to expectations about the pace of their respective financial "enrichment"' (Coutinho and Beluzzo, 2004, p. 60; the original quotation was translated by the author).

Meanwhile, competition could be seen to intensify among banking institutions, with a consequent decline in net interest margins and the associated response, a trend towards financial conglomeration through mergers and takeovers. In this connection, financial institutions have begun to explore different markets, including lower-income ones. On the securities market, for instance, encouraged by growth among institutional investors (hedge funds and pension funds, and so on), securitisation mechanisms were developed where firms and banks financed themselves by 'packaging' receivable earnings. Accordingly, given that securitisation allowed risks to be diluted on the market, financial institutions and institutional investors went on to increase their leverage on the assumption that market self-regulation mechanisms would be able to continue returning correct assessments of the risks inherent to these financial activities.[3]

Ultimately, the crisis on the subprime (high-risk mortgage finance) market laid bare all the contradictions of this process. The existing context of (i) low base interest rates set by the Federal Reserve Bank (Fed) in order to reanimate the United States economy following the collapse of the Nasdaq bubble in 2000 and the terrorist attacks on the twin towers of the World Trade Center in 2001 and (ii) weak financial system regulatory mechanisms – which incidentally even permitted a parallel financial system (institutional investors) to spring up – eventually resulted in a bubble in subprime mortgages (adjustable rate mortgages whose interest rates are reset periodically, starting out low and rising over time, according to a variety of indices). Because of their need to achieve ever greater scale, financial institutions began to take in lower and lower income earners in conditions of 'financial exploitation', resulting in a process of financial strangulation for borrowers. Securitisation was supposed to serve to dilute risks; however, in practice, it served to concentrate on them: securities backed by mortgages were issued by major financial institutions and ranked 'investment grade' by certain rating agencies. As a result of financial globalisation, these assets were purchased in turn by investors of various different nationalities. New financial instruments were created in this way, but were not properly regulated by the authorities. Moreover, market self-regulation mechanisms proved faulty due to the pro-cyclic nature of risk taking, i.e. projects that had been regarded as poor risks during the economic slowdown came to be seen as good risks during the boom.

It is worth noting that the subprime crisis was initially diagnosed as being a problem restricted solely to the institutions that had involved themselves with high-risk mortgage loans. That diagnosis proved mistaken, however, because an injection of liquidity and lower interest rates[4] were not enough to avert the fallout from the crisis. Now why was that? It was because, eventually, given the extensive, interconnected financial network that had been put in place at the global level by the process of 'financialisation', the subprime crisis ended up turning into a systemic crisis – that is, a situation where the liquidity crisis comes to precipitate a crisis of confidence. In that regard, in a situation where no abrupt movements in asset prices had been expected – neither rising United States basic interest rates[5] nor falling housing prices as a result of defaulting mortgage debtors – financial institutions became insolvent.

There could only ever have been one outcome: on the one hand, the systemic crisis meant that bank credit was cut off, because the financial system came to prefer liquidity and, on the other hand, the scarcity of credit came to constrain levels of consumption and investment, thereby impacting the 'real economy'.

2.2 Consequences[6]

The international financial crisis affected economic activity dramatically, both in the developed countries and in the emerging economies, casting doubt on the very notion of decoupling the emerging countries.

The developments from the crisis were observed not just in the financial system, but most importantly in the real realm of the economy. After a long period of prosperity in the world economy running from 2003 to 2007, the United States, the countries of the *Euro zone*, Japan and some of the leading emerging countries, such as Argentina, Brazil, Chile and Mexico, went into recession from the last quarter of 2008 onwards.[7] The scenario that unfolded from September 2008 onwards in terms of economic downturn, shrinking trade flows and asset deflation caused the world economy to go into collapse. In this connection, it is worth remembering that the International Monetary Fund (IMF)'s *World Economic Outlook* of October 2009 held out both a pessimistic forecast for world GDP in 2009 (that is, recession) and also the expectation of a period of slow recovery in the world economy starting in 2010.[8]

It should be stressed that the world recession expected for 2009 might have been much worse had it not been for the actions of the Monetary Authorities of both the G7 countries and the emerging countries: aware that the international financial crisis had stemmed from inaction by the State and not from its purported proactive role, as supposed by the theoreticians of neoliberalism, these countries' Monetary Authorities took an active part in mitigating the impacts of the international financial crisis on the productive sphere of the economy. To that end, they implemented counter-cyclical fiscal policies and expansionist monetary policies, mainly through the activities of their central banks as lenders of last resort, in order to reverse the steadily deteriorating state of expectations among economic agents. In that regard, the injections of liquidity and substantial reductions in interest rates practiced by central banks, as well as fiscal incentives, along Keynesian lines, were important in reducing the impact of the crisis on the 'real economy' and seeking to restore agents' confidence in the workings of the markets.[9]

In parallel, the governments of the G7 and the main emerging countries in the group known as the G20 met in April 2009 and proposed a total restructuring of the international monetary system grounded in greater transparency and regulation[10] and in international financial cooperation. On that occasion they also approved the creation of an emergency line of credit of about US$1.1 trillion to boost the volume of funding by the IMF and multilateral development banks to finance world trade, in addition to which the governor of the People's Bank of China suggested replacing the US dollar as the universal reserve currency by creating a new global currency that would be independent of the decisions of national central banks. In short, the G20 proposed to avert any worsening of the world recession, to monitor and regulate the financial system and to negotiate a 'new architecture' for the international monetary system so that financial markets could return to performing their primary functions, which are to finance productive investment and consequently expand effective world demand.

Unfortunately, the conservatism and conflicts of interest among the participants have prevented any progress towards the possible restructuring of the international monetary system, at least for the present.

2.3 Lessons

The international financial crisis has left us some lessons,[11] which briefly are:

1. Financial (and currency exchange) crises are more and more recurrent in a context of financial deregulation and liberalisation of foreign exchange and capital flows.
2. Markets, especially financial markets, are not efficient, self-regulating and self-balancing, as has been argued by conventional economists.
3. Financial crises are endogenous. On this point, drawing on Minsky (1986) and the idea of a 'financial instability hypothesis', a continuous and dynamic cycle of economic prosperity, such as occurred in

the world economy between 2003 and 2007, lead the economy inevitably to instability, because in times of prosperity economic agents – consumers, firms and financial institutions – take decisions to consume, invest and lend and/or leverage themselves that are essentially speculative ('suicidal' attitudes). In other words, the boom makes the economy inherently unstable; therefore, financial (foreign exchange) crises are associated with the peaks of economic cycles.

4. In a globalised world, the economic and social implications of financial crises are far more dramatic.

5. Solutions to the problem of excessive financial wealth in relation to the 'real economy' usually come at a high price.[12]

6. Lastly, the present world international financial crisis occurred because of deficiency in the regulatory frameworks and excessive leverage in the financial system, dynamised globally by the development of derivatives contracts and credit 'securitisation'. Accordingly, Lehman Brothers, Fannie Mae, Freddie Mac and American International Group, as well as other institutions, *propagated* the crisis, but *were not its origin*.

Utopically, if there were convergence among economists' ideas and world views, we might perhaps be able to add one more item to this list of lessons from the international financial crisis; that is, that eventually we all learn from our past errors. Unfortunately, however, for the conventional theorists, once the crisis has passed, the 'invisible hand of the market' will return to conduct the economy to its natural condition of overall equilibrium. On this point, as Keynes (1936/1964, p. viii) wrote in his *The General Theory of Employment, Interest and Money* (GT), '[t]he difficulty lies, not in the new ideas, but in escaping from the old ones, which ramify, for those brought up as most of us have been, into every corner of our minds'.

3   The conventional and post Keynesian views of financial crises[13]

3.1   The conventional theory

In general, the conventional theory presumes that financial (and foreign exchange) markets are efficient; that is to say, efficient market theory claims that economic agents analyze past and present market data, which means that price signals are presumed to provide enough information about forming rational expectations as a basis for making utility maximising decisions. Thus, financial (foreign exchange rate) crises occur *only* if there is any sort of 'market fundamental' essentially associated with a current or foreseeable future deterioration in economic fundamentals.

Assuming an ergodic world,[14] in which market fundamentals determine the conditional probabilities of future outcomes, financial (exchange rate) crises are explained by the possibility of irrational behaviour involving bandwagon effects. In other words, financial (exchange rate) crises are explained by 'anomalies' (i.e., unsound economic fundamentals). Moreover, using ad hoc micro-fundamentals to explain 'irrational' crises, conventional theory is always trying to find an *ex post* explanation for each 'new' financial or currency crisis.

With the foregoing ideas as their frame of reference, conventional economists uphold the arguments that financial (foreign exchange) crises occur because of random, external events ('sunspots') or because of 'asymmetrical information', or even for reasons of 'moral hazard' (Mishkin, 1992).[15]

In this context, how does the conventional theory explain the current international financial crisis?

For example, a book written by John Taylor (2009) called *Getting off Track* seems to summarise the conventional theory's view of the international financial crisis. Taylor regards the crisis as having resulted, on the one hand, from the adoption of excessively lax monetary policy in the early 2000s, which he considers to have contributed to inflating real estate prices in the United States. According to Taylor, if between 2003 and 2005 the Fed had held short-term interest rates at levels suggested by 'Taylor's rule' – that is, at higher levels than it actually did – the expansion of the United States real estate market would have been far more moderate. On the other hand, still according to Taylor, the United States government's hesitant actions to tackle the crisis merely heightened agents' insecurity. In this connection, both the announcement of the 'Paulson Plan', which suggested buying up the 'rotten' mortgage assets of financial institutions in difficulties, and the United States MAs' mistaken diagnosis of the crisis as simply a problem of liquidity, not perceiving the extent of the banks' solvency problems, contributed to aggravating the crisis. On this latter point, Taylor sees the failure of Lehman Brothers, and also the interventions in Bear Stearns, American International Group, Fannie Mae and Freddy Mac, along with other financial institutions, as just one more step in the confused strategy for dealing with the crisis, where the government's intervention actually worsened the situation, because it spread insecurity and the fear of bankruptcies on the financial market.

Alan Greenspan (2009), former chairman of the Fed, developed a different interpretation of the crisis: the subprime crisis was not determined by the reduction in the Fed interest rates between 2002 and 2005, given that the correlation between the mortgage interest rate and the Fed rate was insignificant, but rather by the sizeable current account surpluses of various emerging countries, especially China, which ultimately pressured the long-term interest rate to steadily lower levels, thus contributing to a global housing price bubble. In other words, the creation of a kind of endogenous currency associated with international liquidity is regarded as having been decisive in the simultaneous drop in global interest rates.

Faithful to his liberal principles, however, Greenspan did not perceive permissive deregulation as one of the main causes of the international financial crisis. He thus provides an interesting explanation for why the housing bubble burst, but is unable to take a more comprehensive view of the crisis. Why after all should a real estate crisis in a secondary sector of the financial system (the subprime market) ultimately contaminate the overall system as a whole?

One critical aspect of Taylor's argument, going beyond the remarks offered by Greenspan, is to suggest that ultimately the propagation of the international financial crisis resulted from excessive, undue interference by the United States government, on the old liberal argument that action by the government, when all is said and done, tends to be ineffective. Now, that does not seem to be a convincing explanation for the international financial crisis, because it confuses relations of cause and effect.

Taylor and Greenspan share a common faith in the free workings of the market – regulated financial markets tend to be inefficient and not very innovative. They also consider the financial system is unstable due to problems of asymmetric information.

In this same direction, Gordon (2008) shows that the origin of the international financial crisis is related to asymmetric information and how the risk was spread to the security and derivative markets.

However, as section 3.2 shows, it has to be understood that financial systems, at the same time as they can help leverage growth, are inherently unstable (Keynes, 1964, Chapter 12).

In short, the conventional explanation for the international financial crisis is that (i) the low rates of interest practiced by the Fed in the early 2000s in order to mitigate the effects of deflating the 'New Economy' bubble eventually gave rise to the housing bubble and (ii) misplaced interventions in the financial market by United States Monetary Authorities constituted problems of asymmetrical information and market irrationality, thus generating situations favourable to the actions of foolish 'noise traders'. In other words, the international financial crisis resulted from exogenous economic variables.

3.2 The post Keynesian perspective

As stated before, according to the efficient market theory, economic agents with rational expectations make the best use of the available information, so that stock prices always reflect fundamental values. Thus, the efficient market theory supposes the axiom of an ergodic economic environment.

As we know, Keynes and post Keynesians reject the ergodic axiom of efficient market theory to explain financial (exchange rate) market behaviour because, in an uncertain world, future market valuations are always uncertain since the future is subject to sudden and violent changes and fundamentals do not provide a reliable guide to the future.[16] As a consequence, economic decision making cannot predict the future based on any statistical analysis of past market information. In such a world, speculation is not an 'anomaly' but results from how financial (exchange rate) market operations actually work.

In different works, Keynes distinguished uncertainty from probable events. By uncertainty, he points out that 'human decisions affecting the future, whether personal or political or economic, cannot depend on strict mathematical expectation, since the basis for making such calculations does not exist' (Keynes, 1964, pp. 162–3), which means that 'there is no scientific basis on which to form any calculable probability whatever. We simply do not know' (Keynes, 1937/1973, p. 114).

It is because uncertainty exists that economic agents, in both financial and exchange rate markets, have heterogeneous expectations, since whatever data sets exist today, they can never be expected to provide a reliable guide to future outcomes. In this light, the expectations that drive spot financial (exchange rate) markets are not rational, because conventional valuation based on psychological market forecasting cannot be held as statistically reliable.

Also, Keynes argues that the expectations of both investors and speculators are governed not by real long-term fundamentals relating to expected earnings from an investment over coming years, but rather by the value the market expects the asset will have in the future. In the words of Keynes (1964, pp. 154–5),

Most of these persons are, in fact, largely concerned, not with making superior long-term forecasts of the probable yield of an investment over its whole life, but with foreseeing changes in the conventional basis of valuation a short time ahead of the general public. They are concerned, not with what an investment is worth to a man who buys it 'for keeps', but with what the market will value it at, under the influence of mass psychology, three months or a year hence.

Thus, speculation is forecasting the psychology of the market.

Keynes shows, in his GT (Chapter 12), that in an entrepreneurial economy – in a context under incalculable uncertainty, money can be held as a safety asset by virtue of its characteristics of transporting purchasing power over time[17] – the organisation of financial markets faces a severe trade-off between liquidity and speculation: on the one hand, the financial market encourages the development of productive activity by making assets more liquid, thus freeing investors from the irreversibility of investment; on the other hand, it increases the possibilities of speculative gains. Thus, in establishing a connection between financial and real markets in the economy, Keynes (1964, p. 159) writes that 'the position is serious when enterprise becomes the bubble on a whirlpool of speculation. When the capital development of a country becomes a by-product of the activities of a casino, the job is likely to be ill-done'.

Echoing Keynes, the activities of present-day global players in markets that are increasingly deregulated and integrated reduce financial markets to a kind of vast global casino. Thus, in a global economy, speculation is by nature disruptive of not just domestic markets, but of whole countries, creating a kind of over-sized financial casino.

From a Keynesian standpoint, financial instability is not regarded as an 'anomaly', but as an outcome of the very way financial markets operate in a system where there is no safeguard structure to perform a global market-maker function. Thus, the specific institutional format of the financial markets determines the possibilities of there existing an environment in which speculation can flourish. Financial crises are not just 'irrational' behavior by agents, but result from the very way deregulated global financial markets operate in a system without appropriate regulation (Alves Jr, Ferrari-Filho and Paula, 1999–2000).

Taking as its frame of reference the ideas of Keynes about how financial markets operate in monetary production economies, the post Keynesian approach regards the international financial crisis as a consequence of processes of financial deregulation, capital flow mobility and intensifying competition among financial institutions, which ultimately constitute a financially globalised world in which finances, instead of leveraging (creating funding) in favor of productive activity, come to increase essentially speculative operations, thus valuating the financial wealth derived from capital.

To sum up, according to Keynes and the post Keynesian approach, in a globalised economy and an uncertain world, financial (exchange rate) crises (i) are an endogenous phenomenon, (ii) stimulate economic agents' preference for liquidity and (iii) lead to a lack of effective demand, as a result increasing the rate of unemployment.

4 A post Keynesian proposal for reforming the international monetary system

The international financial crisis recommends reflection on two counts. In the first place, it calls into question the supposed concrete benefits of financial globalisation with financial markets deregulated everywhere, including in the developed countries. In the second place, given the fiscal and monetary measures implemented by developed and emerging countries to mitigate the world recession, it prompts a rethinking of the very role of the State in the economy, as regards the need both to regulate domestic financial systems and to restructure the international monetary system.

On the first count, as deregulated financial markets are not efficient, in the absence of rules to stabilise such markets, speculative activities and the financial valuation of wealth eventually become routine, because the liberalisation of financial markets and the existence of new financial instruments (such as derivatives) increase the likelihood that speculative activities will be pursued. In that connection, there is a need to regulate 'exotic' derivatives operations and the other practices (excessive leverage by financial institutions) that made the 'party' for investors and banks.

On the second point, the key lesson from the international financial crisis is not only that state action is fundamental in preventing or remedying crises, but that, particularly at critical moments, it is important there be greater global coordination among the various different national policies, especially in the developed countries. In this regard, the role of the State is fundamental to restoring macroeconomic balance and to creating an 'institutional environment' favorable to 'animal spirits'. As stated by Keynes (1964, p. 378), 'I conceive (...) that a somewhat comprehensive socialisation of investment will prove the only means of securing an approximation to full employment'. For that purpose, Keynes suggests fiscal, monetary and income policies.[18] In that direction, the macroeconomic policy of national economies should be coordinated in such a way as to: (i) operationalise fiscal policies designed to expand effective demand and reduce social inequalities; (ii) make for more flexible monetary policy so as to galvanise levels of consumption and investment; and (iii) coordinate and regulate financial and foreign exchange markets in order to stabilise capital flows and exchange rates. In short, taking up the idea of Minsky (1986), there is a need for state intervention and regulation through *Big Government* and *Big Bank*.

Moreover, as regards the need to restructure the international monetary system, a degree of consensus can be said to exist among economists and policymakers as to what measures are indispensable to restoring stability to the system. Nonetheless, there is no consensus as to how the international monetary system is to be restructured.[19]

To conventional economists, an efficient international monetary system is one made up of flexible currency exchange regimes, more capital mobility and greater financial liberalisation on markets. According to Edison, Levine, Ricci and Slok (2002), the benefits of a flexible exchange rate, unregulated capital flows and financial liberalisation to the world economy is that these 'policies' (i) reduce the sources of external vulnerability, (ii) increase the autonomy of monetary policy, (iii) allocate domestic and foreign savings efficiently, (iv) discipline macroeconomic policies and (v) improve economic growth performance.

Meanwhile, the need to preserve the autonomy of countries' fiscal and monetary policy – which are essential to assuring sustainable economic growth trajectories – has reinforced the Keynesian economists' point of view that it is necessary to introduce an international market maker in order to: (i) ensure the international liquidity indispensable to enable the flow of world trade, (ii) stabilise the currency exchange regime and (iii) control short-term capital flows. Issues (ii) and (iii) are particularly important for developing countries, given that these countries suffer from more volatility than developed countries, and this contributes to recessions of longer duration (Hausmann, Pritchett, and Rodrik, 2004).

In terms of proposals, it should be noted that a number of ideas have been formalised in recent decades in the endeavour to signpost this restructuring of the international monetary system. These include: (i) 'Target Zones for Exchange Rates' (Williamson, 1987), the essence of which is to establish rules and goals that limit the fluctuation of nominal exchange rates, with a view thus to establish a relatively stable real rate of exchange which will permit internal and external balance;[20] (ii) 'Fixed Nominal Purchasing Power Parity Exchange Rate System' (McKinnon, 1988), which consists of creating optimal monetary areas where the fixed rate of exchange rests on parity purchasing power among the main international currencies; (iii) the 'Tobin tax', developed originally by Tobin (1978), the idea of which is to introduce a world tax on all – but especially short-term – exchange transactions, with a view to curbing the destabilising action of financial speculation on currency exchange markets, and the resulting exchange crises it occasions; and (iv) 'International Money Clearing Union', a proposal presented by Davidson (2002), which will be explored further below.[21]

Now, as seen in section 2.2, at a time when counter-cyclical macroeconomic policies have come back into the picture and the G20 and multilateral institutions, such as the IMF and the Bank for International Settlements, are signalling the possibility of architecting a new international monetary system, Keynes's ideas on the operationalisation of fiscal, monetary and currency exchange policies to stabilise world effective demand and his proposal for reform of the international monetary system should be reconsidered, because they are essential to surmounting the international financial crisis and, more importantly, to preventing other crises in the future.

What can then be done to prevent the instability of financial (or exchange rate) markets and thus address financial crises in the global economy? Keynes' revolutionary analysis provides us a starting point for designing a new international monetary system that may be able to reduce the current financial crisis and at the same time promote full employment and economic growth in the global economy. Accordingly, post Keynesian theory, basically in the work of Davidson (2002), builds on Keynes' ideas and proposals about an international monetary system[22] in order to offer a proposal for reforming the international monetary system.

In many of his writings, Keynes discussed and suggested schemes to reform the international monetary system, such as:

- In *A Tract on Monetary Reform* (1923/1971), he proposed abandoning the gold standard, due to the fact that 'the gold standard is already a barbarous relic' (Keynes, 1971, p. 138).[23]
- In *A Treatise on Money* (1930/1976, pp. 399–400), Volume 2, Keynes proposed an arrangement set up in a

> Supernational Bank ... [in which] assets [of the central banks of the world] should consist of gold, securities and advances to central banks, and its liabilities of deposits by Central Banks ... call Supernational Bank-Money (SBM) ... SBM should be purchasable for gold and encashable for gold at fixed prices.

In other words, he outlined a proposal for operating a supranational central bank to maintain the stability of international price levels, to increase international asset liquidity and to expand effective demand.

• In *The Means to Prosperity*, published in March 1933, he proposed an international monetary agreement ('gold-notes', under fixed, but alterable, exchange rates) to expand the elasticity of the international currency. According to Keynes (1972, p. 358), '[t]here should be set up an international authority for the issue of gold-notes [a maximum of $5,000 million], of which the face value would be expressed in terms of the gold content of the U.S. dollar'.

• Finally, in his proposal for an International Clearing Union (1944/1980), Keynes developed a scheme based on an international currency, *bancor*.

However, it is Keynes's revolutionary analysis in the International Clearing Union that deserves special attention.

Before examining the proposal Keynes set out in his International Clearing Union, it is important to emphasise that, as in Ferrari Filho (2006, Chapter 3), Keynes's proposals for restructuring the international monetary system have one common goal, which is, through an 'International Market Maker', to create an international reserve currency that cannot be hoarded by economic agents and whose prime function is to enable and encourage real and financial relations in the world economy. In other words, Keynes's proposals seem to converge to a project of 'institutionality' in which, as supposed by the universe of classical theory, currency is *neutral*.[24]

The main idea of Keynes's International Clearing Union is 'the substitution of an expansionist, in place of a contractionist, pressure on world trade' (Keynes, 1980, p. 176). Thus, Keynes (1980, pp. 168–9, emphasis added) suggested a scheme set out in an international agreement as follows:

> We need an instrument of international currency having general acceptability between nations ... We need an orderly and agreed method of determining the relative exchange values of national currency units ... We need a *quantum of international currency*, which is *neither determined in an unpredictable* and irrelevant manner ... *nor subject to large variations depending on the gold reserve policies of individual countries*; but is governed by the actual current requirements of world commerce, and is also capable of deliberate expansion and

contraction to offset deflationary and inflationary tendencies in effective world demand. We need a system possessed of an international stabilizing mechanism, by which pressure is exercised on any country whose *balance of payments* with the rest of the world is departing from *equilibrium in either position*, so as to prevent movements which must create for its neighbours an equal but opposite want of balance ... We need a central institution ... to aid and support other international institutions.

Keynes, moreover, with a view to reducing entrepreneurial uncertainties, proposed (1) an international agreement under a fixed, but alterable, exchange rate, and (2) control of capital movements. In his words:

> The proposal is to establish a Currency Union, here designated an *International Clearing Union*, based on international bank money, called (let us say) *bancor*, fixed (but not unalterably) in terms of gold and accepted as the equivalent of gold (...) The central banks of all member states (and also non-members) would keep accounts with the International Clearing Union through which they would be entitled to settle their exchange balances with one another at their par value as defined in bancor. (1980, pp. 170–1)
>
> ... control of capital movements, both inward and outward, should be a permanent feature of the post-war system. (1980, p. 185)
>
> The advocacy of a control of capital movements must not be taken to mean that the era of international investment should be brought to an end. On the contrary, the system contemplated should greatly facilitate the restoration of international credit for loan purposes ... distinguishing (a) between movements of floating funds and genuine new investment for developing the world's resources; and (b) between movements, which will help to maintain equilibrium, from surplus countries to deficiency countries, and speculative movements or flights out of deficiency countries or from one surplus country to another. (1980, pp. 186–7)

It is important to note that, as explained in Ferrari Filho (2006, chapter 3), Keynes was aware that the organisation of financial markets in monetary production economies poses the dilemma between liquidity and investment: such markets encourage the development of economic activity, but at the same time increase the likelihood of speculative gains. Accordingly, the central idea of Keynes's International Clearing Union was to guarantee the international liquidity necessary to expand world effective demand. To that end, the *bancor*, together with a system of managed exchange rates and curbs on the destabilising influence of capital flows, would reflect the conventions necessary to stabilise economic agents' expectations, which by reducing the degree of uncertainty as to the future behaviour of the prices of assets and/or contracts, would be fundamental to enable them to make decisions to spend, whether on consumption or investment, as a result expanding economic activity and the level of employment.

In this direction, Davidson (2002, p. 231) presents 'the theoretical foundations for comprehending the need for (a) reforming the world's money in the twenty-first century and (b) update[s] Keynes' original proposal for a postwar international monetary scheme'.

Like Keynes, Davidson argues that the international monetary system must be rooted in the following basic elements: a new international currency to assure the elasticity (quantity of international liquidity) to expand global effective demand, a stable exchange rate system to protect domestic currencies and the international currency from speculative activity, and an agreement clause to eliminate the balance-of-payments disequilibrium in either position.

After defining a specific taxonomy to explain the economic dynamism of an open unionised monetary system (UMS) and an open nonunionised monetary system (NUMS),[25] Davidson attempts to present eight provisions required to operate an international monetary agreement according to a UMS. The provisions are as follows (2002, pp. 232–6):

- The International Money Clearing Union (IMCU) would be the unit of account and reserve asset for international liquidity;
- Each nation's central bank would have to guarantee one-way convertibility from IMCU deposits at the clearing union to its domestic money.
- Contracts between economic agents in the various different nations would be denominated in their domestic currency;
- The exchange rate between the domestic currency and the IMCU would be set by each nation's central bank;
- An overdraft system would be built into the clearing union rules, so as to finance the productive international transactions of countries who need short-term credit;
- A 'trigger mechanism' to put more pressure for balance-of-payments adjustments on the creditor countries than on the debtor countries;
- The exchange rate between domestic currencies and IMCU would be fixed to stabilise the long-term purchasing power of the IMCU;

- A creditor nation would be encouraged to spend its surplus credits in three ways: buying products from any other country in the international payment system, investing capital in deficit countries and providing foreign aid to deficit countries.

Provisions 1, 2 and 4 are preconditions to reduce and/or avoid people holding the international asset, IMCU, as a store of value. As a consequence, the IMCU would be used only for international financial and commercial transactions. Provisions 3 and 7 are necessary conditions to stabilise the long-term purchasing power of IMCU. At the same time, they restrict private speculation regarding the IMCU; that is to say, there is no possibility of the IMCU losing its purchasing power. Finally, provisions 5, 6 and 8 are the main instruments to guarantee that 'export–import imbalance is eliminated without unleashing significant recessionary forces' (Davidson, 2002, p. 236).

To sum up, Davison presents the rules required to operate an international monetary agreement according to a UMS to: (i) avoid a lack of global effective demand; (ii) 'induc[e] the surplus nation(s) to bear a major responsibility for eliminating the imbalance' (Davidson, 2002, p. 237); (iii) provide nations with the ability to control movements of capital; and (iv) expand the quantity of international liquidity.

The post Keynesian proposal can thus be seen to create the conditions necessary to alter the present logic of financial globalisation – that is, for displacing the dynamics of international speculative capital in favor of the process of international production – and, as a consequence, it can reduce the uncertainties facing entrepreneurs, which is necessary to expand global effective demand. As Keynes points out, an international monetary system built in such a way "could use its influence and its power to maintain stability of prices and to control the trade cycle" (Keynes, 1980, pp. 190–1).

5 Summary and conclusions

The globalisation process has limited action by macroeconomic policies and nation-states to stimulate effective demand and consequently increase the level of employment. In addition, international speculative capital flows have created serious exchange rate and monetary and financial problems, such as the European exchange rate crisis in 1992–93, the Dow Jones Industrial crash in 1987, the Mexican peso crisis in 1994–95, the Asian exchange rate crisis in 1997, the Russian exchange rate crisis in 1998, the Brazilian *real* crisis in 1999, the Nasdaq crisis in 2000, the Argentinean *peso* crisis in 2001 and, recently, the sub-prime crisis, in 2008, leading to high rates of unemployment, recession, exchange rate imbalances, persistent balance-of-payments disequilibrium, and so on.

The present international financial crisis has come to have dramatic adverse effects on economic activity, on a larger scale in the developed countries, but also in the emerging economies. It has demonstrated that, on the one hand, the international institutions, such as the IMF, and *ex post* fiscal policies are insufficient to solve the financial problems and consequently avert crises of effective demand – *ex post* fiscal policies merely mitigate impacts of the crisis of effective demand. On the other hand, it has generated consensus as to the need to restructure the international monetary system, as a necessary condition for the world economy to see a return to periods of stability and rising levels of output and employment. In this regard, it raises the possibility of replacing the United States dollar as the 'universal currency' on the world stage, as proposed by the governor of the People's Bank of China at the G20 meeting in April 2009.

One of the key principles of liberal capitalism – non-intervention by the state – was set aside in order to prevent the international financial crisis from developing into a situation similar to the Great Depression of 1929. Now, given that the state has gone on to gesture towards a 'socialisation of investment' (through counter-cyclical fiscal and monetary policies and, going even further, its explicit intervention in the 'real economy' by taking control of both financial institutions and companies in order to pave the way for economic recovery), what can be expected from here on?

In this context, the question arises: is it possible that changes are under way in international financial markets?

If we accept that the liberalised, integrated market arrangements of the *global era* may be dangerous to economic stability and that they hinder sustained attainment of a full-employment economy, some sort of global institutional arrangement is necessary to exert control over capital flows in order to prevent the disruptive real effects of speculative whirlpools. Davidson (1997, p. 672) writes: 'what is necessary is to build permanent fireproofing rules and structures that prevent "beauty contest" induced currency fires. *Crisis prevention rather than crises rescues must be the primary long-term objective*'.

Despite the fact that the international monetary problems we now face are more difficult than those faced during the period of Keynes, his revolutionary analysis regarding the reform of the international monetary system can once again be deployed to help us understand the necessity of creating an international standard currency in order to promote full-employment economic growth, as well as to maintain long-run price stability.

In this direction, Davidson (2002) argues that, with a view to overcoming the problem of financial market volatility, market-maker institutions with sufficient resources to assure market price stability are necessary to prevent the volatility associated with bandwagon phenomena. For this purpose, it is a socially desirable policy to build a buffer stock exchange rate market institution to fix price movements. In other words, to avert future balance-of-payments current account crises and financial crises, it is necessary to create the essential conditions for implementing a new global currency reserve system.

To conclude, efforts should concentrate on pursuing creative policy options to reduce the real disruptive outcomes deriving from speculative activity in financial markets. This is one of the key legacies of Keynes's ideas.

Notes

1. According to Minsky (1986, chapter 13), the failures of capitalism can be solved only by creating the *Big Bank*, a lender-of-last-resort function, to avoid financial system collapse, and *Big Government*, to assure fiscal stimulus and state intervention to stabilise output and employment.
2. This section is based, particularly, on Ferrari Filho and Paula (2009).
3. For an analysis of financial globalisation trends see Palley (2008). Cardim de Carvalho (2008) describes the chronological evolution of the subprime crisis and Eichengreen (2008) shows the origins of the international crisis and responses to it. Kregel (2008) presents an interesting analysis of the subprime crisis based on Minsky's financial instability hypothesis.
4. Right after the onset of the crisis, the interest rates charged by the major central banks were reduced significantly. At the end of 2009, the base interest rates of the central banks of the United States, United Kingdom and Japan and the European Central Bank stood, respectively, at 0.25 per cent, 0.5 per cent, 0.1 per cent and 1.0 per cent per year.
5. In 2004, the base interest rate set by the Fed was 1.4 per cent, yearly average, as against 2007 when it rose to a yearly average of 5.2 per cent. Mean rates calculated by the author on the basis of IMF (2010).
6. The main arguments of this section were presented initially in Ferrari Filho and Paula (2009).
7. Of the main emerging countries, only China and India did not fall into recession.
8. Corroborating the IMF's somber forecast for 2009, the growth rates for the United States, the euro zone and Japan, recently published for that year,

were -2.4 per cent, -4.0 per cent and -5.1 per cent, respectively. Moreover, according to the World Trade Organization (2010) in 2009 the volume of world trade decreased by 12 per cent.

9. As regards the synchronised actions of central banks around the world, whether in injecting liquidity into the financial system or reducing base interest rates, it is worth calling attention to the fact that were it not for action of a lender of last resort (Minsky's *Big Bank*), the systemic crisis in the financial system was likely to have led to meltdown in the system of payments and a run on the banks, similar to the Great Depression of the 1930s. In this particular, Eichengreen and O'Rourke (2009), for instance, present an interesting parallel between the Great Depression and the current international financial crisis.

10. The G20 proposed to regulate hedge funds, private equities and derivative markets, as well as putting an end to offshore tax havens.

11. Lessons 2 and 5 are explored by Gontijo and Oliveira (2009).

12. For example, according to estimates by multilateral institutions, by the end of 2009 some US$15.0 trillion had been injected in order to reduce the present international financial crisis, while the public deficits of the G7 countries had expanded abruptly.

13. This section is based mainly on Alves Jr., Ferrari Filho and Paula (1999–2000) and Ferrari Filho and Paula (2009).

14. In an ergodic world, according to Davidson (1994, p. 89) 'future events are always [calculable] and predictable by using a probabilistic analysis of past and current outcomes'.

15. For instance, Rogoff and Reinhart (2008), analyzing eight centuries of international exchange rate and financial crashes in different countries, have a similar view about the origins of them. Moreover, they argue that, in general, economic crises are originated from financial markets with transmission through commodity price collapses.

16. See, for instance, Keynes (1964, chapter 12) and Davidson (1997).

17. Keynes's concept of an entrepreneur economy is developed in his article 'The distinction between a co-operative economy and an entrepreneur economy' (Keynes, 1979, pp. 76–87). See also Davidson (1994, chapter 6).

18. Cardim de Carvalho (1992, chapter 12) presents the policy instruments for stabilising the economy, from a post Keynesian perspective.

19. Concerning this specific point, recently, two different views about the necessity of reforming the international monetary system were presented: on the one hand, some essays collected by Eichengreen and Baldwin (2008) argue that government intervention to stabilise and to create regulatory reforms to the financial market, as well as rethinking the financial architecture are essential; on the other hand, The Group of the Thirty (2008) presents a report addresses to policies related to redefining the structure of prudential regulation and improving the governance, the risk management, the transparency and the accounting practices of the financial system. In other words, the first one emphasises a global action in terms of macroeconomic policy, while the second one explores the idea of reforming the microeconomic framework to stabilise the financial system.

20. Internal balance, on the conventional theory, is understood as the situation where economic policy is framed by a non-accelerating inflation rate of

unemployment, while external balance has to do with current transactions balance of payments stability compatible with the rate of expansion of economic activity.

21. A summary of the main proposals and other contributions with regard to restructuring the international monetary system can be found in Eichengreen (1999, chapter 6 and chapter 7), Eatwell and Taylor (2000, chapter 7), Davidson (2002, chapter 14) and Isard (2005, chapter 7 and chapter 8).

22. Markwell (2006, particularly chapter 6) presents an interesting analysis of Keynes's thinking related to international relations.

23. The reasons that led Keynes to propose a golden-exchange standard type of international monetary system were probably: (a) the need to make international liquidity more flexible and enable monetary policy to work more actively in stabilising price levels and galvanising levels of income and employment, given that under the gold standard it was essentially passive; and (b) his scepticism towards the gold standard's automatic adjustment mechanism.

24. This 'idea' can be associated with the operational principle of the 'International Market Maker' (i.e., the International Clearing Union proposed by Keynes) in which, similar to the banking system, credits would necessarily balance debits. In his words (1980, p.171), '[i]f no credits can be removed outside the clearing system, but only transferred within it, the Union can never be in any difficulty as regards the honouring of cheques drawn upon it'.

25. According to Davidson (2002, chapter 8), in an open unionised monetary system (UMS) the contracts are expressed in the same monetary system – i.e., the exchange rate is fixed – while in an open nonunionised monetary system (NUMS) the contracts are expressed in different currencies and, as a consequence, the exchange rate is flexible.

References

Alves Jr, A., Ferrari Filho, F. and Paula, L.F. (1999–2000) 'Post Keynesian Critique of Conventional Currency Crisis Models and Davidson's Proposal to Reform the International Monetary System', *Journal of Post Keynesian Economics*, 22(2), 207–25.

Cardim de Carvalho, F.J. (1992) *Mr Keynes and the Post Keynesians: Principles of Macroeconomics for a Monetary Production Economy*. Aldershot: Edward Elgar.

Cardim de Carvalho, F.J. (2008) 'Entendendo a recente Crise financeira global', in F. Ferrari Filho and L.F. Paula (eds), *Dossiê da Crise*. Curitiba: FIEP/Associação Keynesiana Brasileira, pp. 16–22.

Coutinho, L. and Belluzzo, L.G. (2004) '"Financeirização" da riqueza, inflação de ativos e decisões de gasto em economias abertas', in F. Ferrari Filho and L.F. Paula (eds), *Globalização Financeira: ensaios de macroeconomia aberta*. Petropolis: Vozes, pp. 59–77.

Davidson, P. (1994) *Post Keynesian Macroeconomic Theory: A Foundation for Successful Economic Policies for the Twenty-first Century*. Aldershot: Edward Elgar.

Davidson, P. (1997) 'Are the Grains of Sand in the Wheels of International Finance Sufficient to Do the Job When Boulders are Often Required?', *Economic Journal*, 107(442), 671–86.

Davidson, P. (2002) *Financial Markets, Money and the Real World*. Cheltenham: Edward Elgar.

Edison, H., Levine, R., Ricci, L. and Slok T. (2002) 'International Financial Integration and Economic Growth'. *Journal of International Money and Finance*, 21, 749–76.

Eatwell, J. and Taylor, J. (2000) *Global Finance at Risk: The Case for International Regulation*. New York: New Press.

Eichengreen, B. (1999) *Towards a New International Finance Architecture: a Practical post Asia Agenda*. Washington, DC: Institute for International Economics, February.

Eichengreen, B. (2008) *Origins and Responses to the Crisis*. Manuscript, Berkeley, University of California, p. 9.

Eichengreen, B. and Baldwin, R. (ed.) (2008) *Rescuing Our Jobs and Savings: What G7/8 Leaders Can Do to Solve the Global Credit Crisis*. http://www.voxeu.org/index.php?q=node/2327.

Eichengreen, B. and O'Rourke, K.H. (2009) *A Tale of Two Depressions*. http://www.voxeu.org/index.php?q=node/3421, 1 September.

Ferrari Filho, F. (2006) *Política Comercial, Taxa de Câmbio e Moeda Internacional: uma análise a partir de Keynes*. Porto Alegre: UFRGS Editora.

Ferrari Filho, F. and Paula, L.F. (eds) (2004) *Globalização Financeira: ensaios de macroeconomia aberta*. Petrópolis: Vozes.

Ferrari Filho, F. and Paula, L.F. (2009) 'Crise financeira e reestruturação do sistema monetário internacional'. *Indicadores Econômicos FEE*, 37(1), 113–17.

Gontijo, C. and Oliveira, F.A. (2009) *Subprime: os 100 dias que abalaram o capital financeiro mundial e os efeitos da crise no Brasil*. Belo Horizonte: CORECON-MG.

Gordon, G. (2008) 'The Subprime Panic', *NBER Working Paper*, no. 14398, October.

Greenspan, A. (2009) 'O FED não causou a bolha habitacional', *Valor Econômico*, 12 March.

Hausmann, R., Pritchett, L. and Rodrik, D. (2004) 'Growth Accelerations'. *NBER Working Paper, no. 10566*, June.

International Monetary Fund (2009) *World Economic Outlook*. October, http:/// www.imf.org (accessed in January).

International Monetary Fund (2010) *Data and Statistics*. http://www.imf.org (accessed in January).

Isard, P. (2005) *Globalization and the International Financial System: What's Wrong and What Can Be Done*. Cambridge: Cambridge University Press.

Keynes, J.M. (1936/1964) *The General Theory of Employment, Interest and Money*. New York: HBJ Books.

Keynes, J.M. (1923/1971) *A Tract on Monetary Reform*. London: Macmillan, 1971 (*The Collected Writings of John Maynard Keynes*, vol. 4).

Keynes, J.M. (1933/1972) 'The Means to Prosperity'. In *Essays on Persuasion*. London: Macmillan (*The Collected Writings of John Maynard Keynes*, vol. 9), pp. 335–66.

Keynes, J.M. (1937/1973) 'The General Theory of Employment'. In: *The General Theory and After: Defence and Development*. London: Macmillan (*The Collected Writings of John Maynard Keynes*, vol. 14), pp. 109–23.

Keynes, J.M. (1930/1976) *A Treatise on Money*, vol. 2. New York: AMS Press.

Keynes, J.M. (1933/1979) 'The Distinction Between a Co-operative Economy and an Entrepreneur Economy'. In: *The General Theory and After: A Supplement*. London: Macmillan (*The Collected Writings of John Maynard Keynes*, vol. 14, edited by D. Moggridge).

Keynes, J.M. (1944/1980). *Activities 1940–1944: Shaping the Post-War World, the Clearing Union*. London: Macmillan (*The Collected Writings of John Maynard Keynes*, vol. 25, edited by D. Moggridge).

Kregel, J. (2008) 'Minsky's Cushions of Safety: Systemic Risk and the Crisis in the U.S. Subprime Mortgage Market', *The Levy Economics Institute of Bard College*, No. 93.

Markwell, D. (2006) *John Maynard Keynes and the International Relations: Economic Paths to War and Peace*. Oxford: Oxford University Press.

McKinnon, R. (1988) 'Monetary and Exchange Rate Policies for International Financial Stability: A Proposal', *Journal of Economic Perspectives*, 2(1), 83–103.

Minsky, H. (1986) *Stabilizing an Unstable Economy*. Binghamton: Yale University Press.

Mishkin, F. (1992) *The Economics of Money, Banking and Financial Markets*. New York: Harper Collins.

Palley, T. (2008) 'Financialization: What it is and Why it Matters'. In: E. Hein, T. Niechoj, P. Spahn and A. Truger (eds), *Finance-Led Capitalism? Macroeconomic Effects of Changes in the Financial Sector*. Marburg: Metroplis-Verlag, pp. 29–60.

Rogoff, K.S. and Reinhart, C.M. (2008) 'This Time is Different: A Panoramic View of Eight Centuries of Financial Crises', *NBER Working Paper*, no. 13882, March.

Taylor, J. (2009) *Getting Off Track: How Government Actions and Interventions Caused, Prolonged, and Worsened the Financial Crisis*. Stanford, CA: Hoover Institution Press.

The Group of Thirty (2008) *Financial Reform: A Framework for Financial Stability*. Washington, DC: The Group of Thirty.

Tobin, J. (1978) 'A Proposal for International Monetary Reform', *Eastern Economic Journal*, 4(3–4), 153–9.

Williamson, J. (1987) 'Exchange Rate Management: The Role of Target Zones', *American Economic Review*, 77(2), 200–4.

World Trade Organization (2010) http://www.wto.org (accessed in February).

11

Neoliberalism, Income Distribution and the Causes of the Crisis

Engelbert Stockhammer

1 Introduction[1]

The financial crisis that began in summer 2007 has since turned into the worst economic crisis since the Great Depression. Its immediate causes are to be found in the malfunctioning of the financial sector: securitisation of mortgages allowed for the rapid growth of credit and lowered credit standards as banks believed they had passed on credit risk; this fuelled a property bubble; statistical models, which turned out to be based on short time samples, were promised to reduce risk by constructing ingenious portfolios; well-paid rating agencies decorated the new assets with triple A ratings; banks shifted credit off their balance sheets into structured investment vehicles; finally, capital inflows from Asian countries that wanted to accumulate reserves provided ample liquidity for this process. Obviously, the financial system needs to be fundamentally overhauled. While these mechanisms were indeed important, this chapter argues, they are only half the picture. The focus on the flaws in the financial system may hide other causes of the crisis. The polarisation in income distribution, in particular, tends to get glossed over as a potential cause of the crisis. This is not to deny the importance of financial factors. The crisis erupted as a financial crisis for very good reasons. The underlying accumulation regime had financial expansion as one of its key building blocks. However, what is at stake is more than the financial system. This chapter will thus argue that the present crisis should be understood as a crisis of neoliberalism. Financial deregulation is one of the components of neoliberalism, the polarisation of income distribution is another one; it is their interaction that provided the grounds for the crisis.

In a nutshell, our story is as follows. Neoliberalism has led to a shift in power relations between capital and labour. As a consequence, income distribution has shifted sharply in favour of capital. Economically this has a dampening effect on domestic demand (as demand is wage led in the world as a whole), which provides the background in front of which the macroeconomic imbalances that erupted in the present crisis have to be understood. Remarkably, increased profits have basically nowhere translated to an investment boom. The change in distribution has interacted with macroeconomic changes caused by financial deregulation, or, more broadly speaking, by financialisation. Financial deregulation has a international as well as a domestic dimension. Deregulation of international capital flows has allowed countries to temporarily sustain large current account deficits – as long as financial markets were willing to provide the corresponding capital inflows. Indeed, capital flows rather than trade flows have become the prime determinant of exchange rate movements and for many countries, boom–bust cycles driven by capital inflows and consequent abrupt outflows (and currency crises) have been the most important feature of the finance-dominated accumulation regime.

As some countries have been able to run substantial current account surpluses (while others run deficits) international financial liberalisation has created new scope for different trajectories across countries. In a first group of countries domestic financial deregulation has provided a key driving force of growth by giving households improved access to credit. This has – typically in conjunction with real estate bubbles – led to a *credit-driven consumption growth*. These credit-led economies have proven the main engine of growth by means of a consumption boom. They have also run substantial current account deficits. A second group of counties has relied on *export-driven growth* (and subdued domestic consumption) and run substantial current account surpluses. Two key sources of the crisis, debt-driven consumption and international imbalances are thus linked to the interactions of financial liberalisation and the polarisation of income distribution.[2]

The remainder of this chapter is structured as follows. Section 2 gives an overview of the present crisis and its metamorphoses. Section 3 discusses neoliberalism and highlights different interpretations. Section 4 analyses changes in income distribution. Section 4 presents the characteristics of the finance-dominated accumulation regime, in particular its effects on investment, consumption and net exports and also highlights the emergence of two different growth models. Section 5 concludes.

2   The crisis 2007–2010

In mid-2006 house prices in the US started to decline. With hindsight, that marks the beginning of the crisis, even if it attracted relatively little attention at the time. Rapidly rising house prices, and the mortgage lending that came with it, had been the basis of a boom driven by credit-financed consumption and construction investment in the US. As will be discussed later, the structural causes of the crisis include the deregulation of the financial sector which gave rise to a wave of financial innovation, i.e. new ways of creating debt, and the polarisation of income distribution. It came with international trade imbalances and huge capital inflows to the US. But this section will give a brief overview of the unfolding of the crisis itself.

The crisis broke out in a seemingly obscure niche of the US financial system: the subprime market, that is the market on which derivatives on low-quality mortgage credit; thus the initial labelling of the crisis as a *subprime crisis*. This is a rather small segment of the overall mortgage market, though it accounted for a substantial part of the growth in the years before the crisis. As subprime credit is, by definition, of low quality, it was the natural field for the kind of financial engineering – securitisation – that was supposed to reduce risk. What was going on here was the extreme form of what happened on a much broader scale in the entire mortgage industry. In August 2007 the crisis spilt over into the interbank market, where banks lend to each other, usually very short term. The interbank market is at the very centre of the modern financial system. Interest rose to more than one percentage points above that on government bonds. This increase in the risk premium of lending meant that banks did not trust each other. And rightly so, as it turned out. Central banks reacted quickly and pumped billions (of dollars and euros) into the market to maintain liquidity.

However, while things stabilised the crisis evolved. In the spring of 2008 Bear Stearns, one of the leading investment banks, was bankrupt and could only be sold with the Fed guaranteeing some US$20 billion worth of assets. A first (small) fiscal stimulus packet was implemented in the USA, but the impact on the real economy outside the US was limited. In August/September 2008 the crisis turned into a full-scale *financial crisis* – and it did so with a big bang: Lehman Brothers, one of Wall Street's leading investment banks, went bankrupt. The end of the world (or at least of big finance) as we knew it, seemed to have arrived. Interest rates soared (interest spreads rose to several percentage points) and liquidity froze.

Again economic policy reacted. The principles of neoliberal free-market economics were suspended for a few weeks. Central banks provided more liquidity, but that proved insufficient to stabilise markets. Governments had to intervene directly: AIG, an insurance firm that had insured huge volumes of credit derivates, was taken over by the state as were Fannie Mae and Freddie Mac, the two state-sponsored mortgage refinancing giants. Within a few weeks the recapitalisation of financial institutions and massive guarantees for interbank credits became mainstream economic policy. Recapitalisation meant that governments were effectively being nationalised (fully or partly) financial institutions – but contrary to private shareholders they were eager to abstain from interfering with management priorities. In late October 2008 a EU summit issued a statement that no systemically important financial institutions would be allowed to fail – a capitalism without bankruptcies was declared!

By the fall of 2008 the financial crisis had turned into a full-blown *economic crisis*. Income in most developed countries shrank at a speed not witnessed since the 1930s (in most countries by around 5 per cent). And it hit not only those countries that had experienced property bubbles, but also countries like Germany and Japan (where property prices had been practically flat) and it spread to the emerging countries. Eastern European countries were hit particularly badly, with the Baltic countries suffering GDP declines of around 20 per cent. The IMF had to be called in to save Hungary, Pakistan and the Baltic States. But the most conspicuous symbol of the downturn was certainly the fall of the carmaker GM: once the world's largest firm and employer, it now had to rescued by the state.

While complete meltdown seemed imminent in the fall of 2008, in the course of spring 2009 it became clear that the – historically unprecedented – scale of government intervention had prevented total collapse. A cascade of bank breakdowns could be prevented by rescue packages that amounted to 80 per cent of GDP in the US and the UK (UNCTAD 2009, Table 1.8) and by the Fed expanding its balance sheet by US$1 trillion, mostly by acquiring assets that it would not have touched in normal times. Risk premia remained elevated, banks were making phenomenal losses, unemployment started rising, but normality of a sort returned. And, apparently, the pressure to reform the system had receded. Earlier declarations of a fundamental restructuring of the financial system had been forgotten and the debate on reform turned into specialists' debate of technicalities, with all but private bankers and central bankers being excluded from the decision-making circles. The arrogance of the financial elite, however, is best captured by the debate over bankers' pay. Despite the obvious disaster in finance, its leaders wanted to cash in again.

But the normality that was about to be re-established was not quite the normality of before the crisis. After all, the crisis was by no means past. Indeed, for large parts of the population, it had only just begun, when for the bankers it was almost over. Production fell and unemployment rose. In the USA foreclosures were rising. People lost their jobs and their homes. And there was another devastating effect of the crisis: budget deficits were increasing, in many case surpassing 10 per cent of GDP. So in the course of 2009 the crisis thus took its next turn: a *fiscal crisis*. This has been lingering for several months and had already erupted in central and eastern European countries, but its most prominent victim in the winter of 2009/10 was Greece and with it the euro system.

In January/February 2010 Greece faced punitive interest rates on its (public) debt issues. Greece had fudged public debt statistics (with the help of leading Wall Street banks) and now had difficulties refinancing its debt. But Greece was not alone, since the other Mediterranean members of the euro area faced similar problems. Indeed, what had been exposed was fundamental flaw in the construction of the euro system. With exchange rates frozen, the southern countries had, despite having much lower inflation rates since the adoptiong of the euro, slowly, but steadily lost competitiveness to Germany and its economic satellites. Germany's net exports (mostly to other euro countries) amounted to more than 5 per cent of GDP. This was achieved by ruthless wage suppression and, consequently, low inflation rates (Lapavitsas et al. 2010). The euro area had no instruments to deal with internal imbalances, other than trusting labour market flexibility to adjust the price levels. The other EU countries vaguely promised support and asked specifically for austerity.

The Greek problem was also the tip of an iceberg in another sense. Most countries now face sharply increasing levels of government debt due to the crisis and it is not clear when and how a solution could be found to the fiscal problems. The budget cuts that are envisioned in many countries will imply a cut back in welfare states, a paradoxical outcome for what started as a speculative financial crisis has ended up as a crisis of the welfare state. After the banks have been saved, it is the lower classes that are asked to pay the bill of the crisis.

3   Neoliberalism

The decades after the Second World War were characterised by what has been called the Fordist accumulation regime, which was based on a social-Keynesian mode of regulation.[3] Partly in response to the Great

Depression, partly in response to the rise of socialist labour movements, governments assumed an active role in managing the economy, the welfare state was expanded and the financial system regulated. Full employment was a policy goal and, in many cases, was approximately achieved. As a result, capitalism experienced what has sometime been called a 'golden age' of prosperity – and this prosperity was widely shared. Wages grew in line with productivity and income distribution was relatively even. Fordism was as a accumulation regime characterised by mass production and mass consumption.

Fordism came into crisis in the course of the 1970s. While the debate on its deeper causes is still going on, its symptoms were clear: waves of labour unrest, a (by today's standards: mild) recession, rising inflation and rising unemployment. Roughly from the mid-1970s trend productivity growth was substantially lower than before. Economic growth rates should not recover to the 'golden-age' rates and, in particular in Europe, unemployment would remain elevated thereafter. Whatever the reasons, with hindsight it is clear that the late 1970s/early 1980s mark watershed, the switch to neoliberalism. Neoliberalism began with the change in monetary policy and a sharp increase in interest rates, but it ushered in a much broader change in government priorities: a return to orthodox economic policies that regards low inflation and balanced budget as the key policy goals and, claiming that government could do nothing to lower structural unemployment, effectively accepted high unemployment rates.

Over the course of the next two decades neoliberalism turned into a full mode of regulation.[4] It was characterised by a retreat of labour, deregulation of the financial sector and globalisation. In the Anglo-Saxon countries neoliberalism came with an outright attack on organised labour. The miners' strike in Great Britain and the air traffic controllers' strike in the US marked bitter defeats for labour. In continental Europe the organisational strength of labour was eroded by two decades of high unemployment, welfare state retrenchment and globalisation. The effects of this on income distribution will be discussed in the next section.

Financial deregulation has two dimensions: the liberalisation of international capital flows and the deregulation of domestic financial systems. This led to fundamental changes in the financial landscape. At the international level capital flows were liberalised. Domestic changes in the financial framework gave rise to a rapid pace of financial innovation, eventually increasing the scope for speculation. Both developments strengthened the influence of the financial sector. Real interest rates rose well above the growth rates of real GDP. Financial ratios such as stock market capitalisation, derivatives turnover or cross-border lending soared. Overall the income shares of financial capital increased considerably (Duménil and Lévy 2001; Power et al. 2003). Moreover, the influence of financial investors on non-financial businesses has increased substantially under the so called shareholder value revolution (Lazonick and O'Sullivan 2000). These structural changes have been summarily called financialisation and will play a key role in our analysis of the structure of accumulation (section 5). Globalisation is a fourth characteristic of the neoliberal mode of regulation. Its financial dimension, the liberalisation of international capital flows, has already been mentioned. This was complemented by a free trade regime.

In continental Europe neoliberalism came, at least as far as economic policy is concerned, often in the guise of European integration and EU policies. In particular, the free trade agreements of the Single European Act, competition policy, and, later the services directive reflect the liberal creed. The Maastricht Treaty and the Stability and Growth Pact combined an anti-inflation priority with a restriction on fiscal policy without offering adjustment mechanisms for the imbalances that it gave rise to (see section 5.3).

The financial and economic crisis that began in 2007 has been a forceful reminder that free markets come with violent boom–bust cycles. By historical standards, government intervention has been relatively quick and extensive. This may suggest that neoliberalism has been abandoned. Such a conclusion interprets *neoliberalism* essentially *as a laissez-faire program*, a political project, which seeks to do away with state regulation and state intervention. While this is certainly a tempting interpretation, and is indeed warranted by some of the neoliberal rethoric, there are also other interpretations. Harvey highlights a tension in neoliberalism: 'We can ... interpret neoliberalization either as a utopian project to realize a theoretical design for the reorganization of international capitalism or as a political project to re-establish the conditions for capital accumulation and to restore the power of economic elites' (Harvey 2005, p. 19). Indeed, *neoliberalism a project to restore class power* is a hallmark of the Marxist interpretation of neoliberalism as (for example, Duménil and Lévy 2001, 2004). In this approach the anti-etatism of neoliberalism is instrumentalist, but not essential. It will be pursued when it is conducive to profitability, but not as an end in itself.

As early as the late 1970s Michel Foucault (2007) had suggested a third interpretation of neoliberalism, which we might call neoliberalism as form of *governance by competitive subjectification*. Based on a careful reading of the German ordo-liberal school and the US-American Chicago School Foucault argues that neoliberalism differs radically from classical liberalism in that it does not aim to liberate markets, but rather to *create* markets and subordinate government activity under this goal. Markets don't create themselves, if left on their own, but have to be constructed and maintained. In contrast to classical liberalism, therefore, neoliberalism requires permanent and profound state intervention. Stockhammer and Ramskogler (2009) reach a similar conclusion based on an analysis of recent economic policy and ('New Keynesian' and Neo-Institutionalist) developments in mainstream economics and label these developments *'enlightened neoliberalism'*. This approach is encapsulated in the title of the 2002 World Development report: *Creating Institutions for Markets*. As in the Marxist interpretation, state interventions do not constitute a break with neoliberalism.

4 Changes in income distribution

One of the hallmarks of neoliberalism has been the polarisation of the distribution of income. The shift in power from labour to capital is reflected clearly in wage developments. Wage shares have been falling across Europe and in Japan and, to a lesser extent, in the USA and the UK (see Figure 11.1). The Anglo-Saxon countries have, however, witnessed a strong increase of inequality in personal income distribution (Figure 11.2). Arguably, the exorbitant management salaries in the Anglo-Saxon countries should be considered to be a form of profits rather than wages. Indeed, subtracting the top 1 per cent of wage earners from the US wage share, a strong decline can be observed. According to (CPI-adjusted) data available from OECD (2008), median weekly wages in the US have grown by a mere 2.8 per cent between 1980 and 2005, the bottom quartile of wages fell by 3.1 per cent and the top10 per cent increased by 21 per cent.

Recently, mainstream economic policy institutions have shown a renewed interest in the determinants of *functional* income distribution. IMF (2007a) and EC (2007) conclude that technological change has been the main cause of the decline in the wage share and that globalisation has been only a secondary cause. In a panel analysis for OECD countries Stockhammer (2009) shows that the findings of these studies regarding technological change are not robust and that financial globalisation, trade globalisation and the decline in union density have been the main forces behind the falling wage share. The

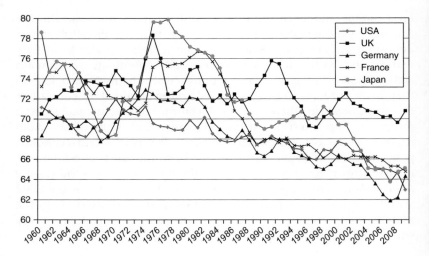

Figures 11.1 Adjusted wage share
Source: AMECO.

influence of globalisation (of trade and production) and have been demonstrated in the mainstream literature (e.g. IMF 2007) as well as in the heterodox literature (e.g. Milberg and Winkler 2009 for the USA). ILO (2008) argues that financial globalisation has contributed to the decline in the wage share, but does not provide econometric evidence. Rodrik (1998) and Harrison (2002) have included measures of capital controls and capital mobility. Remarkably, IMF (2007b) in a study on *personal* income distribution within countries finds that increases in foreign direct investment increases inequality.[5] Onaran (2009) shows that financial crisis have long-lasting distributional effects for several developing countries.

What are the likely macroeconomic effects on aggregate demand of this redistribution? From a Kaleckian point of view, one would expect a dampening effect on aggregate demand. As wage incomes are typically associated with higher consumption propensities than profit incomes, this ought to lead to a decrease in the consumption share. Stockhammer et al. (2009) find a saving differential of around 0.4 for the euro area.[6] Given that wage shares have declined by some 10 percentage points since 1980, consumption shares ought to have declined by some 4 percentage points (of GDP) over this period due to changes in income distribution. The background for macroeconomic developments in the neoliberal era is that of potentially stagnant demand.

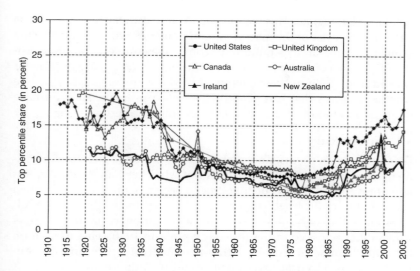

Figure 11.2a Income share of the top 1% in English-speaking countries

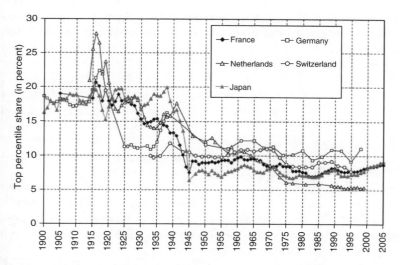

Figure 11.2b Income share of the top 1% in Continental Europe and Japan
Source: Atkinson, Piketty and Saez (2010), Figures 7A and 7B.

5 The finance-dominated accumulation regime

Stockhammer (2008) suggests that since the early 1980s a neoliberal mode of regulation has emerged that is complemented by a finance-dominated accumulation regime. This section will explore the characteristics of the latter. The analysis of the macroeconomic structure will be guided by the standard Keynesian expenditure function. Aggregate expenditures consist of private consumption, investment, net exports, and government expenditures. Each of these components will be investigated to analyse whether changes that can plausibly be linked to financialisation have occurred and modified the relevant behavioural pattern.

5.1 Investment

Given the rise in profits, one might expect a dynamic growth of investment expenditures. However, this is not what has happened. The disappointing performance of investment becomes most evident, when compared to profit levels (Figure 11.3). The decline in the investment-to-profits ratio can be observed in all major economies, even if the peak values differ across countries (the mean peaks in 1980). Financialisation brought about several changes that potentially affect business investment (that is, physical investment by firms). Admittedly, however, it has been hard to pin down these effects as business investment has always been the macroeconomic variable that is hardest to explain for economists. One of the most important changes in investment behaviour is due to the increased role of shareholders. Lazonick and

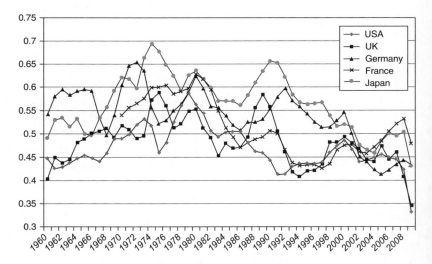

Figure 11.3 Investment to operating surplus
Source: AMECO.

O'Sullivan (2000) argue that a shift in management behaviour from 'retain and reinvest' to 'downsize and distribute' has occurred. More formally, Stockhammer (2004) shows that an increase in shareholder power will modify the desired profit-growth frontier for the firm. His estimation results suggest that financialisation may explain a substantial part of the slowdown in accumulation. However, results vary widely across countries (strong effects in the USA and France, weak effects in Germany). Orhangazi (2008) finds evidence for this channel based on firm-level data for the US. As the measure of operating surplus used in Figure 3.3 (as well as in the National Accounts) is a broad one that consists basically of all non-wage incomes, part of the reason for the declining trend in the investment operating surplus ratio is due to a change in the composition of the operating surplus. Interest and dividend payments have increased (Duménil and Lévy 2001; Crotty 2003). However, only for few countries, namely for the US, is data readily available. Onaran et al. (2009) present econometric evidence for the negative effect of dividend and interest payments on investment.

A second change for investment behaviour has been in the economic environment that firms face. The volatility on financial markets has increased substantially in the course of financial deregulation. As a consequence firms face a higher degree of uncertainty which may make physical investment projects less attractive. In particular, the volatility of exchange rates seems to have had some effects on manufacturing investment. However, uncertainty is hard to measure and estimation results from the existing literature are not conclusive enough to suggest a clear order of magnitude of the effect (Carruth et al. 2000; Stockhammer and Grafl 2008).

Overall, financialisation has had a dampening effect on business investment, probably as the result of negative effects of shareholder value orientation and increased uncertainty. Notably, there has been no renewed interest in the effect of share prices on business investment (quite in contrast to the research on consumption expenditures and share prices). As in the early 1990s (Chirinko 1993; Ford and Poret 1992), most empirical economists would probably agree that share prices have little, if any, effect on investment. Nor is there much evidence that other than in Ireland (and maybe in the Netherlands) residential investment has been strongly affected by rising household debt levels.

5.2 Consumption expenditures

There are two conflicting effects on consumption expenditures. First the deterioration of income distribution puts a downward pressure on consumption, because working-class households have a higher consumption propensity than earners of capital income. The background for macroeconomic developments is one of potentially stagnant consumption demand. Second, financialisation has increased the access of households to credit. In combination with real estate booms this has often led to credit-financed consumption booms.

In the US consumption expenditures have become the main driving force in GDP growth in the 1990s. Indeed, the consumption share in GDP had been increasing since about 1980 (see Figure 11.4). The trend is similar in the UK, but opposite in Germany and France. There consumption ratios have declined since 1980. There has been a remarkable divergence between countries. Mainstream economists try to explain this increase in consumption assuming rational behaviour (in Anglo-Saxon countries). The falling saving rates were first explained as arising from a wealth effect due to the rise in the value of financial assets because of the stock market boom.[7] In the late 1990s a 5 per cent marginal propensity to consume out of financial wealth was often quoted (with some more qualification for European countries; e.g. Boone et al. 1998). The stock market crash in 2000, however, did not result in a slowdown in consumption growth. The unabated consumption boom in the US was then explained by booming house prices. Residential property was now identified as the key source of the wealth effect as is more frequently

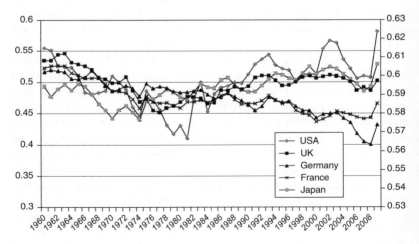

Figure 11.4 Consumption to final demand ratio
Source: AMECO.
Note: All countries except USA left scale; USA right scale

accepted as collateral. Case et al. (2001), Catte et al. (2004) and Girouard et al. (2006) find substantially higher marginal propensity to consume out of property wealth than out of financial assets.[8]

More generally speaking, financialisation has given households increased access to credit. Access to credit, of course, is not restricted to mortgages, but also includes other forms of consumer credit, credit cards and overdraft bank accounts. One of the key disagreements between the mainstream economics and heterodox approaches is the question of whether or not people behave in a rational manner. Much of the mainstream literature assumes that households rationally increased their debt ratios as their wealth levels rose. From a heterodox point of view a substantial part of the accumulated debt is due to households maintaining consumption levels that are unsustainable (and thus could be considered irrational). As wages have stagnated in many countries consumption norms as represented in mass media have arguably increased, and many households could have been driven into debt (Cynamon and Fazzari 2009). From this perspective it is misleading to speak of a wealth effect; it should rather be a *credit access effect*. Either way, in the USA, the UK, Ireland and Spain property bubbles were accompanied by strong increases in household debt ratios.

Household debt is difficult to measure and international comparisons chronically suffer from deficiencies in comparability of data due to different financial institutions and practices in different countries. Girourard et al. (2006) report a wide variation in household debt-to-income ratios. European countries display a wide range of debt to income ratios. However all European countries (for which data is available) have experienced rising debt ratios since 1995. Notably the (unweighted) average of the debt ratios of the European countries is similar to the USA.

OECD data also show that (household) savings rates are falling throughout the OECD countries, with the most pronounced fall occurring in the USA. Surprisingly, however, it turns out that this is not mirrored in the consumption data. While the USA (and Japan) have experienced a substantial and consistent increase of consumption compared to disposable income since the mid-1980s, the same is not true in Europe. In most countries, notably France and Germany, the changes in the consumption share are in the order of magnitude that are within the range of a business cycle. There was a strong increase in Greece and a strong decrease in Ireland. The (unweighted) average of the EU15 is unambiguously flat with no change in the consumption ratio of economic significance (Stockhammer 2008).

Overall, there is clear evidence for consumption as the driving force of growth only for a few countries. The USA appears to be the exception rather than the rule. Moreover, while household debt clearly increased in all countries, it did so to very different degrees, with the Anglo-Saxon countries (as well as Denmark and the Netherlands) showing the largest increases. European countries experienced a sharp decline in wage shares, which should translate into falling consumption If so, increased debt may have compensated this decline even in continental Europe.[9]

5.3   Net exports and capital flows

Over longer periods net exports ought to be balanced. However, financial liberalisation and globalisation have allowed countries to sustain current account deficits at higher levels and for longer periods than previously. The flip side of the current account is net capital flows. Abstracting from changes in central bank reserves net exports have to equal (net) capital outflows. Inversely, a current account deficit corresponds to capital inflows. Financialisation has thus allowed countries to run larger current account deficits, provided that they can attract the corresponding capital inflows. Figure 11.5 plots the standard deviation of the current account as a ratio to GDP (for OECD countries) as a measure of international imbalances. This shows that international imbalances have increased substantially since the mid-1980s.[10] Two things are remarkable about Figure 11.5. First, imbalances in the early 2000s were above the levels of the mid-1970s when the oil price shock gave rise to strong changes in

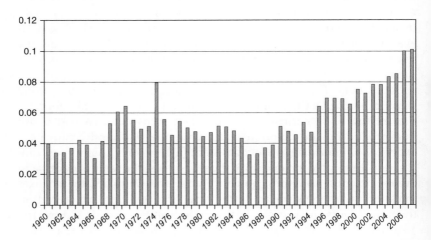

Figure 11.5   Standard deviation of the current account as % of GDP across OECD countries
Source: AMECO.

current accounts across many countries; second, the rise in international imbalances has been gradually building up since 1980.

The imbalances in international trade have also played an important role as a precondition in the building up of the bubble in the USA. The corresponding capital flows have provided vast amounts of capital in search of yield in US$ assets. These they found in various derivatives based on mortgage and commercial credit, thereby fuelling the credit-financed consumption boom. In the absence of capital inflows the bubble in the USA would probably not have inflated as strongly.

Financial liberalisation and globalisation have, ironically, increased the potential for different developments across countries – if only as long as international financial markets remain calm. However, the capital flows that underlie the trade imbalances may abruptly halt or reverse and thereby cause a severe crisis. The macroeconomic dangers of volatile capital flows have so far been felt most acutely in emerging economies. Mexico 1994, Turkey 1994 and 2001, several countries in the course of the South East Asian crisis 1997/98, and Argentina 2001 are all examples of such crises related to capital flows. Each of these led to a severe recession (at times with double-digit declines in real GDP), with some of them being long-lasting, while others were more short-lived.[11] However, the EMS crisis 1992/93 also shook developed economies (although the exchange rate devaluations were not as strong, nor were the following recessions).

The reason why changes in the exchange rate have such a devastating effect is that in liberalised international markets it is usually profitable to engage in interest arbitrage – that is to borrow in one currency and invest or lend in another (often called carry trade). If, say, interest rates in Turkish lira are higher than those in euros (with exchange rates expected to be stable), it is tempting to take out a euro credit and lend in Turkish lira. By implication, assets and liabilities will then be denominated in different currencies (a related risk is that of the maturity of assets). Abrupt exchange rate realignments may then have disastrous effects on firms' or banks' balance sheets.

International exchange rate arrangements seem key to understanding the accumulation and growth dynamics in the finance-dominated accumulation regime. For Europe, the most important institutional change in this area of course was the EMS (which effectively ended with the 1992/93 crisis) and European Monetary Unification. The introduction of the Euro was a reaction to the EMS crisis, where several countries had to devalue their currencies by some 20 per cent (vis-à-vis the Deutsche Mark). At first, the euro appears to have been a success. Not only was the new currency accepted by the public, but the euro system also eliminated (nominal) exchange rate fluctuations and thereby the possibility of exchange rate crises. It also substantially decreased inflation and (real) interest rates in the former soft-currency countries. However, since inflation differentials persist across European countries, there have been creeping changes in real exchange rates that have accumulated over the years. Real exchange rates have diverged since the introduction of the euro.[12] Germany has devalued by more than 20 per cent in real terms vis-à-vis Portugal, Spain, Ireland or Greece since 1999. It is in this context the recent crisis around Greek government bonds has to be seen.

The flaw in the euro system is essentially as follows: There is a common monetary policy and there are severe restrictions on fiscal policy. Exchange rate realignments are, by definition, not available to adjust divergences across the euro zone. So how can countries adjust? Essentially through a process of wage moderation. However, this fails to work in practice. First, labour markets simply are not as flexible as economic textbooks and EU treaties would like them to be. Second, the adjustment via labour markets has a clear deflationary bias – the country with the current account deficit will have to adjust and it has to adjust through wage restraint and disinflation. However, as overall inflation is limited to 2 per cent, any country that wanted to make a serious attempt to improve competitiveness would have to go through an extended period of deflation, which would require mass unemployment and falling wage levels. The present model requires that the deficit countries restrain inflation and growth whereas the surplus countries are allowed to continue to run surpluses. But in addition to its failure to deliver stability, this arrangement also has severe distributional consequences. Simply put, under the present arrangement Greek wages have to fall, but German wages do not have to rise. The system puts a downward pressure on wages.

Europe has reacted to the liberalisation of capital flows by introducing a common currency. While this has ended the risk of exchange rate crises, trade and cost-related imbalances have been building up within the euro area and there is currently no mechanism for resolving these imbalances.

5.4 The finance-dominated accumulation regime: fragile and low growth

While there is evidence for a consumption boom in the USA (and previously for limited periods in some developing countries), for continental European countries one does not find the strong evidence of a consumption boom (related with a property price bubble) – despite the fact that household debt levels increased substantially. However, given that income distribution has changed at the expense of labour, which should have decreased consumption ratios, it is plausible that debt-driven consumption has also fuelled demand in Europe to some extent.[13] Investment performance has been weak. In particular rising profits have not translated into rising investment. Presumably (but hardly conclusively) this is related to shareholder value orientation and increased uncertainty due to volatile financial markets. The liberalisation of capital flows has relaxed current account constraints on countries and led to volatile exchange rates, which however, have not translated into a severe crises in Europe (with the exception of the 1992/93 EMS crisis) as they did in South East Asia, Latin America or Turkey. The euro system has effectively prevented currency crises. However, the euro came with a policy package, the Maastricht Treaty and the Stability and Growth Pact, that has fostered neoliberalisation within Europe and led to a creeping divergence within Europe.

Overall, the effects of financialisation thus give rise to a finance-dominated accumulation regime that is one of *slow* and *fragile* accumulation. There are two related reasons to expect the finance-dominated accumulation regime to come with more volatility in output growth (and other macroeconomic variables). First, macroeconomic shocks from the financial sector have become more severe and more frequent. There is ample evidence that financial markets generate highly volatile prices. Overshooting is well established for exchange rates and the boom–bust cycles of share prices has become evident (again) in recent years. Second, because of high debt levels, there has been an increase in the fragility of the economy. Financialisation has encouraged households to take on more debt. This debt presumably either has fuelled consumption expenditures or was necessary to buy property in the face of soaring house prices. Either way, debt has to be serviced out of current income (or by ever-increasing debt). Even temporary reductions in income may thus escalate if households have to default on their loans. While this need not happen necessarily, the *fragility* of the system has increased as the resilience of households against temporary shocks has decreased.

One would expect that this combination of more frequent crises on financial markets and high fragility of households would translate into macroeconomic volatility. IMF (2007c) presents evidence that business cycles have become more *moderate* since the 1970s. The devil, however, lies in the detail. While 'output volatility ... has been significantly lower than during the 1960s' (IMF 2007c, p. 85), recessions have become harsher in the post-Bretton Woods era than in the Bretton Woods era

(IMF 2002, Table 3.1). As output growth (and expansion) was much higher in the Fordist era than in the post-Fordist era, the IMF is correct in concluding that volatility has decreased. But this does not mean that recessions have become less severe! Moreover, financial crises have become more frequent and more severe (Eichengreen and Bordo 2003).[14] The present crisis is not a rare exception, but only one of many in the age of deregulated finance.

It is important to note that state shares in GDP are still substantially higher than at the time of the Great Depression. Automatic stabilisers are thus in place and government consumption forms a sizable part of value added. Moreover, central banks in developed countries (in particular, the Fed) have been proactive in reacting to dangers of financial crisis. The resilience of a sizable government sector and (by historical standards) a functional welfare state combined with adept monetary policy may be the reason, why financial crises have so far not had a devastating effect on (advanced) economies (Stockhammer 2008).

6 Income distribution and the underlying causes of the present crisis

Two of the main characteristics of neoliberalism are the polarisation of income distribution and the deregulation of the financial system. Both have interacted in complex ways to provide the preconditions of the present crisis. The polarisation of income distribution is closely linked to the international imbalances that underlie the present crisis. In most developed countries the median working-class household has experienced stagnant wages. Certainly consumption norms (as spread through mass media) have increased faster than median wages. Combined with a weak investment performance this has led to a shortfall in private demand. Effectively (but not necessarily by intention) two different strategies have emerged: In Anglo-Saxon countries the shortfall of disposable income has been compensated by credit and increasing debt levels. The property boom allowed households to take out loans that they could not afford given their income, but that seemed reasonable to banks which assumed that property prices would continue to increase. These countries developed a *credit-financed consumption boom* that came with current account deficits. The resulting capital inflows again fuelled the property bubble and bubbles in other financial markets.

In the second group of countries median working-class households faced a similar stagnation in wages. In these countries private consumption expenditures remained weak. Here net exports played the key component of demand growth. Thus these countries developed an *export-led growth model*.

The same phenomenon, a stagnation in real wages, had different effects in different countries. Moreover, the two growth models rely on each other: the credit-driven consumption model implies current account deficits and thus will only work if there are surplus countries. Inversely, the export-growth strategy will only work, if there are deficit countries that absorb their exports. The current account imbalances were made possible by financial globalisation and the liberalisation of capital flows.

The roots of the crisis are thus only in part to be found in the financial sector. Given the severity of the economic crisis it is tempting to infer that it must have profound structural roots. Our analysis suggests that this is indeed the case. All of the building blocks of neoliberalism – financialisation, rising inequality and globalisation – are implicated in giving rise to creating the imbalances that have erupted in the present crisis. In this sense it is very much *a crisis of neoliberalism*.

This diagnosis is not to be confused with forecasting the imminent demise of neoliberalism, even if the stocks of free market ideology have suffered long-lasting damage. The Marxist as well as the Foucaultian interpretation indicate that neoliberalism is about power relations (or govermentality) rather than about free markets. Looking at the policy debates in the aftermath of the crisis, the absence of a serious attempt to regulate finance, the reluctance of governments to use nationalised banks for industrial policy, the persistent taboo of increasing the taxation of the super-rich that neoliberalism has created and the severe cuts in public services that look likely to follow the fiscal crisis can only conclude that in a political sense this is *not* a crisis of neoliberalism. We are in an uncomfortable situation where neoliberalism has resulted in a major economic crisis, but is still hegemonic in policy making.

7 Summary and conclusions

This chapter has argued that the causes of the present crisis are deeply rooted in neoliberalism. Neoliberalism entailed a deregulation of the financial sector (as well as of other areas of the economy) and a polarisation of income distribution. While the former is widely associated as an important cause of the present crisis, the latter is not. Median wages have lagged behind productivity growth, which has led to sluggish growth of consumption expenditures. The polarisation of income distribution and the deregulation of finance have interacted to create macroeconomic imbalances and bubbles as some countries have relied on credit-driven consumption as a growth engine. Highlighting the role of wage moderation in this process also lends itself to policy conclusions: As wage moderation has been one of the structural causes underlying the present crisis, one condition for re-establishing a viable growth regime is a change in wage policy. Wages have to increase at least with productivity growth. This would stabilise domestic demand in the surplus countries and avoid a collapse of consumption demand in the deficit countries. A more egalitarian income distribution is not a luxury that can be dealt with once the economy has been stabilised – it is an integral part of a sound macroeconomic structure.

Notes

1. Some sections of this chapter build closely on previous work by the author, in particular on Stockhammer (2008), Stockhammer and Ramskogler (2009), and Stockhammer (2010).
2. Horn et al. (2009) develop a very similar argument.
3. Regulation theory regards the macroeconomic dynamic (described as the 'accumulation regime') as embedded in a particular institutional setting (the 'mode of regulation'). While there is an agreement that the Fordist accumulation regime has come to an end in the course of the 1970s, there is no agreement on how to characterise the post-Fordist regime. Classical works of the (French) Regulation Theory include Aglietta (1979), Lipietz (1985) and Boyer (1990). Similarities between the Regulation Theory and the (American) Social Structures of Accumulation approach (Gordon, Edwards and Reich 1982; Bowles, Gordon and Weisskopf 1983) are now widely recognised (e.g. McDonough and Nardone 2006). The question how national accumulation regimes interact has received limited attention within the regulationist approach. Becker (2002) and Becker and Blaas (2007) highlight differences along the axes of 'intraverted' versus 'extraverted' accumulation and 'productive' versus 'fictitious' accumulation.
4. This, of course, is the author's interpretation. The label neoliberalism is used to highlight that a mode of regulation is ultimately a *political* project. It is the outcome and institutionalisation of various compromises and (in their intention often provisional) arrangements that acquire a certain degree of coherence. Within the framework of regulation theory the mode of regulation is comprise of the wage-labour relation, the forms of competition, the monetary regime, the forms of state intervention and the insertion into the international regime. This chapter only sketches the changes in these area, but clearly falls short of an exhaustive analysis.
5. FDI flows illustrate the difficulties in distinguishing between financial globalisation and globalisation in production.
6. This value is in line with comparable studies for other groups of countries (Naastepad and Storm 2006/07; Hein and Vogel 2008).

7. Brenner (2003, p. 191) argues that most of the fall in the savings rate (in the late 1990s) occurred in the top income groups, who also benefited most from the increase in financial wealth. This, admittedly, fits uneasily with the argument made here. Evidence for the early 2000s, however, suggests that the debt burden has grown fastest for middle class households (which is in line with our argument) (State of Working America 2006/2007). This issue requires further research.

8. While there is substantial evidence for the USA (albeit based on a short period of observations!) to back up this story, the evidence on European economies was always much thinner. Typically the wealth effects estimated for European economies were not statistically significant and/or much smaller.

9. There is an additional channel through which financialisation may have affected consumption expenditures. In many countries the 'pay-as-you-go' pension systems are being reformed or have been questioned. Typically some version of a capital-based system is envisioned in which households have to invest their savings (usually via funds) in the stock market. This should lead to an increase in savings as households have to put more aside for retirement. I am not aware that this channel has been investigated empirically.

10. As our measure only includes OECD countries China as well as some other South-East Asian countries that run substantial current account surpluses are not included. Our measure thus underestimates the full extent of international imbalances.

11. The fact that some countries recover quickly after a deep recession, does not imply that everything returns to pro-crisis. Onaran (2009) argues that financial crises often lead to lasting changes in functional income distribution.

12. Presumably not all countries entered the euro with the 'correct' exchange rate. In particular Deutsche Mark is often thought to have entered over-valued. However, if the real exchange rate realignments since 1999 were a correction of the initial values, one would expect the real exchange rates to stabilise after a while. As of now there is no indication for that.

13. There is little evidence however, that this debt, much of which is mortgage debt, has caused a substantial increase in residential investment. The latter is falling as a share of overall investment.

14. In particular Eichengreen and Bordo report that there had been *no* banking crises in the 1945–73 period.

References

Aglietta, M. (1979) *A Theory of Capitalist Regulation: The US Experience*. London: Verso.

AMECO (2010) AMECO (Economic and Financial affairs, Annual Macroeconomic Indicators online database), April 2010. Available at: http://ec.europa.eu/economy_finance/db_indicators/ameco/index_en.htm.

Atkinson, A, Piketty, T. and Saez, E (2010) 'Top Incomes in the Long Run of History', *Journal of Economic Literature*, forthcoming. http://elsa.berkeley.edu/~saez/atkinson-piketty-saezJEL10.

Becker, J. (2002) *Akkumulation, Regulation Territorium. Zur kritischen Rekonstruktion der französischen Regulationstheorie*. Marburg: Metropolis Verlag.

Becker, J. and Blaas, W. (2007) 'Introduction', in W. Blaas and J. Becker (eds), *Strategic Arena Switching in International Trade Negotiations*. Aldershot: Ashgate.

Boone, L., Giorno, C. and Richardson, P. (1998) *Stock Market Fluctuations and Consumption Behaviour: Some Recent Evidence*. OECD Economics department working papers no. 208. Paris: Organisation of Economic Cooperation and Development.

Bowles, S., Gordon, D. and Weisskopf, T. (1983) *Beyond the Waste Land. A Democratic Alternative to Economic Decline*. Garden City, NY: Anchor Press.

Boyer, R. (1990) *The Regulation School: A Critical Introduction*. New York: Columbia University Press.

Brenner, R. (2003) *The Boom and the Bubble*. London: Verso

Carruth, A., Dickerson, A. and Henley, A. (2000) 'What Do We Know about Investment Under Uncertainty?', *Journal of Economic Surveys*, 24(2), 119–53.

Case, K., Shiller, R. and Quigley, J. (2001) *Comparing Wealth Effects: The Stock Market Versus the Housing Market*. NBER Working Paper no.w8606 November.

Catte, P., Girouard, N., Price R. and André, C. (2004) *Housing Markets, Wealth and the Business Cycle*. OECD Economics Working Paper 394. Paris: Organisation of Economic Cooperation and Development.

Chirinko, R. (1993) 'Business Fixed Investment Spending: Modeling Strategies, Empirical Results and Policy Implications', *Journal of Economic Literature*, 31(4), 1875–911.

Crotty, J. (2003) 'The Neoliberal Paradox: The Impact of Destructive Product Market Competition and Impatient Financial Markets on Nonfinancial Corporations in the Neoliberal Era', *Review of Radical Political Economics*, 35(3), 271–9.

Cynamon, B. and Fazzari, S. (2009) 'Household Debt in the Consumer Age: Source of Growth – Risk of Collapse', *Capitalism and Society*, 3(2), Article 3.

Duménil, G. and Lévy, D. (2001) 'Costs and Benefits of Neoliberalism: A Class Analysis', *Review of International Political Economy*, 8(4), 578–607.

Duménil, G. and Lévy, D. (2004) *Capital Resurgent: Roots of the Neoliberal Revolution*. Cambridge, MA: Harvard University Press.

Eichengreen, B. and Bordo, M. (2003) ''Crises Now and Then: What Lessons for the Last Era of Financial Globalization?', in P. Mizen (ed), *Monetary History, Exchange Rates and Financial Markets. Essays in Honour of Charles Goodhart*, vol. 2. Cheltenham: Edward Elgar.

European Commission (2007) 'The Labour Income Share in the European Union', Chapter 5 of: *Employment in Europe*. Brussels: European Commission, pp. 237–72.

Ford, R. and Poret, P. (1991) 'Business Investment: Recent Performance and Some Implications for Policy'. *OECD Economic Studies 16*. Paris: Organisation of Economic Cooperation and Development, pp. 79–131.

Foucault, Michel (2007) *The Birth of Biopolitics: Lectures at the College de France, 1978–1979*. Basingstoke: Palgrave Macmillan.

Girouard, N., Kennedy M. and André, C. (2006) *Has the Rise in Debt Made Households More Vulnerable?* OECD Economics Working Paper 535 (ECO/WKP(2006)63).

Glyn, A. (2006) *Capitalism Unleashed: Finance, Globalization and Welfare*. Oxford: Oxford University Press.

Gordon, D., Edwards, R. and Reich M. (1982) *Segmented Work, Divided Workers: The Historical Transformation of Labour in the United States*. Cambridge: Cambridge University Press.

Harrison, A. (2002) 'Has Globalization Eroded Labor's Share? Some Cross-country Evidence', mimeo, UC Berkeley.

Harvey, D. (2005) *A Short History of Neoliberalism*. Oxford: Oxford University Press.

Hein, E. and Vogel, L. (2008) 'Distribution and Growth Reconsidered – Empirical Results for Austria, France, Germany, the Netherlands, the UK and the USA', *Cambridge Journal of Economics*, 32(3), 479–511.

Horn, G., Dröge, K., Sturn, S., van Treeck, T. and Zwiener, R. (2009) From the financial crisis to the world economic crisis. The role of inequality. English version of IMK Report No. 41 IMK Policy Brief http://www.boeckler.de/show_product_imk.html?productfile=HBS-004528.xml.

ILO (2008) *World of Work Report 2008: Income Inequalities in the Age of Financial Globalization*. Geneva: ILO.

IMF (2002) 'Recessions and Recoveries', chapter 3 of *World Economic Outlook 2002/1*. Washington, DC: IMF.

IMF (2007a) 'The Globalization of Labor', chapter 5 of *World Economics Outlook*, April 2007. Washington, DC: IMF.

IMF (2007b) 'Globalization and Inequality, chapter 4 of *World Economic Outlook*, October. Washington, DC: IMF.

IMF (2007c) 'The Changing Dynamics of the Global Business Cycle', chapter 5 of *World Economic Outlook*, 2007/2 (Washington, DC:IMF).

Jayadev, A. (2007) 'Capital Account Openness and the Labour Share of Income', *Cambridge Journal of Economics*, 31, 423–43.

Lapavitsas, C., Kaltenbrunner, A., Lindo, D., Michell, J,. Painceira, J.P., Pires, E., Powell, J., Stenfors, A. and Teles, N. (2010) *Eurozone Crisis: Beggar Thyself and Thy Neighbour*. RMF occasional report March 2010 http://researchonmoneyandfinance.org/media/reports/eurocrisis/fullreport.pdf.

Lazonick, W. and O'Sullivan, M. (2000) 'Maximising Shareholder Value: A New Ideology for Corporate Governance', *Economy and Society*, 29(1), 13–35.

Lipietz A. (1985): *The Enchanted Word*. London: Verso.

McDonough, T. and Nardone, E. (2006) 'Social Structures of Accumulation, the Regulation Approach and the European Union', *Competition and Change*, 10(2), 200–12.

Milberg, W. and Winkler, D. (2009) 'Financialisation and the Dynamics of Offshoring in the USA', *Cambridge Journal of Economics*, 34, 275–93.

Naastepad, C. and Storm, S. (2006/07) 'OECD Demand Regimes (1960–2000)', *Journal of Post-Keynesian Economics*, 29 (2), 213–48.

OECD (2008) *Growing Unequal? Income Distribution and Poverty in OECD Countries*. Paris: OECD.

Onaran, Ö. (2009) 'Wage Share, Globalization, and Crisis: The Case of Manufacturing Industry in Korea, Mexico, and Turkey', *International Review of Applied Economics*, 23(2), 113–34.

Onaran, Ö., Stockhammer, E. and Grafl, L. (2009) *The Finance-dominated Growth Regime, Distribution, and Aggregate Demand in the US*, Vienna University of Economics & Business. Dept. of Economics Working Paper no. 126.

Orhangazi, Özgür (2008) 'Financialisation and Capital Accumulation in the Non-financial Corporate Sector: A Theoretical and Empirical Investigation on the US Economy: 1973–2003', *Cambridge Journal of Economics* 32, 863–86.

Power, D., Epstein, G. and Abrena, M. (2003) *Trends in the Rentier Income Share in OECD Countries 1960–2000*. PERI Working Paper 58a.

Reinhart, C., Reinhart, V. (2008) Capital Flow Bonanzas: An Encompassing View of the Past and Present. NBER Working Paper No. W14321

Rodrik, D, 1998. Capital mobility and labor. Manuscript. http://ksghome. harvard.edu/~drodrik/capitalm.pdf

Stockhammer E. (2004) 'Financialization and the Slowdown of Accumulation', *Cambridge Journal of Economics*, 28 (5), 719–41.

Stockhammer, E. (2008) 'Stylized Facts on the Finance-dominated Accumulation Regime', *Competition and Change* 12(2), 189–207.

Stockhammer, E. (2009) *Determinants of Functional Income Distribution in OECD Countries*. IMK Studies, No. 5/2009. Düsseldorf: IMK.

Stockhammer, E. (2010) 'Income Distribution, the Finance-dominated Accumulation Regime and the Present Crisis', in S. Dullien, E. Hein, A. Truger and T. van Treeck (eds), *The World Economy in Crisis – The Return of Keynesianism?* Marburg: Metropolis Verlag.

Stockhammer, E. and Grafl, L. (2008) *Financial Uncertainty and Business Investment*. Vienna University of Economics & Business. Department of Economics Working Paper no. 123.

Stockhammer, E., Onaran, Ö. and Ederer, S. (2009) 'Functional Income Distribution and Aggregate Demand in the Euro Area', *Cambridge Journal of Economics*, 33(1), 139–59.

Stockhammer, E. and Ramskogler, P. (2009) 'Post Keynesian Economics – How to Move Forward', *Intervention*, 5(2), 227–46.

UNCTAD (2009) *Trade and Development Report 2009*. New York: United Nations.

World Bank (2002) *Building Institutions for Markets. World Development Report 2002*. Washington, DC: World Bank.

Index